George Vance Smith

The Bible and Popular Theology

A Restatement of Truths and Principles

George Vance Smith

The Bible and Popular Theology
A Restatement of Truths and Principles

ISBN/EAN: 9783337098353

Printed in Europe, USA, Canada, Australia, Japan

Cover: Foto ©Lupo / pixelio.de

More available books at **www.hansebooks.com**

THE

BIBLE and POPULAR THEOLOGY:

A

RE-STATEMENT OF TRUTHS AND PRINCIPLES,

WITH SPECIAL REFERENCE TO RECENT WORKS OF

DR. LIDDON, LORD HATHERLEY, THE RIGHT HON.
W. E. GLADSTONE, AND OTHERS.

BY

G. VANCE SMITH, B.A., Ph.D.,

MINISTER OF ST. SAVIOURGATE CHAPEL, YORK.

THIRD EDITION, REVISED AND AUGMENTED.

LONDON:
LONGMANS, GREEN, READER, AND DYER.

1871.

BY THE SAME AUTHOR.

1 vol. 8vo.

THE PROPHECIES relating to Nineveh and the Assyrians. Translated from the Hebrew, with Introductions and Notes. (Out of print.)

London: LONGMAN AND Co.

In 3 vols. 8vo, price 6s.

THE HOLY SCRIPTURES of the Old Covenant, in a Revised Translation. 1862. By

The late Rev. C. WELLBELOVED,
The Rev. G. VANCE SMITH,
The Rev. J. SCOTT PORTER.

To be had from Mr. H. BRACE, 178, Strand.

Post 8vo, 2nd edition, price 2d.

ETERNAL PUNISHMENT, a Tract for the Times: with Remarks on Dr. Pusey's Defence of the Doctrine. 1865.

London: E. T. WHITFIELD.

Post 8vo, price 6d.

PROVIDENTIAL LESSONS in Christian Doctrine: a Sermon preached at the Annual Meeting of the British and Foreign Unitarian Association, 1865.

London: E. T. WHITFIELD.

Post 8vo, pp. 94, price 2s.

CHURCH COMPREHENSION, a Letter to the Right Hon. W. E. GLADSTONE. 1863. (Being Suggestions for the Re-construction of the National Church.)

London: LONGMAN AND Co.

PREFACE.

It has been my leading aim, in the following pages, to offer to the reader a concise and simply written exposition of the Biblical teachings, in relation to several of the more important questions of Christian Theology.

This design I have pursued with a view more especially to non-professional and unlearned readers,—such persons, I mean, as are not likely to be familiar with theological books, or committed in advance to the maintenance of a particular creed or system of doctrine. I speak thus plainly, without the slightest intention to cast any reflection upon the professional clergy or ministers of religion of the different denominations; but I do not pretend to conceal my conviction that it is chiefly the intelligent laity to whom a theological writer can look hopefully, for an unbiassed judgment upon the various evidences and arguments here brought forward. It is not difficult to understand that those who, either by subscription or by other equivalent forms of "assent and consent" well known to most of the Nonconformist churches, have virtually pledged themselves to very definite conclusions on the subjects which I have discussed, can hardly be expected to pass an impartial judgment on such a book as this, even if they should be willing to give it the degree of consideration fairly due to it.

The character of the volume has necessarily been somewhat affected by a regard to the class of readers for whom I have chiefly written. The references to authorities, for example, will be found to be comparatively few, except in the case of the Scriptures. They are also, for the most part, and purposely, to works easily accessible. Indeed, I may add, the due exhibition of the positive doctrine of the Bible, on the subjects here treated of, does not appear to stand in need of the elaborate erudition which, if a judgment may be formed from Dr. Liddon's work, is indispensable for the exposition and defence of the popular theology. This, it may be presumed, is some advantage both for author and reader. May it not be reasonably appealed to as affording also something of presumptive evidence in favour of the simpler and more unpretending cause?

Yet, while admitting and calling attention to this feature of the present work, I am not without the hope that every point of essential importance in the argument will be found to have been adequately considered. I have wished that such should be the case, and that no evidence of value should be omitted or too lightly passed over.

It is perhaps scarcely necessary to say that the volume does not profess to be anything like a formal or detailed reply to the treatise of Dr. Liddon. So large an undertaking could not have been brought within the limits which I had to prescribe to myself. Nor did it appear to be needed for any practical purpose.* I have thought it well, however, to pursue my principal design with a special reference to that treatise, as well as to the work of Lord Hatherley on the Continuity of Scripture, and to that of Mr. Gladstone on Ecce Homo. The three writers may properly be considered as "representative men;" while they may also be classed among the latest and most interesting expounders of the popular theology. Without, therefore, attempting a detailed or complete examination of all that they have advanced, I have kept in view some of the more important and characteristic parts of their several arguments. I have done this the more readily, on account of the eminent station and learning of the two distinguished laymen whose statements I have made the subject of some of my remarks; and to whom, I may add, I do confidently look for a candid and just consideration of what I have said.

I may further observe, that the present volume is necessarily, to some extent, an *argumentum ad hominem*. It addresses itself more especially to those who are accustomed to a particular idea of the function of the Bible, as the depository and teacher of religious truth;—to those, that is to say, who accept the Protestant principle of the sufficiency of the Scriptures, and acknowledge the right of

---

* I take the opportunity of referring the reader to a lately published work which purports to be "An Examination of Canon Liddon's Bampton Lectures"—(Trübner, 1871). This work came into my hands as the final sheets of my own volume were passing through the press. It appears to be a careful and effective reply to all the principal portions of Dr. Liddon's Lectures, and so far as may be judged from a cursory perusal of parts, it is one of the most powerful modern treatises on the Unitarian side of this controversy. The marvel attending it is, that the author should announce himself, on his title-page, as "a Clergyman of the Church of England." I very willingly admit the force of the testimony which this statement affords against the opinion I have just expressed, to the effect that those who might seem to have committed themselves to foregone conclusions can hardly be expected to give an unbiassed consideration to the contents of my own volume.

private judgment—as Dr. Liddon appears to do, by the fact of having made his appeal so emphatically to the Bible. I have not thought it necessary, however, to enter minutely into inquiries respecting the age or authorship of any of the sacred books. These I have been contented to receive under the character usually attributed to them; while yet I have not refrained, in several instances, from noticing the doubt attaching to many of the writings forming our present Canon of Holy Scripture.

It will not, perhaps, be out of place to mention that these pages were nearly all composed (excepting the last Chapter) early in the summer of the past year, although various circumstances have somewhat delayed their publication. It will therefore be evident that my connection with the New Testament Revision Company, or the discussions of one kind and another to which that circumstance has given rise within the last few months, have had no immediate influence on the preparation of the work. Without this statement, the volume might be supposed to have been occasioned by the discussions referred to. Such is not the case.

At the close of the last Chapter, I have added a few words on a subject not perhaps included within the proper scope of this work, but yet not altogether unconnected with it. What I have said is designed to correct certain strange misunderstandings which appear still to prevail, in some quarters, on the points referred to; and I hope it will answer its purpose! I have explained both what a Unitarian *is*, and What Unitarians *worship*. I venture here to make an addition to these statements, and to give my own opinion as to what Unitarians should *desire*, and *aim at*, as a great end of their denominational existence. It is not, primarily, to make themselves a numerous and powerful sect, with a carefully defined system of doctrine, negative or positive;—of which, indeed, there is very little danger at present. It is, rather,—next to the faithful cultivation in themselves, individually, of the religious and Christlike life, the supreme importance of which should never be lost sight of—*first*, that they should earnestly help to free the common Christianity, held by themselves, and the orthodox churches, from the corruptions of one kind and another which, in the course of ages, have grown up around it and upon it, and the removal of which was by no means completed by the Reformers of the sixteenth century. It is, *secondly,* that they should endeavour to hold up to the nation, as a main principle and aim even of its political life, that the people of this kingdom may yet be united together in Christian brotherhood as members of one comprehensive Church of Christ, that thus an end may be put at length to the unseemly divisions which now discredit our national profession of Christianity, and waste both our material and our moral resources. Will the Unitarians of England accept the "mission" which thus seems to be providentially offered to them? Will they be found equal to the adequate discharge of its duties? or shall the work pass from them to others who are stronger and worthier than they?—No doubt most of my readers will regard the idea here suggested as perfectly Utopian. So be it. I have faith, nevertheless, in the rightness of what I have proposed on this subject, as well as in the religious feeling and good sense of the great mass of the English people. May it not prove at last, and when too late to be remedied, that, in our perversity and narrowness of spirit, we have allowed a great opportunity to come to us in vain!

I must not, in conclusion, omit to acknowledge the pecuniary assistance which I have received from the Trustees of the late Robert Hibbert, Esq., who have defrayed the expenses attending the publication of this volume. I thank them very cordially for it, and at the same time I rejoice to think that it should be in my power to contribute, in this form, to the objects contemplated by their liberal and enlightened Founder.

G. V. S.

York, *April 25th*, 1871.

The present Edition has been carefully revised, numerous alterations having been made in the text, chiefly with a view to increased clearness of expression. Some additions have also been made to the volume in the form of notes.

My best thanks are due to the Rev. A. W. Worthington for his kindness in correcting the proof-sheets of this Edition, which has been printed during my own absence from England.

Lugano, *October*, 1871.

** The following are the Works referred to on the title-page:—

The Divinity of our Lord and Saviour Jesus Christ; Eight Lectures, &c. By Henry Parry Liddon, M.A., &c. (Smaller Edition, 1868.)

The Continuity of Scripture as declared by the Testimony of our Lord, &c. By William Page Lord Hatherley. (Third Edition, with additions, 1869.)

"*Ecce Homo.*" By the Right Hon. W. E. Gladstone. (1868.)

Aids to Faith; a Series of Theological Essays. By Several Writers. (Fourth Edition, 1863.) Essay on the Death of Christ, by Dr. W. Thomson, now Archbishop of York.

CONTENTS.

CHAP.		PAGE
I.	Miscellaneous and uncertain Character of the Sacred Books.	1
II.	Unity and Continuity of Scripture—in what sense admissible	8
III.	Unity and Continuity of Scripture as maintained by Lord Hatherley	18
IV.	The Use of the Old Testament in the New	26
V.	Messianic Passages: Isaiah vii. 14; lii. 13-liii. 12; xi.; ix. 6	4
VI.	Messianic Passages continued: Jeremiah xxiii. 5, 6; Daniel vii. 13 Micah v. 2; Zechariah xiii. 7; xii. 10; the Quotation in St. John xix. 36; Malachi iii. 1	52
VII.	The Knowledge and the Ignorance of Christ—Orthodox Excess in the Use of Old Testament Passages—General Result	64
VIII.	The Biblical Doctrine of One God—the Words Elohim and Jehovah	70
IX.	The Biblical Doctrine of One God—its continued Development—the Christian Doctrine	79
	New Testament Passages supposed to express the Doctrine of the Trinity	90
X.	The Orthodox Argument from Plural Forms of Expression	94
XI.	Jesus of Nazareth—the Charge on which he was put to Death	103
XII.	Jesus of Nazareth, as he appeared to his own Contemporaries—the True Import of the Titles Christ and Son of God	114
XIII.	Mr. Gladstone's Testimony to the Humanitarian Character of the Evangelical Narratives—" Ecce Homo"	125
XIV.	The Christ of the First Three Gospels and of the Fourth—Differences	132
XV.	The Doctrine of the Logos—Philo—Justin Martyr—Earlier Tendencies among the Jews	146
XVI.	St. John's Doctrine of the Logos—its Meaning and permanent Value	158

CHAP		PAGE
XVII.	Remarks on Dr. Liddon's Exposition of the Doctrine of the Logos	173
XVIII.	Jesus the Spiritual Christ—Christian Faith—Justification by Faith	189
XIX.	The Humiliation and the Glory of the Christ in the Pauline Epistles	196
XX.	The Creation of all Things through Jesus Christ	208
XXI.	The Apocalyptic Exaltation of Jesus Christ	217
XXII.	The Worship of Christ	220
XXIII.	The Holy Spirit	231
XXIV.	Sacrifices, their Origin and Purpose—the Hebrew System	243
XXV.	The Death of Christ—Popular Theories founded upon it	252
XXVI.	The Death of Christ—its Purpose and Effect as set forth in the New Testament	263
XXVII.	Relation of the Bible to the Reason and Conscience—Inspiration—True Authority of Scripture	283
XXVIII.	Summary of Results with additional Remarks—the Christianity of Christ—his True Dignity—his Death—the Lord's Supper, what it is—the Function of the Bible: Priestly Authority—the Church and the Churches—Proper Basis of Christian Communion—Question of a National Church—What Unitarians Worship—What is a Unitarian?—A Parting Hope	303

GENERAL APPENDIX:

Note A,—Isaiah vii. 14.		324
,, B,—Isaiah lii. 13-liii. 12		325
,, C,—1 Tim. iii. 16		327
,, D,—Titus ii. 13; 1 John v. 20		328, 331
,, E,—Philip. ii. 5-11		333
,, F,—The Instrumental Force of the Preposition $\Delta \iota \acute{\alpha}$		338
PASSAGES OF SCRIPTURE SPECIALLY NOTICED		342

THE BIBLE AND POPULAR THEOLOGY.

CHAPTER I.

MISCELLANEOUS AND UNCERTAIN CHARACTER OF THE SACRED BOOKS.

It cannot be unknown to any reader of these pages that the Bible is not, properly speaking, a single book, but a collection of many different books or writings, in number not less than sixty-six, without counting the Apocrypha. Yet this fact, familiar as it may be, is one of which certain classes of popular writers and preachers are a little too apt to lose sight. It may, therefore, be desirable briefly to mention a few of the particulars which it involves, or which stand in immediate connection with it.

The Biblical writings, comprising so considerable a number of different documents, come down to us from almost as many distinct points or periods of time, in the long interval of a thousand years and more which separates the earliest of them from the latest. They are, moreover, in great part, compositions of unknown authorship. In other words, their writers, in a majority of the cases, are not known to us even by name; and we have usually little or no knowledge, as to the sources of their information, when they give us various statements which must have been derived, in some way, from others.

As the books now stand, the oldest of them is most probably to be found among the Minor Prophets; Joel, Amos and Hosea having lived in or towards the ninth century before Christ. Some of the Psalms are doubtless still older than this; being, there is sufficient reason to believe, from the pen of King David, "the sweet Psalmist of Israel," who lived in the eleventh century B.C. Others are comparatively modern, and bear upon them traces of the times of the Captivity, or even of a still later age.* The book of Genesis and some other historical books are believed to contain sections, that is, incorporated materials, of a higher antiquity still. Nothing certain, however, is known as to the compiler of the former book. Nor can it be shewn, by any evidence at all adequate to the case, that the Pentateuch comes down to us from Moses, although it may very probably contain laws and documents from his time, and possibly even from his hand.† There is no reliable information respecting the origin of the other historical books, from Joshua to the Chronicles; while yet certain internal marks, in statement or in language, are held to be sufficient to determine the century, if not the king's reign, in which they may have been composed, or, as in some cases we must say, put together from older materials. Job and the Proverbs, Ecclesiastes and Solomon's Song, are in much the same position. The exact age of each, and the author or collector, are alike undeterminable; in other words, they are largely

---

* A few of the Psalms are very probably Maccabæan, though this is not universally allowed.

† "It is certain that the books of Chronicles were thus compiled [*i.e.* from more ancient documents], and probably most of the Historical books. Many scholars have also held that Moses made use of the primitive records of the House of Abraham in composing Genesis. The Book of Psalms too, though not a compilation, is a collection of national poetry from the time of Israel's greatest glory down to the return of the exiles from Babylon."—Dr. Payne Smith, *Prophecy a Preparation for Christ* (Bampton Lectures, 1869), p. 2.

matters of speculation, conclusive evidence bearing on these inquiries being no longer within our reach.

The age of Isaiah and of the principal prophetical books is much less a matter of question, with the exception of the book of Daniel,—which, nevertheless, there is good reason to believe belongs, not to the time in which the ancient person of that name lived, as given at the commencement of the book, but rather to that of the Maccabees, the second century B.C.*

On the composite character of one or two of the books of the prophets, it is not necessary here to dwell in detail. It may, however, be noted that the book of Isaiah consists of at least two principal parts—the earlier and authentic † part, from the pen of the prophet so named; and the later, or non-authentic, extending from chapter xl. to the end of the book. The former (which now contains also a few non authentic passages‡) belongs to the last decades of the eighth century B.C.; the latter, by an unknown author, who is conveniently termed the *later Isaiah*, was written about two hundred years afterwards, and bears many clear traces of the period of the Babylonian captivity. The book of Zechariah is probably the work of that prophet only in its first eight chapters, the rest being of older date, and the work of not less than two unknown writers. These conclusions, it will be found, are among the surest results of modern sacred criticism. In this rapid summary, it is only results which can be stated, and that in the briefest form. The reader is referred for the needful investigation to the works of modern authorities, the most impor-

---

* See Deprez's *Daniel, or the Apocalypse of the O. T.*—1865; and, on the other side, Dr. Pusey's *Daniel the Prophet.*—1864.

† *Authentic*, that is, from the hand of the person whose name it bears—often confounded with *genuine*, which properly means unmixed, or uncorrupted with matter from other sources, not readily or certainly separable.

‡ E.g., xiii. xiv., also xxiv.-xxvii.

taut of whom, English and German, will be found abundantly to warrant the statements just made.*

In the case of the New Testament, the dates of the larger Epistles of St. Paul, including that to the Galatians, are determinable within a few years, and their authorship is not questioned. Other books are less certain, though nearly the whole of the New Testament belongs, without doubt, to the first century, A.D. If there be an exception to this, the one important instance of it is the Fourth Gospel, the authorship of which is by no means to be considered as determinately and finally assigned to the Apostle John. The tendency of modern criticism has been increasingly to question or to deny such an origin, which is, however, accepted and defended by many excellent authorities. If the Gospel be attributed to that Apostle, its composition can hardly be thought to have been earlier than about the last decade of the first century, or the last but one.

The question of age is, on the whole, of less importance than that of authorship—though, indeed, the two points are sometimes very closely connected. In comparatively few instances, out of the whole number of Biblical writings, is there either any sufficient external evidence as to origin, or any claim or affirmation as to their respective authors, made in the works themselves. This statement is largely true even of New Testament books, as for example the first three Gospels; which, as is well known to theological students, cannot, by means of any positive internal evidence, be connected with the authors whose names are now upon them, and to whom they are assigned by the ecclesiastical Fathers who mention them. Such internal evidence as there is sometimes bears, indeed, against the statement of those writers. For instance, that Mark's Gospel is the substance of the preach-

* See in particular Dr. S. Davidson's learned and elaborate *Introductions* to the Old and New Testaments.

ing of Peter, written down by the Evangelist: how is this reconcilable with the verbal correspondences between St. Mark and the other two Synoptics? Again, the statement that Matthew wrote his Gospel in the Hebrew (Syro-Chaldaic) language: whereas our present Matthew is an original, not a translation, and is in very numerous passages verbally coincident with the other Synoptics. Some of the minor epistles of St. Paul are extremely doubtful, or almost certainly not from the pen of the great Apostle, according to the judgment of the most competent and free-minded modern investigators. No one can tell us who wrote the Epistle to the Hebrews;* or the Second Epistle of Peter; or the Second and Third of John. The larger number of the New Testament writings may, in short, be said to be of doubtful or unknown authorship.

And the same statement holds even more decidedly of the older Scriptures. For, beginning with Genesis, and going on through the list of books till we come to Isaiah, there is no reasonable certainty on the point of authorship, with the exception only of some of the Psalms, and of the books of Ezra and Nehemiah. In the prophets we tread upon firmer ground. In their case there is usually no good reason for rejecting the statement as to authorship made, or implied, in the book itself.†
In most cases, at the same time, all that we know of a sacred writer is extremely little; being often limited to his name, and the reigns of the kings under whom he lived. This is the case, for example, with several of the Minor Prophets—as Amos, Hosea, Joel, Micah.

It belongs to our present subject to take notice of another fact

---

* Dr. Liddon says of this Epistle, quite arbitrarily, that it was "written either by St. Paul himself, or by St. Luke under his direction."—B. L., p. 281, Note. There is no adequate evidence for any such statement. See *infra*, Chap. XXIV.

† This is not always true of some minor sections of a book, as Isaiah xiii. 1-xiv. 27, where the inscription has probably been added by some collector. So with the inscriptions of various Psalms attributed to David, as acknowledged on all hands.

of some importance. This is, that no reliable information remains to us as to the principle on which the books of the Old Testament were selected and put together, so as to form the more considerable portion of our existing Bible;—in other words, we do not really know on what principle the Old Testament Canon was formed. Nor have we any better knowledge as to the men by whose judgment the collection was made, although various conjectures on this point may easily be formed. In all probability, the whole was in great measure the growth or accumulation of successive ages, without much design on the part of any person concerned. For anything that appears, no definite principle of selection was followed; except only that all ancient documents relating, or thought to relate, to the national history and religion were preserved, especially those which, when put together, seemed to form a connected historical whole. These, in the course of time, would be accounted sacred, either because of their antiquity, or because written, or believed to have been written, by holy men of old, and in the ancient language of the great lawgivers, heroes and prophets of the nation;—a language, which began after the captivity (B.C. 530) to fall into disuse, and to be superseded by the mixed dialects of later times.

To an early collection, probably made on the return from Babylon, or then already existing,* and comprising books of history, law and prophecy, which had descended from olden times, there would for various reasons, at a later period, be added writings composed by priests and others in the ancient language, such as Chronicles, Nehemiah, Daniel, various Psalms, and some of the later Prophets. Thus the Old Testament comes before us, not as being a collection of writings preserved because they had been well ascertained by duly qualified judges to be "inspired,"— in any modern sense of this word,—while others not so inspired were rejected and left to perish; but simply as being the whole of

* See Nehemiah viii. xiii.

the remaining literature of the nation, written in their ancient language,* the whole that was in existence, so far as we know, when the collection was finally closed. If such were the principle on which the books were preserved, or the great reason for their preservation, it certainly goes far to account for the miscellaneous and, in parts, fragmentary character of the collection,—although it gives but little support to the extraordinary claims in behalf of the Bible occasionally put forth by various modern writers.† Supposing that the book of Daniel and the latest Psalms were not written until the time of the Maccabees, the addition of these compositions to the ancient collection may, perhaps, be accounted for by the intense religious and patriotic feelings of that period. Writings in the Hebrew language, as well as in harmony with such feelings, and giving them a fitting expression, might well be thought worthy of being themselves included along with the older and more sacred books—an honour, it is known, which was not refused by editors, perhaps by translators, of the Septuagint to books which we now consider only apocryphal.

The New Testament writings were preserved on their own special grounds. That part of the Bible comprises what was believed to be apostolic, or from apostolic men, and to be, at the same time, in harmony with the catholic faith of the church, as this was developing itself in the second and third centuries.‡

---

* The portion in Chaldee found in Ezra and in Daniel is hardly an exception to this statement, special causes, in both cases, accounting for the use of the Chaldee.

† Some curious examples may be seen in the Introductory Remarks to Colenso's *Pentateuch*, Part I., and in the Preface to Part II.

‡ These statements may be compared with the article on the Canon in Dr. W. Smith's Dictionary of the Bible. The learned writer of that article observes, "The history of the Canon of the N. T. presents a remarkable analogy to that of the Canon of the O. T. The beginnings of both Canons are obscure, from the circumstances under which they arose; both grew silently under the guidance of an inward instinct rather than by the force of external authority; . . . . . . both gained definiteness in times of persecution."—Article *Canon*, p. 261.

CHAPTER II.

UNITY AND CONTINUITY OF SCRIPTURE—IN WHAT SENSE ADMISSIBLE.

In the midst of the uncertainty, or the absolute ignorance, which thus exists respecting the biblical authors,—remembering also the vast space of time over which the dates of their writings lie scattered, as well as the marked differences in the contents and tone of the books,—we are scarcely prepared for certain statements which have recently been made concerning them, by writers of very eminent name. We are told that an "organic unity" pervades the Bible from one end to the other. "Beneath the differences of style, of language, and of method," writes Dr. Liddon, "which appear so entirely to absorb the attention of a merely literary observer, a deeper insight will discover in Scripture such manifest unity of drift and purpose, both moral and intellectual, as to imply the continuous action of a single mind." The same thing is affirmed by another distinguished person: "The volume of God's word is stamped with the same continuous unity of purpose, as that which marks the volume of God's works."*

The exact meaning intended by these expressions will appear in the next chapter. The general idea which they convey is not a new one. At the same time it is, within certain limits, an interesting and suggestive idea, by no means devoid of truth. We propose, therefore, briefly to notice, first, the sense in which

---

* Liddon, *Bampton Lectures*, p. 44; Lord Hatherley, *Continuity of Scripture*, p. xiii. A more recent Bampton Lecturer writes thus:—"St. Paul affirms the prophetic character of the whole of the Old Testament Scriptures. All these writings combine, and were intended to combine, into a concordant body of teaching, given to man to set before him one and the same great truth."—Dr. Payne Smith, *Prophecy a Preparation for Christ*, p. 24. The remark is made in reference to Romans xv. 4, which obviously does not contain any such meaning.

the words just cited may reasonably be held to be correct; and, secondly, that other and inadmissible sense put upon them in the works from which we have taken them.

That a certain Unity, and therefore Continuity, are traceable in the Scriptures, is a proposition which probably no one who has considered the subject will deny. In the first place, there is an indisputable historical *nexus*, running through the Old Testament, from the beginning to the close of the historical books. Commencing with the creation of the world, that portion of the Bible relates the origin and multiplication of mankind, the call of Abraham, the increase of the Jewish people, their deliverance from Egypt, and their settlement in the land of Canaan. It proceeds from this point, with details which extend through many centuries, giving us a rapid outline, perfectly reliable in its main features, of the foundation of the Hebrew monarchy, the division of the nation into two kingdoms, and the parallel histories of these until the destruction of both, terminating in the Babylonian captivity of Judah. To this, again, follows the restoration of the captive people to their own land, with the re-establishment of their religion and of the temple worship on Mount Zion.

Throughout the older Scriptures, there is thus an evident historical continuity fairly consistent in its different parts. The historical books now in our hands may, in fact, be considered to have been arranged as they are, with a distinct regard, on the part of the collectors, to such a continuity.* It may even be, as we have formerly noticed, that this was the great consideration which secured the preservation of a large proportion of the older Scriptures,—the consideration, namely, that the books of the collection, as we have it, form in effect a continuous narrative;

---

* In the Hebrew text, the prophets (except Daniel) and the poetical books intervene between 2 Kings and the later historical books, Ezra, Nehemiah, Chronicles—Daniel, Ruth and Esther being included with the latter.

many of the prophetic writings serving, again, to illustrate or to confirm the historical representations given in the other books.

And there is a continuity of the same kind,—not always harmonious, however,—in the New Testament; comprising, as this does, the Evangelical narratives of the life of Christ, followed by the account of the foundation of the primitive church, and of the labours of some of the chief apostles; the whole being illustrated and confirmed in this case too, by a series of related documents, in the form of the Epistles.

Again, it cannot fail to be observed that throughout the Old Testament, in nearly all its parts, as throughout the New also, the conception of One God, Jehovah, as the central power and providence of the world, and the especial protector of Israel, is almost everywhere prominent. Thus the Hebrew Scriptures are strongly monotheistic, although such was by no means always the case with the people whose history they preserve. The books deliver, in effect, a consistent and faithful testimony, varied in form, but continuous in spirit, against the idolatrous beliefs of the heathen world; and they have, without doubt, been largely the means through which has been handed down to our times the deep-rooted faith in the One God which now exists throughout Christendom.

Moreover, that He, Jehovah, is a personal Being, of might and wisdom unspeakable, is constantly either taken for granted and implied, or more expressly declared. The same is true in regard to His moral attributes; He is a God of righteousness; One who, as the people are often reminded by their prophets, is not to be propitiated by sacrifices, or other forms of ceremonial worship, but who "desireth truth in the inward parts," and requires from His people a character and conduct corresponding to the supreme justice and holiness of His own nature. Intermingled often with less exalted ideas, and unquestionably, in the early periods, with many purely traditionary and mythological details, such thoughts of God as these are yet the resulting impression from a fair perusal of the Old Testament books; and it may justly be said that the qualities of unity and continuity are, in this respect, clearly traceable in them.

There is another important subject in which the same fact is seen, although, in this case, it is more especially in the prophetical books that it is exemplified. The calamities which from time to time overtake the Hebrew nation are not able to shake the confidence of the more devout minds in the protection of Jehovah. Present evil, they are sure, will lead to future good, to the extirpation of idolatry, to purity of worship, to better times of national prosperity and peace, under the rule of some future Prince of righteousness. Hence the Messianic expectations of the Old Testament, which however natural in their origin, were and have been wonderfully powerful in their influence, not only upon the Jews, but upon the Christian world, and in our modern beliefs. And such anticipations are found scattered through the prophetical books, and in various passages of other books, from the beginning;—not, indeed, in the precise form usually alleged,—the expectation of a definite person like Jesus Christ,—but in a simpler form, one more accordant with the national character, and with the cultivation and circumstances of the Hebrews, in the times of the respective writers.* With Jehovah as their supreme Sovereign and Defender, it could not be that they should sink in despair. Even in the worst periods of Assyrian or Babylonian invasion, the comforting thought is present that the season of trouble or of ruin will pass away, and better days hereafter appear. And in the latter Maccabæan times we know how bravely the nation suffered and resisted, and rose up at last triumphant over the most terrible persecutions.

* See, for example, the promises to Abraham, Gen. xvii.; those to Ahaz, Isaiah vii. 13-16; those to captive Israel, Isaiah xl., *seq.*

Such is undoubtedly the prevailing tenor of many books and sections of books; while yet it cannot be said to be uniformly, or everywhere, present. Jeremiah is very constantly despondent. Some of the Psalms are equally so;* and even various passages in the later Isaiah are not without their tone of sadness, almost of hopelessness:—

> "Oh that thou wouldest rend the heavens,
> That thou wouldest come down,
> That the mountains might be shaken at thy presence!
> * * * * * * * *
> "Be not wroth to the uttermost, O Jehovah,
> Neither remember iniquity for ever:
> Behold, see, we beseech thee, thy people are we all.
> Thy holy cities are a wilderness,
> Zion is a wilderness, Jerusalem a desolation;
> Our holy and our beautiful house,
> Where our fathers praised thee,
> Is burned up with fire,
> And all our pleasant things are laid waste.
> Wilt thou restrain thyself at these things, O Jehovah?
> Wilt thou keep silence and afflict us to the uttermost?"
> Isaiah lxiv. 1, 9–12.

The Messianic expectations, in their earlier forms, were, as before noted, somewhat vague, being fixed upon the thought of national prosperity under a wise and victorious prince, rather than upon any conception of a definite religious leader or Saviour for the world at large.† Yet in the course of time, as such expectations remained unfulfilled, the idea of the deliverer and his work would appear to have been greatly modified, and raised in character. Continued or often experienced adversity might well suggest to the people the futility of ambitious hopes, and lead

---

* Psalms lxxix. lxxx.
† Isaiah ix. 1–7, xi. xii.; Dan. vii. 9–14.

them to look for times of spiritual regeneration, rather than of conquest over enemies and political pre-eminence. Probably a change of this kind had taken place, or had been going on, in many minds long before the Christian era. Hence, although the ancient expectations had never been fulfilled, yet they had doubtless served, in a certain sense, to prepare the way for Christ and the Gospel. In this, again, there is clearly a certain "continuity" between the Old Testament and the New. In this sense, too, the proposition is evidently true—true in a higher and better sense than is usually, perhaps, allowed—that Prophecy was a preparation for Christ.*

It is difficult, however, to say to what extent the more elevated idea of the Messiah and his office was entertained in the time of Christ. Both in the Book of Enoch and in the Gospels themselves, many traces occur of the continued influence of the belief in a temporal Messiah.† It cannot, indeed, in any case, be said that special, direct or adequate preparation was made for Jesus Christ, under the influence of the earlier forms of Messianic belief. Those forms did not, in fact, prepare the people for the acceptance of a humble and despised Messiah. This we plainly see by the result. The mass of his countrymen rejected and crucified the "Nazarene." Even the belief held in later years by the personal friends and early disciples of Jesus, appears long to have included very material ideas—ideas which have never been realized—of his return to take vengeance on his enemies and restore the kingdom to Israel.

Yet in another sense the Hebrew religion, almost from its

---

* This, we apprehend, is the only true sense in which such a proposition holds good. The reader may compare, again, Dr. Payne Smith's work before cited, in which he will find the traditional and dogmatic view of the subject duly stated, and ably defended with the usual arguments.

† Matt. xx. 20, *seq.*; Luke xxii. 24; quotations from the *Book of Enoch*, in Colenso on the Pentateuch, Part IV., Appendix.

origin, may clearly be regarded as a providential preparation for him that was to come. Nowhere else in the world, except among the Jews, trained as they were to a monotheistic faith, and at least influenced, if not powerfully controlled, by the high moral and religious spirit of many of their prophets,—nowhere else in the world of that day but among this people, could such a person as Jesus of Nazareth have made his appearance, or taken his stand to appeal to future generations as the great spiritual teacher of mankind. Nowhere else in the world, it may safely be said, could he have obtained an audience, fit though few, of sympathizing minds, or have found even a small band of ardent and devoted disciples ready to follow him, and to lay down their lives for his sake. This fact certainly forms a valid and remarkable set-off against the narrowness and bigotry which led to his destruction. Nor should it be forgotten, as it too often is, by those who are anxious in modern times for the "conversion" of the Jews.

The New Testament differs from the Old, in as much as it possesses a certain character of completion, or fulfilment, as compared with the latter. Yet in this too there is evident unity as well as continuity of plan. There are preparation and growth in the one, resulting in a corresponding development in the other. The idea of the One Jehovah, the Creator and Lord of heaven and earth, is still there; but it is under the better name of Father, the Father in Heaven. We are now, under the influence of great Christian minds, familiarized with the thought of His universal dominion. He is One who is no respecter of persons; and Jew and Gentile alike, by receiving the Christ whom He has sent, may be equally His children. Here is diversity, indeed, from the old exclusive idea, but springing out of this, nevertheless, by a kind of natural growth and completion. So with the morality of the New Testament. It is the old morality, but raised and purified. In Christ and his Apostle Paul, you have its most perfect ex-

'pression; and when separated from the temporary controversies about the claims of the Law, and a few of the Jewish ideas of the time, it is a morality as perfect as the human mind has yet been able to conceive; a morality which few, indeed, of the children of men have been able practically to carry out in its perfectness and unselfishness, in the whole conduct of a life.

In the New Testament, moreover, the better Messianic ideas of the Old are realized and fulfilled—fulfilled in a certain Christian sense, though not in the sense in which they were entertained by the ancient Hebrews among whom they had grown up, or even by the sacred writers by whom they had been put on record. The Messiah, the great leader and prince foreshadowed of old, is not, it is true, the conquering, temporal prince anticipated by them: on the contrary, he is one who has been despised, rejected and put to death by his own people. But this defeat is only for a time; he shall come again, to sit in judgment on his adversaries, to condemn the ungodly, and drive them from his presence into the punishment which is their due; and shall thus introduce the promised reign of prosperity and righteousness.* Those who thus believed had no difficulty in interpreting the great anticipations of the ancient Scriptures. Poetical expressions of confidence in Jehovah, and of deliverance from heathen enemies; a Psalm of joyful congratulation on the accession of Solomon, or some other king; a nuptial ode on the marriage of a Jewish prince; or a passage descriptive of the persecution of a servant of Jehovah in the olden times,† were now understood, after the

---

* Matt. xxiv. 27, seq., xxv. 31, seq.; Mark xiii. ; Luke xii. 36-40, xvii. 24-37. Also passages in the Epistles passim. It is probable that some of the language attributed to Christ on this subject has been influenced and coloured by the expectations of his disciples. Some of his sayings bear a different character, as Matt. xxii. 23; Luke xxii. 24-27. Such passages most probably express the genuine feeling of the Master. Compare John xviii. 36.

† Pss. ii. xlv. lxxii. ; Isaiah liii.

manner of the day, to have their true fulfilment in the fate and fortunes of the Christ and his followers. Here, again, there is a manifest unity; a growth, development, continuity, which correspond in some sense, though not exactly in the sense intended by their authors, to the two expressions before referred to.

On one great subject, however, there is a notable absence of both the qualities in question, when the Old Testament is compared with the New. The doctrine of a Future Life, so prominent in some passages of the latter, is nowhere set forth in the former. It is very questionable whether that doctrine is even alluded to in the Old Testament,* while in some passages it appears to be denied—as, for example, in Ecclesiastes and Job, especially in chapter xiv.† of the latter, taken in connection with other passages of this book. At all events, the doctrine in question is not expressly or clearly taught in the Old Testament; in so much that it may be a matter of great doubt whether the ancient Hebrews had any general belief in it or not. Indeed, we know that a distinguished prelate of the English Church, holding that they had not, founded upon that alleged fact an elaborate argument for the "Divine Legation of Moses." This is one respect, therefore, in which neither unity nor continuity can be affirmed of the Bible; and there are some other points, less fundamental, in regard to which the same admission must be made.

What, for instance, is the unity, or the continuity, between the book of Leviticus and the prevailing tone of the earlier Isaiah, in particular of his first chapter?—between the book of Job and Solomon's Song?—between the Proverbs and the Sermon on the Mount?—the book of Daniel and the Epistle to the Galatians,

---

* A few expressions in the Psalms have been thought to imply this belief, but they are very doubtful. Comp. Ps. xvi. 10, 11; xvii. 15; xxxvi. 8, 9; xlix. 15.
† Job xiv. 7–12, 14, 18–21.

or the First Epistle of St. John?—between the spirit of the various imprecatory Psalms and the spirit of Christ? In what sense can the unity between the books in such cases be said to be "*organic*"—as Dr. Liddon terms it? The only relation existing is simply one of incompatibility, or of marked antagonism; or else, again, there is no sort of describable relation at all, the one book simply standing apart in absolute independence, and ignoring the existence of the other. To how many of the books of Scripture this remark is applicable, we need not stop to inquire; but that the proportion is not small, admits of no reasonable question.

And yet Dr. Liddon does not hesitate to speak with approval of the old and mischievous practice of "quoting from any one book of Scripture in illustration of the mind of any other;" as he does of the belief that Scripture contains "an harmonious and integral body of sacred truth"*—a belief which is so palpably inconsistent with the facts of the case.

In short, the unity and continuity of the Scriptures are very real, very substantial; but they are such, and only such, as we might expect to find in the somewhat fragmentary remains of the entire literature of an ancient people, which is the true character of the Old Testament. There is in the several parts a certain consistency of historical statement, a certain uniformity of feeling, of religious belief, of prophetic anticipation; but, at the same time, there is a great amount of very important diversity. The books of the Pentateuch† may affirm the doctrine of temporal retribution in a very material form; a Book of Job, as its resultant lesson, may deny it. A prophet, like the earlier Isaiah, may anticipate the time when peace and righteousness shall prevail, and the nation shall be supreme over its ancient enemies, Moabites, Philistines, Assyrians, Egyptians;‡ while the later

* B. L., pp. 45, 46.   † For example, Deut. v. vi. xxviii.   ‡ Isaiah xi.

course of the history, as recorded in Scripture itself, may shew us that such anticipations have never been fulfilled. One Psalmist may give utterance to the most terrible imprecations against his own, or his nation's enemies, while a chapter in a Gospel or an Epistle may tell us to love our enemies, to bless them that persecute us, to overcome evil with good. One book may lay a painful stress on the minute observance of outward ceremonies, and the offering of sacrifices, while another, in its predominant strain, may speak with a clear repudiation of such things as utterly unavailing to win the favour of God, or make atonement for a disobedient, idolatrous life. Such diversities are largely seen throughout the books of Scripture—as in truth we ought to expect when we remember their great number and variety, as well as the very dissimilar states of national civilization to which they correspond. Still, with all this rich and various diversity, they present a degree of unity which is sufficiently remarkable, and which has unquestionably helped greatly to render the Bible capable of being, in an eminent degree, the moral and religious educator of a large portion of the human race. This it has undoubtedly been in times past, and this we may venture to anticipate and to hope it will be still, in days to come, in a better and more rational way than the world has yet seen.

CHAPTER III.

UNITY AND CONTINUITY OF SCRIPTURE AS MAINTAINED BY LORD HATHERLEY.

THE degree or kind of "organic unity," and of "continuity," thus found to exist in the Bible, is not, however, that which is meant by Lord Hatherley and Dr. Liddon. This will be sufficiently seen in the course of the present and three following chapters. Our attention is claimed, in the first place, by the careful exposition given in the Preface to the Continuity of Scripture.

There are three forms, we are here told, under which the unity of the Scriptures is seen: The historical unity of subject; the moral unity; the spiritual unity. These three forms, however, under his Lordship's treatment, are really resolvable into *one*, namely, a theological unity. By " historical unity" he does not mean that consistency or continuity of historical and other statements of which we have spoken as actually exemplified in the Scriptures,—but the " Creation, Fall and Restoration of Man."

" The Bible," Lord Hatherley writes, " contains the history of man's creation, his fall, his miserable degradation, consequent on that fall, and his restoration to favour with his Creator, through a sinless Redeemer."* In unfolding for his readers the character of this unity, he naturally sees and interprets everything included in his survey by the light of his own creed; and finds, of course, fresh confirmation for the latter in the prevailing strain of Scriptural statements. Yet few readers, we imagine, will be prepared to follow his Lordship, whose minds are as free as they ought to be from prepossessions similar to his own, even though the path which he takes may appear to be the broad and easy one, and very many may be found upon it. It is not an easy path, in reality, but one of very serious difficulty. Thus, for illustration, there is nothing in Genesis iii. to show that the writer of that passage had any idea of the " Fall," in the usual theological sense of this term. He does not *say*—though Lord Hatherley says it for him†—nor is it anywhere said in the Scriptures, that the Serpent was Satan, or that Satan was in the Serpent, this being only a theological gloss put upon the narrative in later times.

* *Continuity*, pp. xiv. xv.   † *Ibid.*, p. xvi.

Satan does not make his appearance in any of the most ancient books of the Old Testament, as a reader may easily see for himself.* Nor does the writer of Genesis say that all the descendants of Adam and Eve "fell" in their progenitors, that is, became guilty, because of their transgression. Nor, again, is this supposed fall of the human race ever, we believe, so much as alluded to, in the whole course of the Old Testament history, extending over a long interval of many centuries. It is not noticed by the Prophets in the worst periods of national wickedness and idolatry, although, in such times, occasions without number presented themselves, by which the primeval transgression might well have been brought to their minds. It is not mentioned, nor in any way alluded to, throughout all the words of Christ recorded in the Gospels; and the only instances in the Epistles, in which it can be supposed to have been in the mind of the writer, are afforded by two or three obscure expressions † from the pen of St. Paul. That Apostle does not, however, say that all became *guilty* in Adam, but that all became subject to *death* in him, ‡ inheriting from him the mortality which, according to the old Hebrew idea, was the penalty of transgression.

---

* The conception of Satan occurs in three O. T. books, viz., Job (i. ii.), Zech. (iii. 1, 2), 1 Chron. (xxi. 1),—all of comparatively late origin.

† Rom. v. 12–19; 1 Cor. xv. 21, 22; Ephes. ii. 3.

‡ In Rom. v. 15–19, the idea appears to be, that condemnation and death ensued on the transgression of one. The same passed to others, and to all, because all have sinned. So "through the offence of the one" many died, but only by sharing in the mortality introduced,—nothing is said about their sharing in the guilt. The only words which give an apparent support to the latter idea are in v. 19, "were made sinners." The meaning can only be, were *condemned*, treated as if they were sinners, inasmuch as they became subject to death, the consequence of sin.

In Ephes. ii. 3, the Apostle is speaking of actual trespasses and sins; but again says nothing of the imputation of the guilt of others. In their natural state, *i.e.*, as Jews or Gentiles before their conversion to Christianity, all were "children of wrath," liable to punishment, on account of past sins—but these, the Apostle adds, are now forgiven in Christ.

Thus the fundamental idea of the Fall, which lies at the basis of Lord Hatherley's historical unity, affords the very weakest of foundations for the vast and complicated scheme of salvation which is made to stand upon it. At most, it depends on the construction given to a few difficult expressions of the Apostle Paul; and it is certainly nowhere in the Scriptures held up to us as the one greatest fact in the primitive history of man, to which everything else in the Divine plan of restoration bears reference—as the popular theology holds it up.

The "moral unity" is treated in a kindred manner. It would seem to be especially shewn in the fact that, although the design of the Almighty Providence to bring about certain ends usually *fails*, yet this failure is constantly remedied by some later provision.* Man is created that he may be innocent and happy, but he falls from righteousness. "Seth is born that the evil race of Cain may not alone represent the race of man;" yet, nevertheless, in a few hundred years the whole race of man has to be destroyed from the face of the earth, on account of its wickedness. Noah and his family are saved; but here, alas! we soon have "shameful drunkenness" on the part of Noah, "shocking irreverence" on the part of Canaan. Then we have righteous Abraham, guilty of "timid deceit with reference to Sarah;" we have the usual slighting and hardly just estimate of "profane Esau," "Jacob's fraud," David's crime, Solomon's folly; the whole forcibly shewing that there is a constant failure of events and characters to produce the results which they had been intended to bring about. All goes, of course, to exhibit and illustrate the natural helplessness of man, and his need of a supernatural provision for his "salvation" in accordance with orthodox ideas. We wish Lord Hatherley could have added that even the Christian dispensation had been more successful, from his own point of view,

* *Continuity*, pp. xix.-xxii.

than any of the earlier provisions. But, as is well known, popular preaching does not usually admit this. The devil is still the triumphant power in the universe. We have heard this loudly declared by a much esteemed evangelical clergyman, who told his people that even in Christian congregations the larger part belong to Satan. And truly there is ungodliness enough in the world, unbelief in the orthodox doctrines of the Church, idolatry, sin and misery in every direction, enough of these to make us fear that the last state of mankind is quite as bad as the first—even when due allowance is made for all those, comparatively few at most, who may happen to be "saved," or to believe themselves saved, according to the scheme of salvation propounded by Lord Hatherley.

The third species of unity, "the spiritual unity," is of course theological also. It differs from the preceding in being more specific in its doctrinal statements and allusions. "The atoning sacrifice for the guilt of all mankind," is, we are told, "carried through the whole sacred volume, from Genesis to Revelation." So is the doctrine of the Trinity, mysteriously suggested or involved, as it is, in the "Jehovah Elohim,[*] the one yet plural Lord God;" and in some other forms of expression highly significant to orthodox readers,[†] but in which the doctrine of the Trinity was never understood or suspected to exist, by the Jews, either of ancient or of modern times. So that here, again, it might appear as if the whole providential design of God, in the case even of His own chosen people, had been wonderfully frustrated, and what He intended had never been brought to pass!

It is not necessary to our present purpose to enter further into the examination of Lord Hatherley's Preface. Doubtless very

---

[*] A double form rarely met with after Genesis ii.-iii.
[†] Numb. vi. 22-27; Isaiah vi. 3.

many of his readers will entirely sympathize with the devout and earnest spirit in which it is written. But yet, while granting this, it is impossible to lose sight of the grave difficulties of one kind and another which press upon the whole theological scheme set forth, and which are passed over in silence. The learned author, indeed, expressly avoids, almost repudiates, what he terms "the thorny paths of criticism." But, on the other hand, it cannot be supposed possible to reach any result satisfactory to an intelligent mind by taking everything for granted. If, as the poet tells us, "blind unbelief is sure to err," the same may just as truly be said of blind belief; and it contributes little indeed to the support of rational Christian faith, to begin by giving an unquestioning assent to almost every traditional doctrine of the day popularly deemed evangelical.

Into one mode of argument we are especially surprised to find his Lordship so readily gliding. "Assuredly," he observes, "the two Testaments must stand or fall together; assuredly, if the Old Scriptures be devoid in any part of truth, our Lord's testimony to them must (shocking as it is to say so) be untruthful; and if so, then, indeed, the moral world is again a chaos, and the Christian's hope a dream."* Such a saying as this appears to us to be, indeed, "shocking." The writer of the words, perhaps, has not realized to himself what they amount to. But it is plainly this,—if the particular view of the subject taken by him, the writer of this Preface, be not correct, "our Lord's testimony" is "untruthful." This is not an uncommon form of orthodox asseveration. Dr. Liddon offends in the same point more than once. "*Christus, si non Deus, non bonus*,"—thus he summarizes the contents of one of his pages, in which occur these words, "If he (Christ) is not God, he is not a humble or an unselfish man. Nay, he is not even sincere; unless we have recourse to a suppo-

* *Continuity,* p. lx.

sition upon which the most desperate of his modern opponents have not yet ventured, and say with his jealous kinsmen in the early days of his ministry, that he is beside himself."*

Such is the modesty of modern orthodoxy! Either the view which it takes of Christ and his work is the true one, or else the Christian Apostles and Christ himself were little better than deceivers, the Scriptures are without value, and Christianity is an imposition upon the world. We humbly submit that it is not absolutely necessary to accept either of these alternatives. We believe that there exists a far truer *via media*, and this we hope to shew before finishing our present task.

The prefatory exposition of doctrine referred to in these observations is followed by a series of extracts from the Old Testament, set over against certain New Testament passages in which the former are quoted, or alluded to. Nearly every book of the Old Testament, we are reminded, is referred to in the New, by our Lord himself, or by an Evangelist or other writer. "I believe," says Lord Hatherley, "very few persons know how many books of the Old Testament have been stamped with the approval of this really 'high criticism.' For instance, our Lord has not only recognized the whole body of the Old Testament. included by the Jews in the threefold division of ' the Law, the Psalms, and the Prophets,' has not only told us that 'they testify of him,' but has cited or directly referred to passages from every book of the Pentateuch, and has in like manner borne testimony to the following Books:— to the First of Samuel, the two Books of Kings, the Second Book of Chronicles, the Psalms, and to the Prophets Isaiah, Jeremiah, Daniel, Hosea, Joel, Jonah, Micah, Zechariah, and Malachi."†
A similar statement is made in reference to "the writers of the New Testament as distinguished from Christ himself." Thus, "we have only seven Books, out of the thirty-nine constituting the Old

---

* Liddon, B. L., p. 203. † *Continuity*, p. xxxiii.

Testament, which are not referred to in the New." But, moreover, Christ himself, and the New Testament writers, refer to the Old Testament as a *whole;* and hence it is clear, in a word, that a certain "testimony" is "borne by the New Testament to the Old."

These are facts which, we apprehend, only require stating to be admitted by most persons. But yet the conclusion to be drawn from the references to the Old Testament in the New, and in general from the use made of it by the Christian writers, is not very clearly defined by his Lordship. What does the "approval" spoken of amount to?—the "testimony" to the books, what exactly does it attest beyond the fact of their general reception as the sacred books of the Hebrews, perhaps under the name of a particular author, at the time when they were so referred to? Lord Hatherley does not pronounce an explicit judgment on these weighty points. He affirms, however, that "if Christ be Very God, his word must be conclusive on either the authenticity or the value of the writings of the Old Testament."* Doubtless by this proposition the least we can understand is this, that the citation of an Old Testament book by Jesus Christ in the Gospels ought to be regarded as conclusive evidence of authorship and of the "value" of the book, whatever difficulties or impossibilities may lie in the way of admitting the conclusion to which that evidence appears to lead. This position, strange as it is, is doubtless held by many religious persons besides the author of the Continuity; and therefore it will be well, in this connection, to examine, as briefly as may be, the use made of the Old Testament in the New, and how far it bears out the popular ideas on this subject.

* *Continuity,* p. xxxii.

CHAPTER IV.

THE USE OF THE OLD TESTAMENT IN THE NEW.

THERE can be no doubt that the Jews of our Lord's time, as well as their ancestors for many generations, held their sacred books in the greatest reverence. Those books were read in the synagogues, and constituted the chief literary nutriment of the great bulk of the nation. They were to the Jew the depository of almost all knowledge, recording the history of his people, and the wonderful deeds which Jehovah had done for them in times of old. The mind of a devout Hebrew was stored with thoughts and expressions drawn directly from the ancient Scriptures, and the Messianic hopes cherished by the nation were believed to be firmly based upon the words of prophets included within the sacred volume. That volume contained, moreover, the national code, under the sanction of which the religious institutions of the State existed; and no better argument or evidence could be adduced in any doubtful case than the citation of its testimony, the statement of any fact which it might afford, or be supposed to afford, applicable to a point in discussion.

That such value as this was attached to the Old Testament by the Jews of the primitive Christian age, there can be no doubt.* But whether or not they were always *right* in their interpretations, in their ascription of a sacred book to an author, or in their application of the words of ancient prophecy, — this is another question altogether.

It is not to be forgotten that the Apostles and Evangelists, and Christ himself, born and brought up as Jews and among the

---

* The high terms in which Philo speaks of the Old Testament Scriptures may be seen in Gfrörer's *Philo*, capp. 4, 5. The words of Josephus are well known. It is natural, he tells us, to all Jews to adhere to their sacred books, and if it were necessary, even to die for them.

Jewish people, would necessarily share their feelings and opinions in reference to the ancient Scriptures. We have no reason to think that on this subject they had any special knowledge. At least they never *tell* us that they had; and any one who supposes such a thing is bound to give some positive evidence, beyond mere inferences from his own dogmatic theories, or those of ancient Fathers.* It is, indeed, easy to gather from the Evangelical accounts that Jesus Christ, and *à fortiori* his followers, most probably partook of the common views of their countrymen, in this respect. We read of his being a child, and a boy, and living with his parents in Nazareth; and we are told that he "increased in wisdom and in age."† In another Gospel, we read that Jesus himself spoke of the limited nature of his own knowledge. He did not know, he said, of the day of his second coming: "Of that day, and that hour, knoweth no man; no, not the angels which are in heaven, neither the Son, but the Father."‡

Dr. Liddon is naturally very anxious to make it plain that omniscience and ignorance might co-exist at one time in the same person. The problem, it will be found, has not yet received its solution, even at his hands; and it is probably destined to remain, as a test of faith, may we not say, almost as trying to some minds as the Athanasian Creed itself? We need not dwell upon the point, and refer the reader to Dr. Liddon for such alleviation of the difficulty as he has found it possible to offer.§

---

* Compare Liddon, B. L., p. 458, *seq.*, and the quotations there given from various Fathers, who were evidently as much perplexed by the ignorance of Christ in Mark xiii. 32, as Dr. Liddon himself—and no more successful in explaining it, on the orthodox supposition of the two natures.

† Luke ii. 43, 52.

‡ Mark xiii. 32. In this verse, a slight variation in the MSS. ("an angel in heaven") does not materially affect the sense.

§ B. L., pp. 458–472.

There is then, on the face of the Gospels, no reason to suppose that even the Lord Jesus Christ had any special enlightenment on the subject of the authenticity and genuineness of the sacred books. It is certain that he never *informs* us that he had; and it only tends to involve his character and authority in the gravest doubt, to set up for him claims of this kind, which he does not make for himself, and which cannot be substantiated. We may reasonably conclude, therefore, that Christ and his disciples would regard and use and speak of the sacred books exactly after the manner of other Jews of their own time.

In those days, it is hardly necessary to say, critical science was little known. A book, especially a sacred book of ancient descent, was usually, so far as we know, received without inquiry under the name of its reputed author. We believe that there is no instance in which the claims, or reputed claims, of any Old Testament writer are called in question, or discussed on critical grounds, by any authority of the time of Christ, or in previous centuries. A book of Moses, a book of Samuel, a book of Isaiah, would be each read and circulated, and attributed to the supposed author without difficulty, even though it might contain matter which he could not have written.* Critical investigation in reference to such points was simply not thought of.

Hence it is not to be doubted that most of the Old Testament books are referred to in the New Testament exactly as Lord Hatherley has stated, and with precisely the same ready acquiescence as to their authorship which is exemplified by his Lordship himself. But how far this acceptance of the older Scriptures by the personages and writers of the Christian books should be admitted, or can be admitted, by us of modern times, as a substitute for critical inquiry on our part, as a valid reason for shutting our eyes to every literary, or historical, or philological

* Comp. for example, Gen. xii. 6; xiii. 7; Deut. xxxiv.

difficulty involved in a given case, and for putting precisely the same meaning upon cited passages which the Christian writers put upon them,—this may still be a very weighty question. Certainly the anxiety usually shewn by orthodox writers to prove, by considerations of every available kind, that the Pentateuch, for example, or the whole Book of Isaiah, is rightly attributed each to the author whose name is now upon it, allows us easily to see that even the most ready faith is not as yet quite satisfied to believe, on such matters, without some show of reasonable evidence.

Let us take, in illustration of these statements, one of the simplest forms in which the case occurs, that presented by the Psalms. There is reason to believe that this book was popularly received, in our Lord's time, as mainly a book of King David. Many of the Psalms are ascribed to him by name in the book itself; and in the New Testament the collection is sometimes referred to under his name, whether he be spoken of in the original as the author of the Psalm quoted or not.* The inscriptions, or titles, of the Psalms are known to be ancient. It is also probable that they were received in the early Christian times as of equal authority with the rest of the Psalms.

It is well known, however, to the student that it is not always possible to admit the authorship of the Psalms as given in the titles. This is fully admitted by the best modern critics, from De Wette and Ewald downwards, and indeed upwards too; and so the reader will find it substantially stated, even by the very conservative writer referred to in the note.† Thus, for example,

* See Mark xii. 36 (Luke xx. 42); Rom. iv. 6; xi. 9: also Acts i. 16; ii. 25, compared with Ps. xvi. 8; iv. 25, compared with Ps. ii. 1; Heb. iv. 7, compared with Ps. xcv. 7, 8.

† Article *Psalms*, in Dr. W. Smith's Dictionary of the Bible, pp. 954, 955. It may be observed that the writer of this article contradicts himself, in first declaring that the superscriptions are "fully trustworthy," and then telling us that many

Psalms xiv. xxv. li. lxix.* contain references to the captivity; yet the titles attribute them to David. Psalm cxxxix. is also called "a Psalm of David." It belongs to a much later period, containing distinct traces of this in the Chaldaic character of the language. Similar remarks apply to many others in the collection, besides those we have now specified.

Before passing on to speak more in detail of the use made in the New Testament of various Old Testament expressions, we may observe that the ancient Scriptures are, without doubt, occasionally quoted and referred to by way of accommodation † simply. Lord Hatherley, it is true, objects in advance to this idea. "Accommodation or adoption," he observes, "has been *talked of*, as the explanation of our Lord's citations from the Old Testament."‡ And it is evident that he dismisses such a suggestion as hardly worthy of consideration. Let us, nevertheless, endeavour to ascertain a little more exactly how this matter stands, and how far an adequate explanation arises from a reasonable admission of what is thus so summarily rejected.

There is a very remarkable series of references to the Old Testament,—forming, in fact, a kind of clue to the difficulties of the question, and well enabling us to see the use made of the older Scriptures by early Christian writers. This testing passage consists of no less than three chapters in the Epistle to the

---

Psalms with Davidic titles "were written by Hezekiah, by Josiah, by Zerubbabel, or others of David's posterity;" and even saying that many such Psalms are shewn to be of late origin by their Chaldaisms and other indications. "They cannot, therefore," he adds, "be David's own." Then, surely, their superscriptions are *not* "fully trustworthy."

* It has been suggested that the above and other Psalms were altered at, or after, the captivity, to adapt them in use to the altered condition of the people. Such a supposition is uncritical, and in no way necessary except to support a theory.

† By *accommodation* is here, in general terms, denoted the application of a passage in the N. T. to express some sense not intended by the original writer.

‡ *Continuity*, p. xxxiv.

Romans.* It is not necessary for the present purpose to enter minutely into all the cases here presented. The following remarks apply more especially to some of those which occur in the tenth chapter, but might be extended equally to the rest.

Christ, then, the apostle writes, "is the end of the law for righteousness to every one that believeth; for Moses (he goes on to say) describeth the righteousness which is of the law, that *the man that hath done them shall live by them*. But the righteousness which is of faith speaketh on this wise, *Say not in thine heart, Who shall ascend into heaven?* (that is, to bring Christ down): or *Who shall descend into the deep?* (that is, to bring up Christ from the dead); but what saith it?—*The word is nigh thee, in thy mouth and in thy heart*: that is, the word of faith which we preach." †

The sentences here given in italics are quoted partly from Deuteronomy and partly from Leviticus.‡ They are introduced by the Apostle exactly as if he intended to convey the idea that in their original design they were written with a reference to Christ, and the righteousness which is by faith in him, as contrasted with that which came by the law. The words are even explained, in two instances, as expressly referring to Christ (" that is, to bring Christ down;" or again, " to bring Christ up from the dead"). Probably, however, no one can think, or will allege, that St. Paul thus writes in any other sense than by way of *accommodation*, taking words *as if* they originally referred to Christ, although they can have had no such original intention. No one, probably, will go so far as to say that the Apostle himself believed that the authors of Deuteronomy and Leviticus had Jesus Christ in their view, in the words quoted from their respective books. Or will Lord Hatherley go to this length?

Several other quotations occur in the same chapter, from Isaiah

* Rom. ix. x. xi. † Rom. x. 4-8. ‡ Deut. xxx. 11-14; Lev. xviii. 5.

and from other books of the Old Testament. An examination of these yields the same result: and shews that the words cannot possibly have been originally spoken of Christ, or the Gospel, but that they are *accommodated* to them, *adopted* by the Apostle in his own sense, according to the well-understood custom of his countrymen at the time.

The most remarkable of all these applications is, perhaps, that of the words from Psalm xix. 4. Have not the Jews heard the Gospel message? the Apostle asks: Yes, verily, they have heard; for many preachers have spoken to them; and he confirms his assertion by quoting words of the Psalm which speak not of any human messenger at all, not of persons announcing to others Gospel tidings, or tidings of any kind, but of the *heavens* which declare the glory of God, and the firmament which sheweth the work of his hands. *Their* sound, said the Psalmist, is gone out into all the earth, and their words to the end of the world; and the Apostle takes up this declaration, and employs it to express his own immediate idea, to the effect that the Gospel has been made known by preaching throughout the world. What can more plainly prove that, in such cases, we have simply an "accommodation," an adaptation of Old Testament words to the purpose immediately in hand?—that the language of ancient Scripture was sometimes applied by the Christian writers to events and circumstances of their own time, exactly as if it had been so intended to be taken by the original writer; while yet it is impossible to suppose that any such intention can really have been in his mind?

It clearly follows from these facts, that the quotation of a passage, or the application of it to a Christian purpose, is far from being a conclusive proof of the primary intention of the words so employed. This must be ascertained by an examination of the passage itself; its genuine meaning and value being determined by a due regard to its original context. This position will become more abundantly sure as we proceed.

On looking into the Continuity of Scripture for some further illustration of these remarks, we come at once to a passage taken from the prophet Isaiah, and quoted in St. Luke iv. 16-21. In this place we read that Jesus went into a synagogue and began to read in the Book of Isaiah, the words which are found at the beginning of chapter lxi. of that prophet.* At the close of his reading, we are told, " he began to say unto them, This day is this Scripture fulfilled in your ears." On referring to the book from which the words are taken, it is found that they do not correspond to the Hebrew. The passage is probably from the Septuagint. It contains also words from Isaiah lviii.,† incorporated with those from lxi., while omitting some words of the latter;—facts which afford a very significant illustration of the freedom with which these quotations are sometimes made.

A slight examination of the original passage is sufficient to satisfy the reader that the prophet is speaking, not of a personage like Jesus Christ, who was to arise and become prominent in the world five or six centuries, more or less, after his own time, but of the deliverance of his people, then captive before his eyes, or at some time to be so. They shall return home, he says, to rebuild the waste places of Jerusalem, and restore the worship of Jehovah on Mount Zion. The prophet speaks of himself as appointed to announce these tidings to his captive friends and companions, " to proclaim liberty to the captive, and the opening of the prison to them that are bound." These words were, however, *applicable*, in a certain degree, to the spiritual deliverance wrought by Christ, and they are accordingly taken up and applied

---

* *Continuity*, p. 17.

† The words, "to set at liberty them that are bruised"—from Isaiah lviii. 6, in the Septuagint version.

by him to himself, as the suitable medium by which to *express* the leading purpose and spirit of his own ministry. Is it possible, under such circumstances, to suppose that our Lord intended to claim the words as referring to himself in the original and conscious intention of the prophet who wrote them? On the contrary, it appears to be almost too evident to admit of an argument, that we have here a true instance of the "accommodation" or "adoption" which Lord Hatherley rejects, and that the Reader of the words in the synagogue simply applied them in the usual popular way to the particular case and circumstances then existing —as occurs in another Evangelist, in connection with different words.*

Many additional instances of the same kind readily present themselves, and some of these shall be duly considered in the two succeeding Chapters.

CHAPTER V.

MESSIANIC PASSAGES:

ISAIAH VII. 14; LII. 13—LIII. 12; XI.; IX. 6.

In applying the term *accommodation* to the use of Old Testament language noticed in the preceding Chapter, it is not, as before intimated, intended to affirm that no case occurs in which a passage is conceived by the Christian quoter of it to have been originally written with reference to Christ, or the events and circumstances of his life. Such cases, no doubt, do present themselves; and this Christian conception and use it is which is urged upon us as the all-sufficient proof of the original meaning and purpose of each given passage. In opposition to this, how-

* Mark xii. 10, 11.

ever, it is alleged that the real and primary import and intention are to be gathered from the cited words, as these lie before us in their original connection; and that their use by a Christian writer or speaker, their adoption or accommodation to express Christian ideas, should not be held to afford conclusive evidence as to their original signification;—only exemplifying, in fact, as thus used, the way in which the early Christians were accustomed to read and apply their ancient Scriptures.

This position we now propose further to illustrate by the example of several passages in the Book of Isaiah usually considered as Messianic, and adduced as such by Dr. Liddon. To these, for the sake of completeness, shall, in the next Chapter, be added a few instances from the Minor Prophets.

Isaiah vii. 14.—This verse is quoted by the first Evangelist (i. 23), in terms taken nearly *verbatim* from the Septuagint Greek, which differs, though not materially, from the Hebrew. We need not dwell upon this difference, further than to make one remark. It is not an uncommon case, and it shews us that New Testament writers who thus make use of the Septuagint, even when it differs from the Hebrew, and even when they might have quoted the Hebrew (as doubtless several of them, especially St. Paul, could have done), cannot have held those high notions of the "inspiration" of the words of Scripture which are often put forth in our days.* If they had done so, how could they have left the original text and adopted an imperfect, sometimes corrupted, version, as they occasionally do? Or are we to understand that they were ignorant of any difference between the Septuagint and the Hebrew original? If so, what is the value of the "high criticism" so strongly insisted on, as we have seen, by Lord Hatherley?

In the English New Testament (Matt. i. 23) the words of the

* By such writers, for example, as Dr. J. Baylee, *Verbal Inspiration* (1870).

prophet are quoted thus:—" Behold a virgin shall be with child, and shall bring forth a Son, and they shall call his name Emmanuel, which being interpreted is God with us."* In this rendering, the definite article has been neglected by our translators. In the Greek, and in both the Hebrew and the Septuagint, the words are "*the* virgin." In regard to the latter term, it is by no means clear that the original is rightly rendered by the Septuagint παρθένος, and the English "virgin." The idea properly belonging to these words is not in the root meaning of the Hebrew word, and it is at least doubtful whether there is an instance in the Old Testament in which that word ought to be rendered as in the English version. The Hebrew, it is well known, has another term to which the strict sense does belong.†

It thus appears, that the rendering might properly be, "the young woman," or even "the young wife," with the article, as it stands not only in the Hebrew and Septuagint, but in the New Testament text also, indicating that a definite person was within the prophet's view at the moment. The verb following is (in the Hebrew) in the *past* tense; or, rather, what is rendered "shall be with child," may better be regarded as an *adjective*, denoting a present condition, no verbal tense occurring in the original.‡ So that even a future, or predictive, meaning of *these* words in their original connection is excluded; the future import of the prophet's declaration being first indicated, not in this verse, but in the two following verses (15, 16), which speak of an interval between the birth of the child in the time when he shall be old

---

* Most probably the verb should be understood, "God *is* with us," as the word Emmanuel is rendered, Isaiah viii. 10. Comp. Ezek. xlviii. 35. It is scarcely necessary to add that in such expressions no literal presence (incarnation) of Jehovah can have been intended by the prophet, or understood by his readers.

† See Appendix, note A.

‡ As in Gen. xvi. 11, "Thou art with child," which, with the following words, is parallel in form to this verse of Isaiah.

enough to know to refuse the evil and choose the good. The state of the young wife is a something already existing, and it is to result hereafter in that which shall be a *sign* of the coming deliverance.

The meaning of the words of Isaiah may, therefore, be presented thus:—"Behold the young wife *is* with child, and she shall bear a Son, and call his name Immanuel." The sign referred to is to consist in the presence of the child with a significant name; the promise of deliverance lies in the statement that before this child, yet to be born, has reached a certain age, the land shall be delivered from its invading enemies.

It is evident, again, that this verse and its context belong solely to the time and circumstances of King Ahaz. There is nothing whatever to shew that the writer was looking forward to a time which lay many hundred years away from him in the distant future, or that he had any hidden meaning in his mind which belonged specially to that remote and unknown period. Everything indicates that he is wholly and exclusively in the present, or at least in what immediately relates to the present and is shortly to come to pass.* The whole chapter, in short, from beginning to end relates and is suited simply to Ahaz and his people, their feelings, their hopes and apprehensions.

But how, then, does it come to appear as it does in the New Testament? Evidently, in accordance with the usage of the Christian writers; according to which expressions were applied to events and persons of the later times, just as if they had been originally written with reference to them. "All this was done,"

---

* This is allowed by the writer of the article *Isaiah* in Dr. W. Smith's Dictionary of the Bible. He, however, persisting in applying the verse to the birth of Christ, thinks that the prophet may "have misconceived the relations of time in regard to events." Art. *Isaiah*, p. 880. That is to say, the prophet made a mistake of several hundred years in regard to the birth of the Messiah! Of what value, then, was the prophecy to Ahaz or his people?

says the Evangelist. "that it might be fulfilled which was spoken of the Lord by the prophet." The name Immanuel (God is with us) might also be appropriately transferred to Christ—to whom, however, it is never afterwards applied—in whose birth the presence of God with His people was so especially manifested.* But there is nothing to shew that either child *is* or *was* what he is *named;* that his nature mysteriously corresponded to the appellation put upon him for a special purpose. We may, therefore, reasonably understand the quotation as a simple accommodation of the prophet's words to the birth of Christ, according to the usual manner of the New Testament writers.

The presence of a secondary meaning in the words of Isaiah, is assumed by Bishop Lowth, as by many other expositors; but it is a pure assumption. There is absolutely nothing in the context to suggest such an idea, or to render it in any way tenable. Nor is it needed for the full exposition of the prophet's words. What object could he have in announcing so obscurely, to the trembling king and his subjects, that at some indefinite point of time in the remote future a spiritual prince would be born in Israel? What present comfort or encouragement could this afford to men terrified at the speedy approach of hostile armies? Or shall we say, with the writer of the article just referred to, that Isaiah's prophecy of the Messiah was really full of comfort to all who heard it, even though the prophet made a mistake of seven hundred years in regard to the time of the expected advent?

Will it be said, however, in defence of the idea of a double sense, that the deeper secondary meaning may have been intended, not so much for the people of the time of Ahaz, as for later and Christian times, and to assist in establishing the Messianic claims of Jesus of Nazareth? In the way of such an explanation the difficulty is obvious and insuperable. The words do not answer

* Comp. Luke i. 32; ii. 29-32; John iii. 2; 2 Cor. v. 19.

such a purpose. The very discussion of the subject in these pages shews that they do not; that their meaning and intention is left in uncertainty, to say the least—uncertainty, however, only inasmuch as they are supposed to have such a purpose; to the assumption or admission of which the mere fact of uncertainty is altogether fatal. It is needless to add, that Jewish writers of character and learning acknowledge no such force or utility in the words, but reject the common Christian use of them as wholly unwarranted.*

A second passage repeatedly appealed to by Lord Hatherley as "attested" by Christ himself, as well as by the Evangelists and Apostles, is Isaiah liii., or, more exactly, the entire section, Isaiah lii. 13-liii. 12. These verses are usually cited as affording incontestable proof that the prophet looked forward to the days of the suffering Christ, and described his fortunes in language wonderfully corresponding to what actually took place. The section is thus referred to for example, by Archbishop Thomson, in his Essay on the Death of Christ,† and Dr. Liddon is very clear on the same point. "Messiah," he observes, "especially designated as 'the Servant of God,' is the central figure in the prophecies of Isaiah." He at once appropriates the passage as a prophecy of the sufferings and death of Christ.‡

It must be acknowledged that there is a singular degree of correspondence between the prophetic statements and the narratives which have come down to us of the last scenes of our Lord's personal history. There is a remarkable general correspondence. The impression left upon the mind, in reading the prophet, is, in short, strongly favourable to the usual acceptation of his words.

---

* Dr. H. Adler's *Course of Sermons* preached in the Bayswater Synagogue (1869), p. 16, *seq.*—Comp. Liddon, B. L., p. 88, note.

† Aids to Faith, 4th edition, p. 325.   ‡ Liddon, B. L., pp. 85, 86.

It is true, however, that, when we come to examine details, that impression is disturbed. As in liii. 10, what is meant by the words, "He shall prolong his days"?—by the words of verse 9, "He made his grave with the wicked"?—by his "dividing the spoil with the strong,"—if these expressions be applied to the crucified Christ? Still, in spite of several obscure or ambiguous phrases like these, we are left with the feeling that those who have been accustomed to accept the passage as a prophecy of the closing incidents of our Lord's career, have not been without a great appearance of reason in so doing.

Several passages in the New Testament,* as duly cited by Lord Hatherley, appear to justify this application of the words, and clearly shew us that they were thus applied in the early Christian times. One of these passages is Mark xv. 28. We speak first of this, because, in the somewhat vague and general form of the reference, it appears to afford a true expression of the idea under which this and similar quotations from the Old Testament are often made. The Evangelist's words are these: "And the Scripture was fulfilled which saith, And he was numbered with the transgressors."† The Scripture is to be found in Isaiah liii. 12. In this quotation, there is nothing to indicate the Evangelist's belief that the words were originally written with a prophetic foresight of the incidents to which he applies them, and in which he sees that they were "fulfilled." The same remark may perhaps be applied to the use of the words in the third Gospel, and even to the reference made to them in Matthew.

* Matt. viii. 17; Mark xv. 28; Luke xxii. 37; John xii. 38-41; Acts viii. 26-35; 1 Pet. ii. 24.

† It is to be noted that the verse of Mark is omitted by Tischendorf; but it is unquestionably ancient, and serves equally well to illustrate the Christian application of O. T. language. A very similar use is made of the same O. T. passage in Luke xxii. 37, and here by our Lord himself.

Some of the other New Testament references, however, probably imply more, and convey the idea that the prophecy was written with a special view to the suffering Messiah. If this be intended, as in the passage in the Acts, and in that in St. John, it is so, we may, nevertheless, reasonably hold, in accordance with the usual practice of accommodation. The words were seen to be *applicable* to certain incidents; they were therefore "fulfilled" in these: they were even written "that they might be fulfilled." Such appears to have been the train of thought; while yet it is true that the real primary meaning is to be found, not in the Christian use made of the cited words, but simply in the original circumstances to which they relate, and in the context from which they are taken.

Special circumstances in the present case make it perfectly clear that the prophetic writer could not have had Jesus Christ in his contemplation. The passage, in the part supposed to refer to the sufferings of Christ, is not predictive, but simply historical. Various considerations combine to shew that the prophet is speaking of incidents which had already befallen some of the captive people in Babylon, and that the latter are spoken of collectively as the Servant of Jehovah.

Here, however, we come to a question which Dr. Liddon does not dwell upon, but dismisses with a quotation from Bishop Ollivant. It is the question of the authorship and date of the latter part of the book of Isaiah, from chapter xl. to the end. We take it to be one of the surest results of modern investigation, that this portion of that book comes down from the time of the captivity, and from the pen, not of the prophet who lived in the days of Ahaz and Hezekiah (B.C. 750 to 700), but of one who was himself among the captives in Babylon, and who wrote with reference to scenes and persons then before his eyes (B.C. 580 to 530). This conclusion we cannot here attempt to justify in detail, but we may state that it has been accepted by the best Hebrew scholars and critics of recent times—a fact which is sometimes strangely lost sight of by writers of our day.* It is certainly not to be evaded or nullified by the slighting words of Bishop Ollivant.† The Bishop's remark, to the effect that, supposing the assumption of a later Isaiah to be true, " this later Isaiah was not only a deceiver, but also a witness to his own fraud," is it not simply another instance of that form of orthodox argumentation which has been already noticed, and which really amounts to this,—Either our view of the matter is correct, or such and such a prophet or apostle, or even our Lord himself, as the case may be, was a deceiver, wrote or said what was untrue? ‡

Let us, however, next observe the connection and substance of this section of Isaiah. The prophet, it will be found, in the chapters which immediately precede, amidst many alternations of hope and fear, anticipates the restoration of his people to their own land. Their enemies the Babylonians shall be overthrown by the conquering arms of Cyrus, who is mentioned by name;§ the temple worship on Mount Zion shall be restored; and ultimately, through the Hebrew people and their faithfulness to

---

* Dr. Payne Smith, for example, observes that "the theory of a Babylonian Isaiah is dead." We believe the reverse to be the truth, although that theory has certainly been held along with many critical extravagances, as Dr. P. Smith ably points out.— *Prophecy a Preparation*, pp. 320–322.

† "Supposing this assumption," says the Bishop, "to be true [that, namely, of a later Isaiah], this later Isaiah was not only a deceiver, but also a witness to his own fraud; for he constantly appeals to prophetic power as a test of truth, making it, and specifically the prediction respecting the deliverance of the Jews by Cyrus, an evidence of the foreknowledge of Jehovah, as distinguished from the nothingness of heathen idols. And yet we are to suppose that when this fraud was first palmed upon the Jewish nation, they were so simple as not to have perceived that out of his own mouth this false prophet was condemned."—Charge of the Bishop of Llandaff, *apud* Liddon, B. L., p. 83.

‡ Compare *supra*, p. 23. § Isaiah xliv. 28; xlv. 1.

Jehovah, the knowledge of true religion shall be diffused throughout the world (ch. xlix.).

In the earlier verses of ch. lii., we have some of these anticipations clearly expressed. In the language of poetry, the prophet speaks of the Messenger bringing to the now deserted Jerusalem the good tidings of the return home:

> " How beautiful upon the mountains
> Are the feet of him that bringeth good tidings,
> That publisheth peace!
> That bringeth good tidings of good,
> That publisheth salvation!
> That saith unto Zion, Thy God reigneth!" (lii. 7.)

Again he exclaims:

> " Break forth into singing together,
> Ye waste places of Jerusalem;
> For Jehovah hath comforted his people,
> He hath redeemed Jerusalem." (v. 9.)

Then he reverts to the place where he and his people now are, and calls upon them to depart out of the midst of the idolatrous city:

> " Depart ye, depart ye, come ye out from thence,
> Touch no unclean thing;
> Come ye out of the midst of her,
> Be ye pure who carry the vessels of Jehovah:
> For not in haste shall ye come out,
> Nor in flight shall ye pass along;
> For Jehovah shall go before you,
> And the God of Israel shall guard your way."
> (vv. 11, 12.)

These expressions occur in verses immediately *preceding* the section more particularly before us. In the verses immediately following that section, we find the prophet's mind still full of the same theme. He calls upon Judea, now lying depopulated and barren, to break forth into singing, because its population is about to be increased beyond all former bounds by the return of the captives. In a great variety of beautiful expressions the thought is constantly recurring of the future prosperity and happiness of the restored nation:

"O thou afflicted, tempest-tossed, disconsolate,
Behold I will lay thy stones in bright colours,
And thy foundations with sapphires.
And I will make thy battlements of rubies,
And thy gates of carbuncles,
And all thy borders of precious stones.
And all thy children shall be taught of Jehovah,
And great shall be the peace of thy children.
* * * * *
This is the heritage of the servants of Jehovah,
And the reward of their righteousness from me, saith Jehovah."
(liv. 11-17.)

And so verse after verse might be quoted, all to the same effect, —the restoration of the captives to their own land. When, therefore, we find the prophet, both immediately *before* and immediately *after* the section under notice, speaking in such terms of circumstances and events then occurring, or about shortly to occur, are we to suppose that he all at once, in the midst of these expressions, abruptly, and without any apparent occasion, sends his thoughts far away, five hundred years or more in advance of his own time, and goes on mysteriously to speak of the life and death of Jesus Christ?—of one who had no sort of traceable connection with the existing state of affairs, and the introduction of whom in this way could do nothing to encourage or console the captive people, or lead them the more readily to prepare themselves for the labours and hardships of the long march homewards through the desert, from Babylon to Judea? Truly, such a supposition seems but little flattering to the judgment of the prophet, and could scarcely be put forth by reasonable men, except under the pressure of great theological necessity.

The "servant" (Isaiah lii. 13), or the servant of Jehovah, spoken of in this section and in some other places of the later Isaiah, cannot, therefore, be supposed to denote the future Messiah —Jesus Christ—or any personage expected by the prophet to appear some indefinite number of centuries after his own time. There is, indeed, ample evidence in this book itself as to the meaning of the expression referred to. Thus in xlix., at the beginning, we read as follows:—

> "Listen, O isles, unto me,
> And attend, ye peoples, from afar;
> Jehovah called me from the womb,
> From my mother's womb he hath made mention of my name.
> And he made my mouth like a sharp sword;
> In the shadow of his hand he hid me, ...
> And he said unto me, *Thou art my servant,*
> *O Israel,* in whom I will be glorified.
> * * * * *
> And now, saith Jehovah,
> Who formed me from the womb *to be his servant,*
> * * * * *
> Thus he saith,
> It is a slight thing that thou shouldest be *my servant,*
> To raise up the tribes of Jacob,
> And to restore the preserved of Israel;
> I will also give thee to be a light to the nations,
> That my salvation may be extended to the end of the earth."
> (xlix. 1-6.)

The sacred writer immediately adds,—

> "Thus saith Jehovah, the Redeemer of Israel,

And his Holy One,
To him that is despised of men, abhorred by the nation,
To the servant of rulers,—
Kings shall see and arise, princes and they shall bow down,
Because of Jehovah who is faithful,
The Holy One of Israel, who shall choose thee." (v. 7.)

These words are almost parallel to those of lii. 14, 15, and can hardly refer to a different object. Other places occur in which the servant of Jehovah is sufficiently shewn to be the collective Israel, especially the better and more faithful part of the people in captivity, who are to be the means of giving safety and honour to the whole nation.* With these the prophet sometimes identifies himself, speaking in his own name, when he is really speaking in behalf of his people.† As, then, these more faithful worshipers of Jehovah, who were eager to return home to rebuild Jerusalem and the temple, were, probably in consequence of this, subject to persecution at the hands of the more worldly portion of their captive countrymen and perhaps of the Babylonians,‡ we have at once suggested to us the true explanation of the passage, and of some other related places.

Having spoken in the preceding verses of the coming restoration of the captive people, the prophet goes on to contrast their past helpless and despised condition with their future prosperity. Speaking for Jehovah, he says,—"My servant shall be exalted and extolled," whereas he had once been an object of astonishment in his misery:—"His visage was so marred, more than any man's" (as it is figuratively expressed),—"but he shall sprinkle many nations"—or probably, "he shall cause many nations to spring up," that is, with wonder at the change which has taken place; "kings shall shut their mouths at him," in amazement,

---
* Isaiah xlii. 1-9; xliii. 8-15; xliv. 1-5. † xlix. 1-4.
‡ Isaiah l. 4-11; lvi. 9-lvii. 11; lviii. 1-7.

when they see the prosperous return of the captives, and behold the re-establishment and gradual diffusion of the religion of Jehovah. This part of the section is predictive; the tenses used in the introductory sentences are appropriately futures, but they change to preterites as soon as the suffering condition of the people is referred to. So it is very regularly throughout Chapter liii. " Who," the prophet proceeds, " hath believed our report ?" that is, believed what has been announced : and then he goes on to describe,—*not*, be it observed, in terms of prediction, but in those of *history*, and as one speaking of something past,*—the former sufferings of the collective Israel, in particular of that part of the nation which has been steadfast, and by whose piety and obedience Jehovah's cause is finally to triumph. This more faithful part of the people is idealized as Jehovah's Servant, who has been despised, forsaken of men, wounded, oppressed, afflicted, cut off from the land of the living, and put into the grave among transgressors, though he had done no violence and there was no deceit in his mouth. But in these sufferings there was an expiatory efficacy. They were undergone, not for the sufferer's own sins, but for those of his people, the rest of the people :

" He was wounded for our transgressions,
Bruised for our iniquities :
The chastisement of our peace was upon him,
And with his stripes we are healed." (liii. 5.)

These statements, it may be observed, are in accordance with the ancient Hebrew belief, that misfortune and suffering fall upon men in punishment of sin; and are also the means of expiation

---

* This fact is too much overlooked. But any one who will take the trouble to examine the leading tenses of the Hebrew will see that what is here said is fully borne out. In general terms, when the prophet speaks of the sufferings of the " servant " he does so in words which indicate that he is speaking of something *past*. When the results are spoken of to which those sufferings shall lead, the form of expression is different (comp. lii. 13, 14; liii. 10–12). See Appendix, note B.

and purification for transgression. But, then, in this case, the righteous servant of Jehovah had no sins of his own to deserve such visitations. It was an obvious thought that what has befallen him has been the means of expiation for others, for the rest of the people; what he has suffered "shall make intercession for the transgressors." The whole conception is in harmony with the sacrificial ideas which would doubtless be familiar to the writer. The section concludes with the anticipation of the great results to spring from the patient endurance of wrong, the steadfast adherence to Jehovah, the religious faithfulness even unto death, which have been exemplified by a portion of the captive Israel.

It is only, we venture to add, one who can shut his eyes to the historical exposition of this passage, and its connection with the circumstances of the times in which the writer lived, that will be satisfied to find in it a prophetic description of the last scenes in the history of Christ,—a prophetic description, consciously so *intended* by the Hebrew writer. The references to it in the New Testament are in accordance with the habits of thought of the early Christians. Everything in their sacred books which seemed to correspond to the events and characters of Christian history they were ready to consider as "fulfilled" in those events and characters;* but no reliance can be placed on this mode of interpretation, whether exemplified in ancient or in modern times, as evidence that an Old Testament passage originally contemplated that in which it was so deemed to find its fulfilment.

Such considerations as these are applicable, *mutatis mutandis*, to all the Old Testament passages appealed to by Lord Hatherley and by Dr. Liddon as prophecies of Jesus Christ. In saying

---

* There is a curious illustration of this in John ii. 17. Jesus had just driven the money-changers from the temple. After this, his disciples, it is said, "remembered that it was written, The zeal of thy house hath eaten me up;" and doubtless we are to understand that they thought the ancient saying "fulfilled" in the incident which brought it to their remembrance.

this, however, it is by no means intended to affirm that various Hebrew writers, and especially the prophets, did not anticipate a future time of national prosperity and peace, and the wide diffusion of the religion of Jehovah. It cannot be doubted that they did so. But it does not appear that they looked forward to a definite point of time so long after their own as that of Christ, or to a definite person like him; that they ever anticipated such a personage or character as our Lord proved to be. The Messiah expected by the Jews of old, under the influence and training of their own sacred books, was a very different person from Jesus of Nazareth. We see this in many expressions of the New Testament;* and it is especially evident in various Old Testament passages.†

An example to this latter effect is afforded by the eleventh chapter of the genuine Isaiah, which is no doubt a true Messianic passage. It evidently stands in intimate connection with the destruction of the Assyrian army announced in the preceding chapter. The mighty forest of Assyria (x. 33) shall be hewn down, "And there shall come forth a branch out of the stem of Jesse" (xi. 1). This prince is to be a wise and mighty ruler, who shall conquer the enemies of his people, Moabites, Edomites, Philistines, Egyptians (xi. 11–14). He shall re-unite the divided kingdom of the Hebrews; Ephraim and Judah under him shall cease to be rivals; and the dispersed captives of the nation shall be brought back "from the four corners of the earth" (v. 12).

Such sayings find no real application in the founder of Christianity;‡ have never been fulfilled, in any intelligible sense, in *him;* and so it is in each separate case of the kind, when duly examined.

---

* Matt. xvi. 22; xx. 21; Mark x. 35-41; Luke xxiv. 21; John xii. 34.
† E.g., Is. xi.; Jer. xxiii. 5-8; Dan. vii. 13, 14; Mich. v. 1-6.
‡ Dr. Liddon, it may here be noted, while citing this passage to show the high moral and religious character of the expected Prince, including his possession of

Although, then, it must be admitted that some of the New Testament writers appear to have had a different idea, yet in a question which is so largely critical and historical in its character, critical and historical evidence and fact ought to prevail over everything else. We are not obliged to believe that the sun moves round the earth, even though a Scriptural writer may say so, or may take it for granted.

We come in the next place, and in further illustration of these statements, to a passage to which Dr. Liddon attaches the greatest importance. He terms it, "that great prophecy, the full and true sense of which is so happily suggested to us by its place in the Church services for Christmas day." In this prophecy,* he proceeds to say, "the 'Son' who is given to Israel receives a fourfold name. He is a Wonder-Counsellor, or Wonderful above all earthly beings; He possesses a nature which man cannot fathom; and He thus shares and unfolds the Divine Mind. He is the Father of the Everlasting Age or of Eternity. He is the Prince of Peace. Above all He is expressly named the Mighty God." So Dr. Liddon,† but now let us refer to the prophet Isaiah, and inquire what *he* says, and what he meant.

In three instances, in chapters vii. and viii., the prophet introduces us to children with significant names. The first is his own son, Shear-jashub, a name meaning *a remnant shall return*, and expressing the prophet's trust that the care of Jehovah will provide for the restoration of Israel. The second is the child Immanuel, *God is with us;* a name, again, denoting his confidence that Jehovah will be with His people to deliver them from their invading enemies. The third is the case (viii. 3) of a child of

---

"the infallibility of a perfect moral insight," *omits to notice* the verses which refer to him as a victorious warrior, who shall be able to subdue and despoil the ancient enemies of his people!—B. L., pp. 84, 85.

* Isaiah ix. 6. † B. L., p. 87.

his own, called Maher-shalal-hash-baz; another significant name, referring to the circumstances of the time, and intended to denote the speedy despoiling of Damascus and Samaria by the king of Assyria. Yet again, a fourth time, the prophet gives us the same kind of symbolical prophecy. In ix. 6, another child is announced, who is to sit upon the throne of David, to order and to establish his kingdom, "from henceforth, even for ever,"—that is, for a long indefinite period, according to the frequent meaning of such expressions. This child too shall have a significant name. He shall be called, "Wonder, Counsellor, Mighty God, Father of Duration, Prince of Peace."

If the English translators had followed the same mode of rendering as with the other significant names in this context, they would have given this name also in its Hebrew form, and would have said, "His name shall be called Peleh Joetz El-gibor Abi-ad Sar-shalom." This long compound name means, without question, what we have given above as the English rendering. We have thus a significant name made up of eight words, as in the case of Maher-shalal-hash-baz we have one made up of four. But, just as before, what is to shew us that the child *is* or *was* what he is named?—that because his *name* shall be called either "Mighty-God,"* or "Father of Duration," he is to be a person corresponding in nature to these words?

But, again, *this* child, we are told, is Jesus Christ! Such is the assumption of orthodox writers,—an assumption which is wholly without warrant from the New Testament; for there is not an instance in which any New Testament writer refers to this verse as one that was "fulfilled" in the birth or life of Christ. And it is evident from the the context that the prophet is speak-

* Exactly the same word (El) is used of Nebuchadnezzar in Ezekiel xxxi. 11, disguised in the English rendering as "mighty one." The words of Isaiah denote that the expected ruler shall be a mighty conquering prince, as in xi. 11-14. "Father of duration" may indicate simply the durable and paternal character of his government, under the protection of Jehovah.

ing of a child of his own time, under whose rule the nation is to become prosperous and happy. The preceding verses relate to an invasion by the Assyrians, which must have fallen especially upon Galilee and the northern parts of the country, "by the way of the sea" (or lake).* Isaiah doubtless refers, therefore, to a prince already born,† who shall be mighty and victorious, and give peace to the distracted land under his own government.

Whether the words were or were not fulfilled in Hezekiah, as many authorities, Jewish and Christian, have supposed, it does not here concern us to determine. There is no proper evidence for understanding the passage of Jesus Christ. On the face of the matter it would seem impossible, except for one who is entirely carried away by a foregone conclusion, to find in the words a reference to a person whose birth was to be at least seven hundred years after the time in which they were written, and whose life could have no imaginable connection with the fear and misery of which the prophet was speaking, and the alleviation of which was the very object of his writing.

CHAPTER VI.

MESSIANIC PASSAGES (*continued*).

JEREMIAH XXIII. 5, 6; DANIEL VII. 13; MICAH V. 2; ZECHARIAH XIII. 7; XII. 10; THE QUOTATION IN ST. JOHN XIX. 36; MALACHI III. 1.

THE words above quoted from Dr. Liddon, in connection with Isaiah ix. 6, introduce the following propositions, made

---

* See Isaiah viii. 19–ix. 7. A portion of this passage is applied in the N. T. (Matt. iv. 14-16) to the commencement of the ministry of Christ, in the same northern part of Palestine. The original reference of the whole is unquestionably to the distress caused by a hostile invasion, and to the subsequent deliverance. The Evangelist's use of the words is surely another suggestive example of the practice of accommodation.

† The tenses are *past*—" is born," " is given "—literally, *has been*.

in reference to Christ: "...... Jeremiah calls him Jehovah Tsidkenu, as Isaiah had called him Emmanuel. Micah speaks of his eternal pre-existence, as Isaiah had spoken of his endless reign. Daniel predicts that his dominion is an everlasting dominion that shall not pass away. Zechariah terms him the Fellow or Equal of the Lord of Hosts; and refers in the clearest language to his Incarnation and Passion as being that of Jehovah Himself. Haggai implies his Divinity, by foretelling that his presence will make the glory of the second temple greater than the glory of the first. Malachi points to him as the Angel of the Covenant, Jehovah, whom Israel was seeking, and who would suddenly come to his temple."*

Of the passages referred to for these assertions, *four* are quoted by the Evangelists. Of these, therefore, we will more particularly speak: but, before doing so, let us briefly notice the use made, not by any New Testament writer, but by Dr. Liddon, of two of the others.

Jeremiah (xxiii. 5, 6) writes—"Behold the days come, saith Jehovah, when I will raise unto David a righteous branch, and a king shall reign and act wisely, and shall execute justice and righteousness in the land. In his days Judah shall be saved, and Israel shall dwell safely: and this *is* his name whereby he shall be called, Jehovah Tsidkenu [Jehovah *is* our Righteousness]."

This passage is not referred to in the New Testament. The application of the words to Christ is simply an assumption of orthodox writers; and it is easily shewn to be wholly unwarranted. The prophet is speaking of a deliverance for his people which was *soon* to come—a deliverance of captives "out of the north country" (v. 8), referring to persons who had been carried away in those times by Assyrian or Babylonian invaders.

---

* Liddon, B. L., pp. 88, 89—referring to Jer. xxiii. 5, 6; Mich. v. 2: Dan. vii. 14; Zech. xiii. 7; ii. 10-13; xii. 10; Hag. ii. 7, 9; Mal. iii. 1.

If the words, then, are referred to Christ, are we again to be told that the prophet was mistaken by five or six hundred years in his anticipation of the advent? But, indeed, even supposing that they are to be so referred, how do they shew that Christ *is* Jehovah? They only say that the *name* wherewith he shall be called is "Jehovah is our righteousness;" just as the prophet afterwards says the same thing, in the same words, of Jerusalem —"this is the name wherewith she shall be called, Jehovah is our righteousness."* The Hebrew prophets were evidently fond of these symbolical names—as, indeed, we know that every Hebrew name was significant. If, then, the words in question ought to be referred to Christ, which is a purely gratuitous supposition, still they can prove nothing respecting his *nature*, any more than do the significant names given to other persons and objects.

The passage in Daniel (vii. 13) refers to the Messiah as expected by the writer of that book, probably in the second century B.C. He speaks (v. 13) of "one like a son of man,"† who "came to the Ancient of days," and to whom are given "dominion, and glory, and a kingdom"......"his dominion is an everlasting dominion, which shall not pass away." Such is the vision seen by Daniel. Two or three points are noticeable in it. First, the distinction, here as often elsewhere, between the Eternal Being, "the Ancient of days," and every other existence. The "Son of Man" is clearly one person, the "Ancient of days" another. Secondly, the "everlasting dominion" is said to be "*given*" to the "Son of Man." The latter is evidently conceived of, and represented, as the instrument of the awful Being to whom he comes. And, thirdly, this passage is never referred to

---

* Jer. xxxiii. 16.—More probably, "Jehovah is our deliverance," in both texts.

† "A son of man," so the original, meaning probably *a human being*, as distinguished from the Divine Being mentioned in the same verse.

in the New Testament as a prediction of Christ, to whose life and character it is in fact highly inapplicable. The Messiah expected by the Jews, under the influence and training of this and similar Old Testament passages, was a totally different personage from Jesus of Nazareth.

The words of the prophet Micah, to which we next come, are, in part, reproduced in the first Gospel.* Herod asks of the "wise men" (or Magians), "where the Christ should be born." They reply, "In Bethlehem of Judea; for thus it is written by the prophet, And thou Bethlehem in the land of Judah, art not the least among the princes of Judah: for out of thee shall come a Governor, that shall rule my people Israel." It is noticeable that the wise men do not quote the Scripture correctly, and in fact misquote it; for they insert the negative "not," which is absent in the Hebrew, as in the Septuagint.† Nor do they (or the Evangelical writer) exactly give the words of the Septuagint, as we have it. But these variations do not materially concern our argument. It is clear, nevertheless, that the verse from Micah was considered Messianic in the time of the wise men, and that, in the Evangelist's conception, it had the effect of leading them to Bethlehem to seek for the new-born child. But this amount of Messianic prediction, or meaning, does not satisfy Dr. Liddon. He goes beyond the wise men; and takes the verse as not only foretelling the birth in Bethlehem, but as intimating the "eternal pre-existence" of the child to be born. In this surely he only gives us an example of being wise above what is written; or, at any rate, above what is written in the New Testament; for it does not appear that any New Testament writer ever brings forward the words of Micah to prove, or illustrate,

---

* Matt. ii. 6; comp. Micah v. 2.

† For modes of explaining away this difficulty, see Turpie's *The Old Testament in the New*, p. 190.

or express the "eternal pre-existence" of Christ, or of any one else.

Nor do the words convey any such meaning. "Out of thee, says the prophet, "shall come forth for me *one* to be ruler in Israel; and his comings forth *are* of old, from ancient days." Such is the literal rendering of the Hebrew. The passage is usually admitted to be Messianic; and taking it in this sense, the character of the expected ruler is here, as elsewhere, very different from that of Jesus Christ. In the verses which immediately follow, it is said that after an interval, during which the nation shall be given up to its enemies, he whose coming is spoken of shall "stand and feed in the strength of Jehovah, in the majesty of the name of Jehovah, *his God.*" His people under his protection shall be secure, for he shall be powerful to "the ends of the earth," that is, to the remotest countries known to the Hebrews. He shall be able to protect them "*when the Assyrian shall come.*" His princes (v. 5) shall even lay waste the land of Assyria, with the sword. "Thus," adds the prophet, "he shall deliver us *from the Assyrian.*"* We would respectfully ask Dr. Liddon, whether, on re-consideration, he really thinks this prophecy was fulfilled in Jesus Christ? And we would appeal to the intelligence of the reader, to say whether the whole passage does not manifestly refer to a state of things then existing, or soon to be so,—whether the "Assyrian," with his land and his invading armies, were not objects of actual present fear to the prophet and those for whom he was writing? How then can this verse have referred to Jesus Christ, or be applicable to him, except by the usual licence of accommodation?—or how, again, can it avail to shew the "eternal pre-existence" of Jesus Christ?

* Micah v. 2-6.

In regard to the words "of old" and "from everlasting," (ancient days), the following statement will scarcely be disputed. The Hebrew words thus rendered do not necessarily express eternity of duration. This is evident from the fact that they are not unfrequently used of limited time past. Thus Job xxix. 2, "Oh that I were as in *months past;*" Psalm lxxvii. 5, "I have considered the *days of old*, the years of *ancient times.*" In these places the same Hebrew words occur as in Micah. They are differently translated to suit the connection; but the limitation of meaning is clear in all; and so it is in many other cases.

As to the meaning of the prophet, it may be that he intends simply to allude to the circumstance that the coming of the person spoken of has been determined upon from of old, from ancient days, even from everlasting. Or does the expression only convey, that he who is to come forth is one the antiquity of whose descent, in the kingly line of David, is very great? Neither of these explanations yields us the "eternal pre-existence;" but we venture to say that they are both quite as probable, and quite as suitable to the context.

The prophet Zechariah, we are further told, speaks of the Messiah as "the Fellow or Equal of the Lord of Hosts." The words referred to occur in the anonymous and earlier part of the Book of Zechariah (xiii. 7):—"Awake, O sword, against my shepherd, and against the man that is my fellow, saith Jehovah of Hosts." Of these somewhat difficult and obscure words, it is a very pertinent inquiry, How is it known that they refer to Jesus Christ, or even to the expected Messiah? They are not so applied in the New Testament, nor are they ever quoted there in any form. So that here, again, we have a gratuitous supposition, viz., that *these* words should be referred to Jesus Christ, and indicate his Divine nature. The note, therefore, which Dr. Liddon quotes approvingly from Dr. Pusey * on this expression, has no force or propriety whatever.

The words of this verse which *are* cited by two of the Evangelists are these:—"Smite the shepherd, and the sheep shall be scattered." The words are used in Matt. xxvi. 31 and Mark xiv. 27; these Evangelists agreeing with each other in deviating from the Hebrew text of Zechariah, while not agreeing with the Septuagint. Both Evangelists introduce the words thus: "Then saith Jesus unto them, All ye shall be offended because of me this night; for it is written, I will smite the shepherd, and the sheep shall be scattered." Is it possible to regard such a use of the words of Scripture as anything else than the simple vehicle for expressing the thought in the speaker's mind at the moment—the thought of the fear and scattering of the disciples? † Can we think that *he* regarded the words of Zechariah as having been written with a conscious looking forward on the part of the prophet to *him;* or could have deemed them capable of supplying a link in the chain of elaborate argument to prove that he who so used them was one whose "incarnation and passion" were those of Jehovah himself? Yet even this, it would appear, is what commends itself to the judgment of Dr. Liddon and Dr. Pusey.

There is another verse in Zechariah which is similarly made to act the part of an incompetent witness. In xii. 10 of that book we read thus:

> "And I will pour upon the house of David,
> And upon the inhabitants of Jerusalem,
> A spirit of grace and of supplications;
> And they shall look upon me whom they have pierced,

---

* "The 'Fellow' of the Lord is no other than He who said in the Gospel, 'I and My Father are One.'"—Pusey, *apud* Liddon, B. L., p. 89.

† Comp. Matt. xxvi. 56, "Then all the disciples forsook him and fled."

And they shall mourn for him,
As one mourneth for his only son."

The prophet is speaking, it is plain, of evil days which were to come upon Judah and Jerusalem, followed, however, by a great deliverance to be wrought by Jehovah for His people. This result shall be accompanied by penitence and supplication on the part of the people. Jehovah shall pour upon them "a spirit of grace and of supplications," insomuch that they shall look to (or towards) Jehovah, against whom they have formerly transgressed: "they shall look towards me whom they have pierced, and they shall mourn for him."

A sudden change of person like this is not uncommon in the prophetical books,* the subject spoken of remaining, nevertheless, the same. Grammatical exactness is not so carefully attended to in a primitive and simple language like the Hebrew, as in our modern and more elaborate forms of speech. Jehovah is doubtless meant both by the "me" and the "him;" but in the one case it is Jehovah himself that is conceived of as the speaker, in the other it is the prophet. "They shall look towards me," Jehovah says; "and they shall mourn for Him," adds the prophet. The people then, saved from their enemies, and touched with gratitude and penitence for their deliverance, shall look towards Jehovah whom they have offended, and shall mourn for their transgressions against Him with a great mourning.

The fourth Evangelist † cites the words, and applies them to the literal piercing with the soldier's spear—an instance, it is observable, in which an original metaphorical sense is changed in the application into a literal sense. Can we reasonably suppose that to the Evangelist's mind the crucified man, to whose case he

---

* E.g., Isaiah l. 2-4.

† John xix. 37: "And again another Scripture saith, They shall look on him whom they pierced.

applies the prophet's words, was Jehovah?—can *we* accept so stupendous a conclusion on the ground of his use of these words?—or is not the case to be simply considered as one of those many instances in which the expressions of the ancient Scriptures, being found to be in a sense applicable to a modern event, are used to describe or illustrate the latter, or also said to be "fulfilled" in it? After the instances we have had before us of the way in which the Old Testament language is applied, it is impossible to think that such a doctrine as that of the Deity of Christ ought to be drawn from this kind of evidence. It is impossible to think that such a doctrine could have been left in any degree dependent on so daring and questionable an argument as Dr. Liddon's way of putting the case really amounts to.

The Evangelist, it may be observed, takes no notice, in quoting the words, that the speaker in the Old Testament is Jehovah. It was evidently beside his purpose to do so, and inconsistent with it. An apt quotation of Scripture words, suitable to the particular case, was what he desired to give—and he found (as it were) on the surface all that he required, without looking deeper, to see the true connection and meaning of the passage.

How entirely this was the case, may be seen in the verse of the Gospel immediately preceding that under notice. "These things were done that the scripture should be fulfilled, A bone of him shall not be broken."* It has not suited Dr. Liddon's argument to refer to this verse, but it is deserving of our especial notice in this place. It is not clear what scripture is thus referred to. It has been supposed to be Exodus xii. 46; Numbers ix. 12; Psalm xxxiv. 20. In the two places in the Pentateuch, it is the Passover lamb that is spoken of; in the Psalm, it is a righteous man whose bones Jehovah keepeth, so that "not one of them is broken." The words in the Evangelist are not an exact quotation

* John xix. 36.

from any of these: but yet they serve well to show how an Old Testament passage could be applied to Christ, or to incidents in his life, and could be said to be thus "fulfilled," while yet it is clear that the original writer cannot have had Jesus Christ in his mind when writing the words. In this case, it is certain, what the ancient scripture speaks of is either the literal Passover lamb, or a righteous man delivered out of his afflictions by Jehovah. In neither case, can it be thought that the future Messiah was contemplated; while yet the words are introduced in the New Testament narrative just as if this had been the purpose for which they were primarily written.

The last of the Old Testament passages belonging to the present Chapter is Malachi iii. 1:—"Behold I will send my messenger, and he shall prepare the way before me" (or, "before my face"). The words are quoted in each of the Synoptics;* but St. Mark, according to Tischendorf's text, introduces them as "written in Isaiah the prophet;"—a singular error on the part of the Evangelist.† This case also exemplifies the somewhat loose way in which these quotations were occasionally made,—the words of two different prophets being joined together and cited as if they belonged to one. It is not the only example of the kind.‡

The three Synoptics agree in the form of their quotation, which yet does not correspond either to the Hebrew or to the Septuagint.§ Passing over this difference, we notice that in each Gospel the words are given as fulfilled in John the Baptist—that is to

---

* Matt. xi. 10; Mark i. 2; Luke vii. 27.
† The English version of Mark i. 2 reads, "As it is written in the *prophets;*"—following a correction probably introduced into the manuscripts by some late copyist.
‡ Heb. ii. 12, 13, and others.
§ In particular, they change the pronouns: instead of the Prophet's "the way," they write "my way;" and instead of "before me," they write "before thee." They also insert the words, "before thy face," which are neither in the Hebrew nor in the Septuagint.

say, they are applied to him, as if they had been originally intended to speak of him. He is the messenger sent before the face of him "that should come," to prepare the way before him. This is the extent to which the Evangelists represent our Lord as appropriating the words, or applying them either to himself or to the Baptist. They do not give us to understand that *they* conceived of him for whom John has prepared, as being Jehovah, nor do they say anything about Jehovah coming to His temple in the person of Jesus Christ. This is only Dr. Liddon's construction of the words of Malachi; or, perhaps we should say, it is only an inference of his by no means infallible judgment.

But the verse, it is certain, can have had no original reference to Christ—in the intention, that is to say, of Malachi. In a later passage of the prophecy (iv. 5), the messenger to come is named by name, and is designated as Elijah the prophet. Hence the passage before us (Malachi iii. 1–6) cannot originally refer to the distant coming of Jesus of Nazareth, and cannot, therefore, be properly used as revealing anything about his rank or nature.

It refers, indeed, manifestly, to some judgment upon the wicked and rebellious nation, anticipated by the prophet as coming to pass in his own generation. Everything in the book of Malachi shows that it was a speedy visitation for which the writer was looking.* A messenger, then, namely Elijah (raised from the dead), is to come and prepare the way before Jehovah, who shall appear in judgment (iii. 5) "to purify the sons of Levi, and purge them as gold and silver is purged" (iii. 3). Jehovah is thus Himself the "Lord" of verse 1, who shall suddenly come to His temple: as in verse 5 also He says, "And I will come near to you to judgment, and I will be a swift witness against the sorcerers. . . . . . For I am Jehovah, I change not" (iii. 6).

The messenger (angel) in the second clause of the verse, is the

* See the whole of Mal. ii.

same, there is no reason to doubt, as the one in the first, and the word rendered "even" in the English version should be rendered *and*. There is thus an obvious parallelism of sense in the three clauses of the verse, which alone might be sufficient to determine its interpretation. Thus:

" Behold I, Jehovah, will send my messenger [Elijah],
 And he shall prepare the way before me;
 And the Lord, [Jehovah Himself,] whom ye [the people] seek
   shall suddenly come to his temple,
 And the messenger of the covenant whom (which) ye delight in;
 Behold, he shall come, saith Jehovah of hosts."

In the second part of the verse, Jehovah speaks of Himself, in the third person, as the "Lord" whom the people "seek"—the latter perhaps alluding to their seeking him in worship.* The change of person, from the first to the third, affords no objection to this exposition. It is not an uncommon change, as noticed before. The last clause of the verse refers to the prophet Elijah, who is to be sent as Jehovah's messenger. It follows, therefore, as the result of the inquiry, that words spoken by the prophet Malachi of Jehovah and his messenger Elijah, are applied by the Evangelists, in the usual way of accommodation, to Jesus Christ and his forerunner John the Baptist, as though fulfilled in them. Does it follow that the Lord Jesus Christ is Jehovah, any more than it follows that John the Baptist was Elijah?

* As, e.g., in Ps. xl. 16; lxix. 6.

CHAPTER VII.

THE KNOWLEDGE AND THE IGNORANCE OF CHRIST—ORTHODOX EXCESS IN THE USE OF OLD TESTAMENT PASSAGES—GENERAL RESULT.

If the cases already examined may be deemed to establish anything like a general principle, in the use made of the Old Testament in the New, it will be unnecessary to dwell at greater length on this part of our subject. It would be easy to multiply examples; and in every instance similar considerations would be found to apply. This will be the case even in such passages as those referred to in the note.* These too must be accepted as exemplifying, more or less directly and completely, the kind of accommodation of which we have spoken. And it is the easier, or rather the more necessary, to say this, even in reference to cases in which our Lord himself is the speaker, because however exalted in one sense may be the nature or dignity attributed to him, it is yet on all hands admitted that he was truly a *man*, possessed, like others around him, of a genuine human nature. He was, therefore, subject to the same laws and conditions of growth, instruction, progress, knowledge or ignorance, which affected other men. He shared in these. As Bishop Colenso has observed,—in words noticed by Dr. Liddon, but certainly not refuted by anything he has advanced,—" he took our nature fully, and voluntarily entered into all the conditions of humanity, and among others, into that which makes our growth in all ordinary knowledge *gradual* and *limited*. We are expressly told, in Luke ii. 52, that ' Jesus increased in *wisdom*,' as well as in ' stature.' It is not supposed that, in his human nature, he was acquainted, more than any educated Jew of the age, with the

* John v. 39; xii. 37-41; Luke xxiv. 44; Heb. i. 5-11, in reference to Pss. ii. and xlv.; Matt. xxii. 41-44, referring to Ps. cx. Comp. Liddon, B. L., pp. 79-83.

mysteries of all modern sciences; nor, with St. Luke's expressions before us, can it be seriously maintained that, as an *infant* or *young child*, he possessed a knowledge surpassing that of the most pious and learned adults of his nation......"* From whatever point of view, therefore, the subject may be regarded, there is no good reason to think that the knowledge or the ignorance of Christ was not of the same character which belonged to his age and country, or that he did not participate in the prevailing ideas and feelings respecting the ancient Scriptures and the use that might be made of them. Everything in his recorded history points clearly to this conclusion.†

Hence, again, it may reasonably be inferred that he too would accept the statements of the Old Testament in popular senses; would take passages as Messianic, because such was their usual acceptation, and because, as the son of devout parents, familiar with the sacred books of their people, he had been educated to do so. We may further understand how it was that he could apply passages usually considered Messianic to the incidents of his own career. So to do was in accordance with the common habit of the time, was justified by it, was its inevitable consequence. It was, we may believe, with Jesus Christ much as with a religious man of our own day and nation. Such a person, trained from childhood to believe the popular theology of the time, will necessarily express himself on religious subjects in accordance with his belief, and quote the words of either Testament according to the meaning which he has been taught to put upon them, and this he will do with perfect truthfulness and innocence. It is far from reasonable, however, to conclude that such a use of the

---

* Colenso, *Pentateuch*, I. p. xxxi.

† E.g., the anticipations, more than once expressed, of his own second coming within that generation : Matt. xvi. 27, 28; Luke xvii. 22, *seq*. Do not these anticipations remain unfulfilled?

F

older Scriptures in the new Testament is to bind their readers, for all ages to come, to accept without inquiry either the authorship or the interpretation popularly attributed to them in the time of Christ. It ought not to be deemed essential to good Christianity to suppress critical investigation into the origin of a sacred book, or into the original meaning of an Old Testament passage, or to discuss such questions with a foregone determination to believe only in one way. It cannot be necessary to good Christianity to do this, any more than it can be so to receive the Christ on false pretences, or to insist on attributing to him a knowledge, or a character, which he does not claim, or rather disclaims, for himself. On this subject, as on every other, doubtless the simple truth is what we ought to seek; and this, we may be well assured, can alone be acceptable to Him whose name is Truth.

It remains to notice another point, more expressly than has yet been done. We have seen how Dr. Liddon takes occasion to quote from Old Testament Scriptures, referred to in the Gospels, a *larger* portion than is really brought forward in the latter. He is not contented to go as far as an Evangelist, and to take the alleged prophecy as it is used by him, but he adds to it something beyond this, so far as it suits his argument to do so.

For example, in Zechariah xiii. 7, the prophet's words are these:

"Awake, O sword, against my shepherd,
And against the man that is my fellow,
Saith Jehovah of Hosts:
Smite the shepherd, and the flock shall be scattered;
And I will turn my hand against the little ones."

The portion of this verse quoted in the New Testament and applied to the circumstances of Jesus Christ, is the phrase, "Smite the shepherd, and the flock shall be scattered." But this is not enough for the quoter of our day: he brings forward the earlier part of the verse also, as though this too, in the Evangelist's conception, had necessarily the same reference. We cannot but ask why he should stop where he does. Why not similarly urge upon his reader the latter part of the verse?—or the preceding verse, or the following one? Of course, he does not do this, because those other verses would not suit his purpose, or might perhaps be unfavourable to it. But such words of the passage as seemed to be available, these he picks out. Not contented with the quotation actually given in the Gospel, he adds the further expression as to "the man that is my fellow" (or *associate*). And this expression, too, he tells us, means Jesus Christ, and the latter is therefore the "fellow" and Equal of Jehovah! But what is the value of this assertion? Is not its real foundation an assumption? Because certain words are quoted in the Gospels as applicable to circumstances spoken of by the Evangelists, does it necessarily follow that *other* words in the same context which are *not* quoted may be equally so applied, at will, by the modern reader?

It is perfectly gratuitous to suppose that the idea in each Evangelist's mind, in citing the prophet's words, was that of Jesus Christ being the "fellow," or equal, of Jehovah, seeing that the quoted words express a totally *different* idea; namely, that of the scattering of the disciples at the crucifixion. Had the former been intended, we must believe that the Evangelist would have done what Dr. Liddon has done; that is to say, he would have introduced the words which might at least bear such a construction.

And not only is this an obvious remark, but let it be further observed that, in several of these cases, that part of an Old Testament verse which would seem most especially available for the orthodox argument, is precisely that which the Christian Evangelist does *not* bring forward. This will be seen in the passages noted below.* Thus, for example, in Micah v. 2, a *part* of this verse is referred to, as we have seen, in the New Testament as indicating the *place* where the Messiah is to be born. That part of it which might have served more certainly to express what Dr. Liddon terms " the eternal pre-existence," that part of the verse which the modern orthodox theory cannot fail to adduce, is not quoted or appealed to in the Gospel. So that here, again, what to a mind pre-occupied with the popular theory, is necessarily the most prominent thing in the original verse, is, by the Evangelist, passed over in silence.

It may, indeed, be replied, that an Evangelist is not to be expected to cite more of a passage than his immediate purpose required. Just so, it may be answered; and therefore his immediate purpose was not that which is attributed to him. It was not to suggest the deity of Jesus Christ, or to help in building up an argument for that doctrine. If such had been his intention, he would have brought forward the words which would best have served such an end. But these are just the words which he passes over. Ought we not, therefore, from the Evangelist's non-use of the words, to conclude that he could not have had the intention to convey or suggest the doctrine supposed?

If, however, it be urged that the citation of some of the words of a verse shews that the *whole* verse must have been in the Evangelist's mind, and ought on his authority to be understood to have referred originally to Christ,—this, it may be replied, is evidently the point to be proved. And it cannot be proved, because

---

* E.g., Hag. ii. 6, in Heb. xii. 26—while verses 7 and 9 are not noticed; Isaiah xl. 3, in Matt. iii. 3, Mark i. 3—while the words of the prophet, "make straight in the desert a highway for our God," are not quoted; so in Luke iii. 4, John i. 23; Mic. v. 2, comp. Matt. ii. 6.

it may be shewn in each case, as we have seen in the cases actually examined, that the passage could not in its first intention have had any connection with Jesus Christ, but had an entirely different reference—relating, if truly Messianic, not to Jesus of Nazareth, but to the personage anticipated, under the character of Messiah, by the ancient Hebrew writers. The words, therefore, as before, can be applied to the former only by a kind of accommodation.

Moreover, if the application of *some* words of a verse in a Hebrew prophet to circumstances in the life of Christ shews that the rest of the verse also related originally to him, why stop at a single verse? The modern division into verses and chapters is an arbitrary one. Why not, therefore, take the whole chapter, or the whole book?* And so we reach a result which is clearly equivalent to a case of *reductio ad absurdum;*—a result at which the most determined upholder of this kind of argument may well be disposed to pause, asking himself whether a doctrine, or a mode of proof, which puts so severe a strain upon common sense can indeed be true.

It follows from the foregoing considerations that there was nothing in the ancient anticipations of a Messiah, to lead to the expectation that that personage would be "divine," in the sense which is commonly given to this word. He was indeed to be a wise and righteous sovereign and warrior, especially under the protection of the Almighty, and enabled by His aid to overcome his enemies. He was one, to whom the highest epithets, short of those reserved for the ineffable Being, might be properly given, whose right it was to have such epithets conferred upon him. But, at the same time, there is no passage producible from the Old Testament, in which he is really described or conceived of as

---

* Thus, in Micah v., verses 5, 6 must evidently be included with v. 2, materially affecting the character of the passage.

Supreme God,* or as, in any sense, equal to him; there is no evidence producible to this effect, which will stand the test of cross-examination. ONE only, to the ancient Hebrew mind, as to the modern, could be so designated; and He it is of whom Jesus himself teaches us to think as "Our Father" in heaven; of whom he himself said "The Lord our God is One Lord;" of whom he spoke as "My Father and your Father, my God and your God;" and whom he is also recorded to have addressed in prayer as "the Only True God."† Such words as these are very plain indeed. Their meaning does not wait to be determined by obscure and doubtful arguments from Old Testament prophecies; and it may well be a question whether not only our own reason, but also our loyalty to God and to Christ, do not require that we should accept and act upon the conclusion which such language, taken in its plain and obvious sense, so clearly conveys and urges upon us.

CHAPTER VIII.

THE BIBLICAL DOCTRINE OF ONE GOD—THE WORDS ELOHIM AND JEHOVAH.

OUR purpose leads us now to speak more in detail of the positive teaching of the Scriptures on some of the principal subjects of theological interest. Of these, the doctrine of the Divine Unity unquestionably holds the chief place among the

---

* The popular or orthodox doctrine unquestionably represents the Son as "Supreme God," as much so as the Father. So it is, for example, in the First Article, and in the Athanasian Creed. The qualifying language, sometimes met with, about the "subordination" of the Son, merely serves to exemplify the gross inconsistencies of statement which are found unavoidable, for the protection, or apparent protection, of monotheistic faith. But, in truth, the distinction between the Father as Supreme, and the Son as Subordinate, is plainly equivalent to a doctrine of *two Gods*, one of whom is inferior to the other.

† Mark xii. 29; John xx. 17; xvii. 3.

fundamental doctrines of the Bible. It is presented to us by the sacred writers in a peculiar and interesting manner. They give us especially to see how, from obscure beginnings, it gradually grew up and assumed a commanding influence among a people long unable to receive it with a cordial assent; and how, finally, it was established after centuries of conflict with idolatrous tendencies, and became the abiding possession first of the Jewish people and then of the Christians. Thus the Bible leaves this doctrine, as it were, to speak for itself, and win its own way to the sympathy and faith of devout minds. It places before us, not so much a creed as a great historical drama, the scenes of which run through many ages, and commend themselves to us by their simplicity, by their truthfulness to human nature, and by the power with which the final result appeals to religious feeling, and vindicates its claims on our acceptance.

Of the two principal terms, ELOHIM and JEHOVAH, by which the Hebrew writers denote the Supreme Being, the former was the older, as it was also the more general in meaning and application. By its etymology, the word Elohim was expressive of power; as though God were thought of as pre-eminently the Mighty One; much, indeed, as we now employ the term Almighty. It was used, however, not only of God, as known among the Hebrews, but also of "other gods."* It is also applied even to human beings, as, for example, princes and judges, and others occupying an eminent position. Thus we read, "And Jehovah said unto Moses, See, I have made thee a god (Elohim) to Pharaoh; and Aaron thy brother shall be thy prophet."†

It has been inferred from the plural form of this word, that in

---

* Exod. xx. 3; xxiii. 13; Deut. v. 7.
† Exod. vii. 1; xxi. 6; xxii. 8, 28; Ps. viii. 6; xlv. 6; lxxxii. 1, 6; John x. 34, 35. In some of these, Elohim is rendered "judges" in the English Bible.

the early, or ante-Mosaic times, it was employed in its proper sense, as a true plural, and that the people among whom it was in use were polytheists. This, however, does not appear in the sacred books. In these, the term in question is usually, and from the first, though with a few rare exceptions,* employed with singular verbs and adjectives, and denotes everywhere as thus used the One Divine Object. Yet that such is the case affords no conclusive argument against admitting the very imperfect, and perhaps polytheistic character of the religion of the early Hebrews. The ancient documents which form the basis of the Mosaic books,† were probably most of them written after the Exodus. Their writers thus lived at a time when the belief and worship of the One God were beginning to prevail among the Hebrews. Hence those writers, and much more the still later compilers of the Pentateuch, and of other historical books, would naturally accommodate their language to the religious belief of their own time. It is, nevertheless, clear from their history, that the Hebrew people were long excessively prone to idolatrous practices and to the acknowledgment of many gods. It is difficult to think that they could have been so, had anything like a pure monotheism come down to them, and been firmly established among them, from the early days of patriarchal history, as this is represented in the Book of Genesis.

The low state of religious belief prevailing in the most ancient times is not, however, a matter of merely conjectural inference from their oldest word for God. Other and direct indications are not wanting to the same effect.

On the face of the narrative which relates the events of the primitive Biblical history for many hundred years, it is plain that the Israelitish people during the whole of this period could have

---

* E.g., Gen. xx. 13; xxxv. 7 Exod. xxxii. 4, 8; 2 Sam. vii. 23.
† Comp. *supra*, p. 2.

had only gross unspiritual ideas on all religious subjects. Doubtless, there were exceptions among the better minds of the nation, including leaders and prophets eager for the acknowledgment and service of the One God; but the statement just made is probably correct of the great majority, even though the people may have been brought at times to believe in their own Elohim as the sole Being entitled to worship and obedience from themselves.

In the books relating to the earliest history, all that is said respecting the Deity and His intercourse with man is highly anthropomorphic in its character. Jehovah Elohim walks in the garden of Eden, and enters into conversation with the primitive pair, as He does afterwards with many of their descendants. After the deluge, when Noah offered his sacrifice of burnt offerings, "Jehovah smelled a sweet savour," and "said in his heart," that he would not "again curse the ground any more for man's sake." It is plain that, in the conception of the writer of such words, He is a God of very human tastes and ideas. So, He speaks face to face with Abraham and Sarah, and goes down from his interview with them to "see whether" Sodom and Gomorrah are as wicked as the cry which had come unto Him had indicated, "and if not," He adds, "I will know."*

In the Book of Exodus, the Almighty converses with Moses. He gives him tables of stone, containing the commandments which He has Himself written. It is even said respecting Moses and others of the elders and nobles of Israel, that they went up to the mountain, "and they saw the God of Israel, ... they saw God, and did eat and drink."†

It is needless to add that these representations continue

---

* Gen. viii. 21; xviii. 21.
† Exod. xxiv. 9-12. The words "did eat and drink" may here mean, *continued to live.*

through later books,—that is to say, books recounting later events. Hence it is evident that for many ages, according to the sacred narrative itself, essentially rude and material ideas of the Almighty Being prevailed among the Israelites, and we cannot wonder that they fell away as they did, from time to time, into positive idolatry and the belief in strange gods. To the great bulk of such a people even Jehovah, it would appear, could only be a national god, the one who favoured and protected them more especially—ideas which are certainly very nearly akin to polytheism, if not identical with it.

This conclusion might easily be confirmed by various other considerations drawn from the books of Genesis, Joshua and Judges. On these, however, it is hardly necessary here to dwell at any length.*

Subsequent historical books present many similar traces of the same disposition. They reveal, in fact, a long continued series of vacillations between the worship of Jehovah and that of the gods of the surrounding nations. Of King Ahaz we read, that "he sacrificed unto the gods of Damascus which smote him, and he said, Because the gods of the kings of Syria help them, therefore will I sacrifice to them, that they may help me."†

Later kings, as Manasseh, and earlier ones also, were equally prone to idolatrous worship. The "high places" and sacred groves and gardens are often referred to; and it is clear that the people, as well as their rulers, were continually guilty of the same great apostasy. Even in the later Isaiah, there are plain allusions to idolatrous practices among the captives in Babylon.‡

This tendency to false worship appears to have prevailed in spite of the prophets who came forward from time to time with

---

* See Gen. xxxi. 19, 30-34; xxxv. 2, 3; Jos. xxiv. 14-23; Jud. xvii. xviii.
† 1 Kings xii. 28-33; xviii. 13, 21; 2 Kings xxi. 3-6.
‡ Isaiah lvii.; comp. i. xxix.; Jer. vii. 17, *seq.*

their faithful warnings and expostulations. It may doubtless be accounted for, in part, by the intermixture among the Hebrews of some of the ancient idolatrous inhabitants of Canaan;* in part, and perhaps more fully, by the fact that the Hebrews were so much surrounded by tribes and nations addicted to very gross and sensual religions—as, for example, the Syrians, the Phœnicians and the Egyptians. Ignorant and uncultivated men, little given to reflection, are easily attracted by outward and visible rites, appealing to them in the sacred name of religion. Such persons among the Hebrews,—that is, indeed, the great mass of the nation —would be constantly liable to be drawn away from a system which, like their own, forbade the making of any sensible image of God, and was, in other respects, of a higher and severer character than the religions of adjoining nations.

Of this statement we may find ample illustration in the religious world of our own day; in the influence of what is termed Ritualism, for example, over certain classes of minds; and in the prevalence of Roman Catholicism among the great masses of the people of many countries, for whom, it is not to be doubted, such forms of Christian faith and worship have far stronger attractions than a simple and comparatively cold and rational Protestantism.

Another and more general cause of the same tendency may be found in the endless variety and diversity seen in the world around us, both in the visible phenomena of nature and in the occurrences of human experience. Even in our Christian times, the belief in Satan is, to many persons, a relief; inasmuch as it seems to take away from God the responsibility for much of the seeming evil that exists in the world. It takes the responsibility from Him, and puts it upon the prince of evil. But this, like polytheism itself, is only a temporary and superficial relief. True science

* See Psalm cvi. 34-38.

and true religion unite to force the mind onward and upward to the thought of One all-sufficient Cause, the central Power, the controlling Providence, of the universe—helping us to think and say of Him, with the Hebrew prophet of old, " I form the light and create darkness; I make peace and create evil; I, Jehovah, do all these things."

The word JEHOVAH differs from the word Elohim in being a singular in form, and in being applied only to one definite object. It is a proper name, and, like other proper names, found in the Old Testament, it has a distinct meaning of its own. It was probably expressive of eternity of existence; and accordingly, in some recent versions of the Old Testament into English, the word is rendered " the Eternal," as it is by the equivalent phrase in various foreign versions.

This name, it is well known, is esteemed so sacred among the Jews, that, for many ages past, they have refrained from uttering it; and always, in reading their Scriptures, substitute another word, namely, either *Lord* or *God*. The true pronunciation of the sacred name is not certainly known to us. It has been long lost, and different accounts have been given in recent times as to what it was, and ought now to be.* This is easily understood, when it is mentioned that the word which we pronounce "Jehovah," properly consists of only four *consonants*, without any original vowel sound to guide us in pronouncing them. The vowel sounds which we now attach to them are comparatively modern—that is, they have been added to the word since the commencement of Christian times, and are, in fact, borrowed vowels.†

---

* See the excellent *Short Dissertation* on this subject by Prof. R. Martineau.—1860. While largely concurring in what is there said, we yet hope that we are not to lose the familiar and euphonious word "Jehovah," for the poor-looking and ill-sounding *Jahveh*—especially when it is not absolutely certain that the latter is the correct form.

† It is scarcely necessary to remind the reader that, in the English Bible, the

There is reason to believe that the name Jehovah was not yet known in the most ancient times of Hebrew history to which we can ascend. At what period it was first introduced, is, however, a doubtful point. We need not dwell upon the considerations which bear on this question; but we may note that they tend to establish the position that the name in question was not in use before the time of Moses. It was long ago pointed out by an eminent German author, that there is no instance in the Pentateuch of a proper name formed by composition with a syllable derived from the word Jehovah—no instance until we come to the time of Moses, whose mother's name was Jochebed, and whose successor's name was Joshua. Many names, on the other hand, occur formed from the syllable *El*, derived from Elohim, or its kindred forms. Hence the inference that while El and Elohim were common in the pre-Mosaic times, the term Jehovah was as yet unknown.*

The absence of the word in the earlier history appears, indeed, to be recognized in the Bible itself. In the Book of Exodus we read, " God spake unto Moses and said unto him, I am the LORD; and I appeared unto Abraham, unto Isaac, and unto Jacob by *the name of* God Almighty; but by my name JEHOVAH was I not known to them."† It is true, nevertheless, that this name

word LORD (in small capitals) represents the original Jehovah, while the form " Lord " is the rendering of a different original word. In so rendering "Jehovah," our translators followed the Septuagint, the Jewish authors of which naturally refrained from repeating or writing the sacred name. Hence the confusion between the word LORD in the Old Testament, and the word Lord in the New, as used of Jesus Christ. The two are by no means equivalent. The one represents the ancient and venerable Hebrew name Jehovah, the other the common Greek word κύριος,—a word often applied to others besides Jesus Christ (e.g., Matt. xviii. 26–34). It is to be hoped that, in the version of the English Old Testament now being made, the name Jehovah will be everywhere introduced where the original has it.

* Ewald, *Geschichte d. Volkes Israels* (1843), II. pp. 145–148.
† Exod. vi. 2, 3 : " the LORD," in v. 2, represents the original Jehovah.

constantly occurs in the Book of Genesis;—a fact which is appealed to as one of the evidences of the composite structure of that book, and as indicative also of the comparatively late origin of many portions of it.

It is possible, as Bishop Colenso maintains, that the name Jehovah was not known so early as Moses; or was not, at least, in common or familiar use in his time, or, indeed, until many hundred years after him.* But, however this may be, we shall probably not be far wrong, if we regard the introduction of it, whenever that took place, as indicating a step forward on the part of the Hebrew people, or their leaders, towards better ideas of the Eternal Being. Their Elohim is now Jehovah, and no other. He is henceforth to be their sole God, their national God; not probably, as yet, in their conception, the One Only Being entitled to that highest of appellations, but at least Supreme among gods, God of gods;—the additional advancement towards the idea of His sole Deity being gradually made and completed at a yet later period in the nation's history.

In the Book of Genesis and throughout the historical books, the two names of Elohim and Jehovah appear together from the first, much as if they had been in use in the earliest times. It is Elohim who "created the heavens and the earth," in the first verse of the Bible; and it is Jehovah Elohim who, in the second chapter, carries on and completes the work of creation. The two words constantly occur afterwards, though not in such close conjunction as this, making a kind of compound form, which is seldom found beyond the second and third chapters of Genesis.†

It has been supposed that the one word or the other is afterwards used from time to time, according as the sacred writer

---

* Colenso, *Pentateuch*, Part II. c. viii. *seq.*

† This remark does not apply to such forms as "Jehovah, God of Israel," which is not uncommon.

deemed the one or the other more suitable to his subject. There is doubtless truth in this supposition; but it has been pushed further than the evidence will warrant. Many cases occur in which the words seem to be used quite indifferently, and without any particular reference or special fitness to the requirements of the context, or to the ideas expressed in it, so far as we can now judge. The term Jehovah, however, is generally employed when the Divine Being is spoken of as the protecting God of Israel, who had entered into special covenants with them, and made them His chosen people.

CHAPTER IX.

THE BIBLICAL DOCTRINE OF ONE GOD—ITS CONTINUED DEVE-
LOPMENT—THE CHRISTIAN DOCTRINE.

THE imperfect religious belief above spoken of prevailed in the nation down to the time of the captivity. The writings of Jeremiah are sufficient evidence to this effect. He frequently speaks of the grievous apostasy of his countrymen, and repeatedly threatens them with captivity and destruction, as the consequences of their "sin." Several other prophets, both of earlier and of later date, bear the same unfavourable testimony respecting their people.*

But, while this is true, it is equally clear that higher and better ideas were now also asserting their sway, and long had done so. In Isaiah, for example, while Jehovah is probably still thought of as the special Protector and God of Israel, it is, nevertheless, evident that the prophet conceived of Him as the One true and living God; nor is there anything to indicate that he looked upon

* Jer. vii. 17, 29-34; xi. 11-13; xv. 6, 7; xviii. 1, 2; Hosea i. 2; iv. 12, 13, and *passim;* Amos ii. 8, and *passim;* Micah i. 5-7; v. 12-14; Zeph. i. 4-6; Mal. ii. 11.

the idols to which he refers as other than the mere creatures of the foolish imaginations of their worshipers.* Indeed, some of his expressions respecting God, and the obedience which is acceptable to Him, are of the highest character; hardly inferior to anything of the same kind to be found elsewhere in the Scriptures. His first chapter is a passage of this kind, and so is much in his second, and in his fifth. The Book of Jeremiah is equally decided, not only in its denunciation of idols, but also in the distinction which it draws between the false gods and Him whose name is "Jehovah of Hosts," who is "the true God," even "the living God, and an everlasting King."†

Similar remarks are true, in perhaps a less degree, of several of the Minor Prophets; ‡ and thus it is clear that, for a long period, and contemporaneously with the often prevalent idolatry, there existed in the nation a powerful tendency of an opposite character. The origin of this is doubtless to be referred to a time long anterior to that of the prophets just mentioned. Not to speak of the Mosaic teaching and legislation,—which, however, no one can doubt were purely monotheistic,—the names of Samuel, Nathan, Elijah, Elisha and others, readily occur to us in this connection. All that is known of these venerable men indicates their zeal for Jehovah, as the God of Israel; and if they had not altogether reached an elevation from which they were enabled to look to Him as the Only Divine Existence, and to think of the gods of the nations as altogether vanity and "the work of men's hands," yet their labours and prophetic teaching must have contributed essentially to this final result.

The hard experience of the captivity, and the lessons which it taught, would tend in the same direction. The unknown author of the latter part of the Book of Isaiah is remarkable for the

---

* Isaiah xvii. 7, 8; i. 29-31; xix. 3; xxx. 22.   † Jer. x. 10, 16.
‡ Amos iii. v. ; Hosea xi. xiii. ; Micah vi. ; Hab. iii.

power with which he proclaims the nothingness of the idols, and the sole Deity of Jehovah.* The Book of Deuteronomy, also, the composition of which may belong to the age of Jeremiah, contains passages which fully correspond to that more advanced period of national intelligence.† The same is evidently true of the Book of Job, and of many of the later Psalms.‡ The latter have frequent passages in which the writer gives utterance to the loftiest conceptions of the greatness and power, as well as of the goodness, holiness and mercy, of Jehovah; passages which, for many ages past, have served as appropriate forms of expression for the best and highest thoughts of Christian devotion. Here is a portion of one of the most remarkable of these:

> " Whither shall I go from thy spirit?
> Or whither shall I flee from thy presence?
> If I ascend up into heaven, thou art there;
> If I make my bed in the grave, behold, thou art there;
> If I take the wings of the morning,
> And dwell in the uttermost parts of the sea,
> Even there shall thy hand lead me,
> And thy right hand shall hold me." (Ps. cxxxix. 7–10.)

We feel, at once, that men who could write thus respecting the All-pervading Presence, that men who could worthily appreciate such writing, could never be led away to the worship of imaginary deities. In this higher faith, an immense step has been secured in the progress of religious knowledge; and good soil has been prepared in which to sow still better seed of Divine truth, whenever any servant of God, even greater than Moses and the prophets, shall be raised up to guide and enlighten mankind.

---

* Isaiah xliv. 9–20; xlv. 5–7.
† Deut. iv. 35–39; vi. 4; vii. 9; xvii. 2–5; xxxii. 39, 40.
‡ Job xi. 7, 8; xxviii.; xxxiv.–xxxix.; Pss. xcv.; xcvi.; xcix.; c.; ciii.; civ.; cxxxix.

In the diffusion of such ideas as these we have, therefore, a true "preparation for Christ"—far better, and more real, than any consisting in supposed predictions, often of mysterious import and doubtful interpretation, to say the least; and which, moreover, from the nature of the case, could be known to comparatively few readers, and were liable to be misunderstood even by the most intelligent.

The advance in religious knowledge which these ideas indicate was doubtless, on the whole, well maintained during the long interval between the close of the captivity and the commencement of the Christian literature. To this period belong a few Hebrew books, the testimony of which, so far as it bears upon the subject, goes to shew that, in the midst of much of mere ceremonialism, the higher faith in Jehovah was by no means lost sight of. Evidence of this may be seen in the prayer of the Levites in the book of Nehemiah; in one or two places even of the apocalyptic book of Daniel;* in the prevailing tone of the prophet Haggai; and in that of the first eight chapters—that is to say, the later portion—of the book of Zechariah.

To the period of which we are now speaking belong also the Apocryphal writings of the Old Testament, including the so-called Sapiential Books, that is to say, the Wisdom of Solomon and Ecclesiasticus—works of great beauty, and abounding in just and noble sentiments respecting both God and man—works, in short, which, although not written in Hebrew and originating under Hellenistic influences, are wholly worthy, not merely, in Dr. Liddon's words, to "lie outside the precincts of the Hebrew canon," but to occupy an honourable place within it. To the same space of time belongs the great struggle, under the Maccabæan princes, against the house of Antiochus. Terrible as this was to the Jewish people, it tended, without doubt, in its after-influences, to consolidate their attachment to their religion, as this now existed among them,

* Neh. ix. 4–38; Dan. ii. 20–23; ix. 3· 19.

in the purely monotheistic form which they had formerly been so unable, or so slow, to receive. This result is seen in expressions occurring both in the Sapiential books and in the books of the Maccabees.*

Still, even with this establishment of a better faith, the whole process is not yet completed. The prevailing tone even of the higher passages of the ancient Scriptures represents the Almighty more especially in the light of Creator and Ruler. The remembrance of His greatness, power and majesty is predominant; although it is also in many cases qualified by the thought of his more beneficent and attractive moral attributes. This necessarily arises from the radical conception of the Hebrew religion, that of a Law imposed by the will of a Sovereign, enforced by sanctions of reward or punishment, as the consequence of obedience or of disobedience. Nor were the people themselves prepared to receive anything higher. They have, therefore, only to obey the law which is given to them, and to observe the appointed rites of worship, simply because they are enjoined by their invisible Lawgiver and King. The conscience and the affections are but little appealed to, and little cultivated. It is rather the fear of punishment. God is a jealous God, who will visit iniquity to the third and fourth generation, and shew mercy to them that love Him and keep His commandments.†

Such ideas are not the highest which it is given to man to attain concerning God. They belong to the earlier rather than the later stages of religious knowledge; and accordingly in the "fulness of time" a better revelation of the Infinite Being is given in the teaching and influence, more especially, of Jesus Christ and of his great Apostle, St. Paul. This appeals more directly to the moral nature of man, and altogether comes nearer

---

* See the beautiful prayer of Solomon, Wisd. of Sol. ix. ; also Ecclus. xlii. 15, seq. ; 2 Mac. i. 24-29.   † Comp., however, Ezek. xviii. 19, seq.

to us than anything contained in the older dispensation. The latter, we feel, was but as a step, slow and hesitating, though firmly made in the results,—a step towards the more perfect knowledge; and it is not until we come to the life and words of the great Teacher, and to the influences immediately springing from them, not until we come to him, and learn from him and see in him[*] how to think of God as the merciful Father of all, who is to be worshiped "in spirit and in truth," that we have obtained the full sum and substance of the Biblical revelation. God is now no longer, as in the ancient times, only Elohim, a Being of inexpressible might and greatness; nor only Jehovah, the true eternal existence, before which everything else is changeable and perishable; but He stands in a far dearer and more intimate relation to us, as the great Parent Spirit, the Heavenly Father of all.

The conception of God as a Father is not unknown to the Old Testament; but it is there usually limited in its application to the chosen people alone.[†] In the Christian teachings, the term is one of wider sweep, and greater depth and richness of meaning. And from this, the characteristic Christian idea of God, a new and clearer light breaks forth upon the path of life, shewing the relations in which men stand not only to God, but to each other.

---

[*] John xiv. 9, "He that hath seen me hath seen the Father." These words, it may here be observed, were recently adduced by the Editor of the *Record* (No of September 8, 1871), as an all-sufficient proof "of the equality and unity of Jesus Christ with the Father." Such is the incredibly superficial or thoughtless way in which a mind long subjected to the hardening dogmatic influences of the established orthodoxy can misinterpret the Scriptures, even while professing to honour them as the inspired word of God! That the words ought not to be taken in the literal sense alleged, may be sufficiently learnt from another expression of this Evangelist, "No man hath *seen* God at any time; the only begotten Son, which is in the bosom of the Father, he hath *declared* him" (John i. 18). Their meaning is evidently to be sought for in connection with the doctrine of the Logos, and for this the reader is referred to the Chapters of this work relating to that subject.

[†] Isaiah xlv. 11; lxiv. 8.

They are placed now, as it were, under a more penetrating and spiritual law, and bound over to live together in peace and mutual goodwill and service, as the children of one family, members of the great Christian brotherhood. "There is neither Jew nor Greek, circumcision nor uncircumcision, Barbarian, Scythian, bond nor free," but all are as "one in Christ Jesus."* So writes the great Apostle of the Gentiles, indicating that now, "in Christ," the grosser distinctions of class and nation are to count for nothing; well applying and developing the idea contained in the words of his Master, as addressed to his immediate disciples, when he told them to aim at being "the children of their Father which is in heaven."

Within the long period over which we have now so rapidly passed, we have seen the gradual establishment among a particular people of the true idea of God. We have seen them advancing, by slow and painful efforts and with a constant tendency to fall back, from the rude beginnings of their early history, and from very unworthy conceptions of the Almighty, to the belief in His eternity, His universal power and dominion, His sole Godhead. We have seen this ancient Hebrew belief resulting in the still more spiritual conception of the Christian Master and his disciples, even in the great faith in "One God and Father of all, who is above all and through all and in you all."

And, throughout this vast space of time, in all the Biblical writings belonging to it, where, let us now ask, is there any trace of a radical change in the mode of conceiving of the Oneness of God? In reply to this question, it is not enough to refer, as Dr. Liddon does,† to "hints," "suggestions," "adumbrations," symbolical "unveilings," not understood at the time by those to whom they are supposed to have been given, and often matter of controversy since. Dark innuendoes of this kind are not what may reasonably be expected in such a case, but some positive declaration, plainly

---

* Coloss. iii. 11 ; Gal. iii. 28. † B. L., p. 48, *seq.*

announcing the new doctrine. But where is this, or anything like this, to be found in either Testament? *When* and *where*, precisely, in the teaching of Scripture, is the new idea of a divine plurality, a divine threeness, first distinctly introduced, as the correction or completion of the older doctrine? Where is the ancient idea of One Jehovah, besides whom there is no other God, modified and changed into a Trinity of persons, each of which is God as much as either of the others? Can Dr. Liddon, or any other person, confidently lay his hand upon the place, and say, Here the doctrine of the threefold nature of the Godhead was first revealed?—or, Here we see the interest or astonishment it aroused in the minds of those who were beginning to apprehend it?—or, Here, again, it is clearly, fully declared, finally established?

What answer Dr. Liddon can give to such questions as these, we shall presently see more fully. Meantime we venture to say that, within the pages of the Bible, an affirmative answer cannot be found. And this is said, not forgetting the passages which are usually thought definitely to express the doctrine of the Trinity.* An answer to such questions is easily found, when we reach the second and following centuries of the Christian era. Then it may be seen how Gentile converts to Christianity brought with them into the new religion certain ideas of their philosophy, and elaborated from them much of the system of the modern orthodoxy. Among these men, we can easily see when and where the doctrine of the Trinity began to be, and how it gradually assumed its now prevailing form.† But this is not to be traced within the pages of Scripture. Here, we have One God at the beginning, and One God at the end, without any limitation or qualification whatever. As, for example, we read in the words of Moses,

---

* Matt. xxviii. 19; 2 Cor. xiii. 14; 1 John v. 7. See Appendix to this Chapter.

† See a clear and concise historical account in Réville's *Histoire du Dogme de la Divinité de Jesus Christ* (English translation, 1870): compare also Donaldson's *Christian Literature*, Book ii. See *infra*, Chapters XVI. to XIX.

"Hear, O Israel, Jehovah our God, Jehovah is one." Christ takes up the same strain, and when he was asked by the scribe which was the first commandment of all, Jesus, we are told, answered him in the same ancient words, "The first of all the commandments is, Hear, O Israel, the Lord our God is one Lord; and thou shalt love the Lord thy God with all thy heart, and with all thy soul, and with all thy mind, and with all thy strength: this is the first commandment."* The Apostle Paul re-echoes this declaration: "To us," he says, "there is one God, the Father, of whom are all things, and we in him."†

Where, then, does it appear that Jews or Christians were ever taught a *different* doctrine respecting God from that of the great founders respectively of Judaism and Christianity?—where does this clearly and explicitly appear?—until indeed, as before observed, we come far down into the post-apostolic times, when there is no doubt whatever either as to the fact of a new doctrine having been introduced, or as to the source from whence it was immediately derived?

In itself, and apart from the necessities of controversial explanation or defence, Christianity is usually declared to be as truly a monotheistic religion as the ancient Judaism. Few persons will deny that such a statement is correct in regard to the Christianity of the New Testament. It ought then to be a matter of the gravest consideration to every Christian mind that the doctrine of the Trinity, as popularly held,—as defined, for example, in the Athanasian Creed,—practically and logically amounts to tritheism. It makes Jesus Christ to be God, as much as the Almighty Father. It constantly speaks of him as such, and so addresses him in the language of prayer, in a manner which is absolutely without precedent in the Scriptures. The popular Christianity, again, makes the Holy Spirit to be God, a distinct and personal being, as much as the Father and

* Deut. vi. 4; Mark xii. 29, 30.   † 1 Cor. viii. 6.   Comp. Ephes. iv. 5, 6.

the Son; telling us that each of the Three, separately and apart, is God, exactly as either of the others is so. And if this does not amount to the assertion of *three co-equal beings*, each of which is God, it is surely impossible to find language in which to make such an assertion. Nor can this conclusion, however unacceptable or repulsive it may be to the devout mind, be effectually hindered or nullified by the few words with which the creeds and their defenders endeavour to protect themselves from the imputation of tritheism, when they append the proposition, or explanations which are equivalent, that "yet there are not three Gods, but only one God." In thus proceeding, they simply exemplify the absurdity of saying that a thing *is*, and is *not*, at one and the same time.*

This tritheistic element, however, or anything really like it, is not to be found in the pages of the Scriptures,—any more than is the worship of the Virgin Mary. The one, in truth, it is very plain, has much the same foundation as the other; that is to say, it is equally founded, not in the teaching of the Bible, but on Church authority,† and on creeds which have come down to us from comparatively ignorant and corrupt ages—ages too of subtle and daring speculation on divine things.

The quality of unreasonableness, therefore, let us finally

---

* Eminent Trinitarian writers have expressed themselves in very similar terms on the great mystery of their religion. Thus:—"When it is proposed to me to affirm, that 'in the unity of the Godhead there be three persons, of one substance, power, and eternity, the Father, the Son, and the Holy Ghost;' I have difficulty enough! my understanding is involved in perplexity, my conceptions bewildered in the thickest darkness. I pause; I hesitate; I ask what necessity there is for making such a declaration. . . . . . But does not this confound all our conceptions, and make us use words without meaning? I think it does. I profess and proclaim my confusion in the most unequivocal manner: I make it an essential part of my declaration. Did I pretend to understand what I say, I might be a Tritheist, or an infidel; but I could not both worship the one true God, and acknowledge Jesus Christ to be Lord of all."—Dr. Hey, Lectures on Divinity, *apud* Wilson, *Concessions of Trinitarians* (1842), p. 34.

† This has been fully *admitted* by a certain class of High Church writers, whose statements it is not necessary here to cite in detail.

observe, which any one may see in the ecclesiastical doctrine of the Trinity, he ought not to impute to the Bible. That volume is not really to be charged with it. The Scriptures, it is needless to observe, do not contain the word Trinity, nor can the idea be expressed in Scriptural terms, or by any combination of Scriptural words. It would perhaps be as easy to describe the electric telegraph, or the parts of the steam-engine, in Biblical language, as to describe the doctrine of the Trinity. How therefore can the latter be really a doctrine of the Bible? That book puts no such strain upon devout faith. On the contrary, in its record of the development of the Theistic belief of the Israelites, it is in remarkable harmony with the dictates of reason and the analogies of human experience.

And not only so:—in that ancient and simple doctrine of one God, the Heavenly Father, "in whom we live and move and have our being," which is the final result yielded by the ages of varied experience through which the sacred history runs, we have that which is in harmony not only with our reason, but with one of the marked tendencies of modern science. For the latter, we know, is constantly seeking and striving to reduce the number of Causes which are at work in producing the visible phenomena of the universe; to rise up, in fact, to One Great First Cause; and to shew that all the various powers and laws of nature are but simple manifestations of that. Natural philosophers will tell us that such things as heat and light and electricity are most probably but various developments, or applications, of one and the same inscrutable primary force. Some may even add to this that the principle of life, and even Thought itself, can be only forms of the same all-pervading original cause. What that Great First Cause may be, they do not presume to define, hardly even to conjecture.

The Bible would lead us to believe that, in the last resort, it is the Living God, or the intelligent, conscious Will of the one

Almighty Creator. And this proposition, however difficult it may be to any one to receive, is certainly neither opposed to reason nor condemned in any way by the moral sense. On the contrary, the rational and spiritual part of our nature will gladly, in most cases, respond to that proposition; and in it, therefore, the devout man may well be contented to rest, until the day comes, if that is ever to be, when scientific research shall be able to give us something better—a day, we must add, which we do not expect, and can hardly desire, to be permitted to see!

APPENDIX TO CHAPTER IX.

NEW TESTAMENT PASSAGES SUPPOSED TO EXPRESS THE DOCTRINE OF THE TRINITY.

Of such passages the number is three;—one of them being, however, the worthless interpolated verse in the First Epistle of John, 1 John v. 7, 8. This passage runs as follows:—"There are three that bear record, [in heaven, the Father, the Word and the Holy Spirit, and these three are one. And there are three that bear witness in earth] the Spirit, the water and the blood; and these three agree in one." The words in brackets are now generally known and acknowledged to be spurious. On this point it is sufficient here to cite the testimony of Dean Alford. He observes that the words "*are omitted by all Greek MSS. (till the sixteenth century)'; all the Greek Fathers; all the ancient versions; and most of the Latin Fathers.*" (Revised Version of N. T., note *in loc.*) The words are evidently without value for any dogmatic purpose.

There are left two other passages which are usually supposed clearly and unquestionably to express the doctrine of three Divine persons—two only, be it remembered, out of the whole extent of the Bible. They are found in Matt. xxviii. 19, and 2 Cor. xiii. 14.

The former of these, in a corrected translation, reads thus: "Go ye therefore and make disciples of all the nations, baptizing them into the name of the Father, and of the Son, and of the Holy Spirit."* In judging whether or not we have here, as alleged, a statement of the doctrine of the Trinity, it should be remembered that, throughout the whole Gospel of Matthew, there is no expression or word, in which that doctrine can be supposed to be conveyed, until we come to this, the last verse but one of the Gospel. So far, therefore, as this Gospel is concerned, it would appear that throughout all the ministry of Christ, in all his discourses, parables and sayings of various kinds here recorded, there is nothing to shew that the Trinity of Persons was ever spoken of between our Lord and his disciples, until we come to the latest moments of his life on earth. And then (we are asked to believe), by using the words now under notice, he revealed the truth to the disciples and to the Christian world of future ages.

Is the supposition a probable one? Could such a doctrine have been withheld by the Master from the disciples and from the world in such a manner—left to be revealed to them only in this slight and accidental kind of way,—and that too, not directly, as a doctrine of supreme importance offered to their faith, but only as something, after all, *implied* or *deducible* by way of inference from the words employed?

For, it will be observed, even this verse does not explicitly declare Three Persons and One God. It does not *say* that the three are each equally God, one as much as the other; it does not *say* that the Son is God, or the Holy Spirit, but simply "Go and baptize into the name" of the Three, whatever these may each severally be.

But what, then, is the meaning of the injunction? To be baptized into the name of any person (or into that person) does not pre-imply that he is accepted as an object of worship, but as one of religious faith. Such baptism makes him the subject of recognition and belief, under some implied or imputed character, whatever that

---

* "Holy Spirit." See note on the words *Ghost* and *Spirit*, *infra*, Chapter XXIII.

may be. St. Paul says of the fathers of his nation that they were "all baptized into Moses" (1 Cor. x. 1, 2). He does not mean that they had been taught to consider Moses as God, or to make him an object of their worship. He can only mean that they recognized and had faith in him as their leader, and adopted the religious system which he gave them. The same Apostle even speaks of baptism into his own name as a possibility (1 Cor. i. 13–15). Whatever his definite meaning may have been, he could not have intended to suggest that those who might have been so baptized would by the act have recognized him as God, or made him an object of religious worship.

Thus, then, it is clear that, although the Father, the Son, and the Holy Spirit, are here placed together in one form of words, as objects into which baptism shall take place, it by no means follows that the three are each a Divine person, and each equally God. It does not follow, therefore, that we have here any statement of the doctrine of the Trinity, or any allusion to it. The most that can be said is this: It that doctrine were certainly established and known by other evidence, this verse might be interpreted in accordance with it. But is it certainly established and known by other evidence? We submit that the contrary is the case;—and that there is in fact no passage of Scripture whatever in which the doctrine of the Trinity is either clearly stated, or even necessarily implied.

Baptism "into the name of the Father," was baptism into the confession of the One God, the Heavenly Father:—no unimportant article of faith to a convert from heathenism, who had perhaps been a believer in many gods, or in none. Baptism into the name of the Son was the distinctively Christian part of the rite. It was baptism into the belief and reception of Jesus as Christ, the Messiah or "Son of God." This was evidently an essential part of the new disciple's confession, and neither Jew nor heathen could become a Christian without it. Baptism into the Holy Spirit was, to the convert of those days, baptism into the confession and participation of those gifts of the Spirit, which in the Book of Acts are stated to have been shed upon the disciples, and are often referred to in the course of that book.*

We must not forget that in the early Christian times it was a disputed question whether the Messiah (the Son) had come or not. Jesus of Nazareth the Jewish nation did not receive in that character. They rejected and crucified him. Hence it was indispensable that converts should make a distinct confession of what was thus denied, and should be baptized into the name of the Son; that is to say, into the belief in Jesus, not as God, but as Christ.† In regard to the Holy Spirit, it will be remembered that there is a passage in the Acts where Christian disciples, imperfectly instructed, are said to know nothing of that object of faith. "We have not so much as heard whether there be any Holy Spirit" (Acts xix. 2). It is impossible to think that they could have been left in such ignorance, when they became Christians, had the term "Holy Spirit" really denoted the third co-equal member of a Divine Trinity, into the confession of which converts were received by baptism. We see what is meant (v. 5) when it is said that they were "baptized into the name of the Lord Jesus"—and that the Holy Spirit then "came on them" (v. 6). The form of baptism here spoken of, "into the name of the Lord Jesus," is the one which, being indispensable, alone occurs in the Book of Acts. What is termed the baptismal formula (Matt. xxviii. 19) is nowhere met with in that book; shewing us plainly that a confession of the doctrine of the Trinity, so far as can be learnt from the New Testament, was never made; that, for some reason not stated, the supposed "formula" was not used, and that Christian baptism in the Apostolical age, was baptism into the name of Jesus alone.

The second instance in which the doctrine of the Trinity is thought to be clearly expressed in the New Testament occurs again in an accidental kind of way, in the last verse of one of St. Paul's Epistles (2 Cor. xiii. 14):—"The grace of the Lord Jesus Christ,

* E.g., Acts ii. 4; iv. 31.   † See *infra*, Chapters XI. XII.

and the love of God, and the communion of the Holy Spirit be with you all." The words are easily shewn to be inconsistent with the doctrine they are supposed to express. For it is plain that the Almighty Being is separated, in the writer's conception, from Jesus Christ and from the Holy Spirit. "The grace of the Lord Jesus Christ, *and* the love of God, *and* the communion of the Holy Spirit:"—three objects of thought, God being one of them, distinctly apart from the others. What the Apostle wishes for his Corinthian friends is simply this, that the grace (or favour) of Jesus Christ (their expected Judge *) may be with them, and God's love, and a participation in the good gifts and influences, constantly denoted in the New Testament by the phrase Holy Spirit.†

CHAPTER X.

THE ORTHODOX ARGUMENT FROM PLURAL FORMS OF EXPRESSION.

THE plural form of the word Elohim has been brought forward as affording evidence in support of the doctrine of a plurality of persons in the Godhead. This appeal to that word we had thought obsolete, like some other arguments for the same doctrine; or, if not obsolete, available only among ill-informed persons.‡ It has, however, been revived in the present instance, by one who certainly cannot be classed among such persons; and it may therefore be desirable here to notice the use which he has made of the word in question.

Dr. Liddon ascribes great significance to this plural, as giving us "intimation of the existence of a plurality of Persons within

---

* Acts xvii. 31. † See *infra*, Chapter on the Holy Spirit.
‡ Bishop Colenso observes that it is "quite a mistake to think of proving the doctrine of the Trinity, as some do, from the fact that Elohim is a plural name." *Pentateuch*, II. p. 256.

the One Essence of God."* It was only in modern times that its full importance to this effect was perceived. "It was not insisted upon by the primitive Church," as Dr. Liddon admits He does not tell us whether it merely escaped the observation of earlier Christian writers, nor how it came to pass, if they attached any value to it, that they should have made no use of it. Most probably they passed it over because it is simply and really devoid of value, and could never, by the nature of the case, have occurred to men who lived near to the ages when Hebrew was a living language. The scholastic subtlety of later times, however, easily found the doctrine of the Trinity in the peculiarities of Hebrew syntax; and following such guidance Dr. Liddon gravely informs us that when "Moses" relates "the primal creative act of God,". . . . . . "he joins a singular verb to a plural noun."†

It is a very large assumption, in the face of modern investigations which cannot be supposed unknown to the writer of these words, to say that it is "Moses" who does this. But letting that pass, it may be observed that the circumstance referred to does not appear to be perfectly satisfactory to Dr. Liddon himself. "The analogies of the language," he candidly says, "may indeed prove that the plural form of the word had a majestic force;"‡ but then, he suggests, would it not have been *dangerous*, in connection with a monotheistic religion like the Hebrew, to use a plural form to express the sacred name?—and could so great a risk have been run, except for some mysterious purpose of foreshadowing the higher truth to come? So easy and self-evident is the orthodox meaning of these forms to one who brings to them a mind already full of the doctrine they are supposed to teach, as it may be learnt from the Creeds and Articles, or from the decrees and speculations of ancient Councils and Fathers. To

* B. L., p. 48. † B. L., *ibid.* ‡ B. L., p. 49.

such a mind it is useless to point out that plural forms occur in Hebrew, in other cases in which a singular might have been expected. For example, when Abraham is spoken of as the Master of Eliezer, the word rendered *Master* is sometimes in the plural. So with the word rendered *Wisdom* in Proverbs, and the word *Behemoth* in Job.* These are plural in form, while evidently used each of a single object of thought; and other cases of the same kind are easily found.

But these simple and obvious explanations are little suitable to the genius of the popular theology. Dr. Liddon accordingly urges that the plural was "necessary in order to hint at the complex mystery of God's inner life." He omits to explain how it was that the hint was so entirely *lost* upon the Hebrew people, both in ancient and in modern times. For is there anything more certain in their history than that they have always, both in the later Biblical times and since, clung to the belief in Jehovah as the One only God, and have never admitted the idea of a distinction of personal existences in His nature?

In regard to such expressions as, "Let us make man in our image," "Let us go down," "become as one of us,"† Dr. Liddon reminds us that the Church Fathers detected the plurality of persons in these too, and he is again willing to follow their example. It would not be correct, however, to say that the earliest Fathers regarded such passages as implying the doctrine of a Trinity. Justin Martyr explained them of the Word or Logos, but says nothing about a third person. It is nevertheless perfectly reasonable to regard these forms of speech as having been used by the ancient Hebrew writer, who was evidently not afraid of anthropomorphism, simply from his conception of the Deity as surrounded by angels;‡ or, again, even to regard them

---

* Gen. xxiv. 9, 10; Prov. ix. 1; Job xl. 15.   † Gen. i. 26; xi. 7; iii. 22.
‡ Comp. Job i. 6-12; xxxviii. 7.

as employed much as similar forms are used in modern times, in documents issued by, or in the name of, sovereign potentates.* At all events, the judgment of the ancient writer of Genesis is clearly to be commended, when, in speaking of the Deity, he used his plural forms of expression, and avoided the corresponding singulars. Literary taste alone, to say nothing of religious feeling, might well lead him to prefer the former as alone suitable to the greatness of his theme. How then can a weighty theological argument be built with any confidence upon so slight a foundation?

Some difficulty, however, is felt, and not unnaturally, in regard to the words " our image," or " likeness," in which man is said to be created. How could it be a likeness common to God and angels? It can only point, therefore, Dr. Liddon thinks, both to a plurality of persons in the Godhead and also to " Their participation in an Undivided Nature." But what if it appears that the sacred writer conceived of a likeness between God and man of the literal kind? That he did so, may be gathered from another passage in Genesis, in which it is said that God created Adam " in the likeness of God," and that Adam " begat a son in his own likeness." The phrase and the original word are here the same as in the first chapter of Genesis.† So that there can be no doubt that the resemblance meant was one of form and feature; that the ancient writer regarded man as having been literally made in the likeness of God, as Adam's son was in that of his father; and that he conceived of Elohim, as Himself in bodily form and organs like the man whom He had called into existence. There is excellent Scriptural warrant for thus thinking. For, as we are told, the Deity " walks" in the garden of Eden,

---

* Examples of this use of the plural occur in the Bible. See Ezra iv. 18; vii. 21, 24.
† Gen. v. 1-3; i. 26, 27.

Adam and Eve hear his " voice" speaking to them, and He also " made coats of skin" for them and clothed them.*

But Dr. Liddon has another great class of plural forms of expression, by which the future unfolding of the nature of God is foreshadowed, though here too, alas! to blind eyes; for there is nothing to shew that the expressions in question were ever understood in this way, until the later days of Trinitarian speculation. The priest is directed to repeat the Holy Name three times, in the blessing which was to be given to the children of Israel: so in some of the Psalms, there is, we are told, a threefold rhythm, or recurrence of prayer or praise.† It will be found, however, that in some of the passages referred to, the rhythm is only twofold, or that it is also fourfold or more.‡

But passing from this point, the crowning significance of such passages is to be found in the vision of Isaiah.§ Here we have unquestionably the threefold cry, "Holy, holy, holy;" and in a subsequent verse does not Jehovah say, "Who will go for us?" "What a flood of almost Gospel light," Dr. Liddon exclaims, is here "poured upon the intelligence of the elder church" ‖—only again, as before, the elder church did not, could not see it! It is reserved for the modern church alone, it would seem, to read these passages in their true sense, and the modern church, in the abundance of other instruction, does not need that ancient light; so that it really appears to have been shed upon the world in vain.

The argument advanced is, in any case, so purely " subjective," that we have difficulty in meeting it, except with the remark that we do not see or feel its force. We must therefore be contented to make Dr. Liddon, and such of his readers as are satisfied with

---

* Gen. iii. 8, 21.   † Num. vi 23 26; Ps. xxix. 4, 5, 7, 8 ; xcvi. 1, 2, 7, 8.
‡ E.g., Ps. xxix. 1, 2 ; also vv. 10, 11 ; xcvi. 11, 12.   § Is. vi. 2-8.
‖ B. L., p. 51.

it, a present of it, such as it is. He has certainly the merit of having put it extremely well, and drawn from it as much support probably as any one would venture to take.*

Similar considerations apply to what Dr. Liddon next says about the "Theophanies" of the Old Testament. These remarkable appearances of the Divine Being to the patriarchs and others, are very curiously related in the books of Genesis and Judges. There is, in one place, some little confusion of persons, it is true; but this may not amount to much in a theological argument: as where "Jehovah appeared to Abraham" in the plain of Mamre, "and he lifted up his eyes and looked, and lo, *three men* stood by him." The narrative goes on to tell us how Abraham and Sarah prepared food for these men, and stood by them under a tree, in the heat of the day, "and they did eat." One of the men proves to be Jehovah, or, at least speaks under his name; and after giving the promise of a son to Abraham, and rebuking Sarah for laughing, the same speaker says, in reference to Sodom and Gomorrah, "I will go down, now, and see whether they have done altogether according to the cry of it, and if not I will know."†

It would have been more consistent, theologically, if the speaker had here said WE; especially as three persons are present.‡ To this extent, therefore, Dr. Liddon's argument from the passage unquestionably fails; but he has an abundance of instances at command to make up for this§ and to establish the conclusion to which he desires to lead us. Granting the large, and really

---

* It may be well to remind the reader that the monotheistic Koran frequently attributes to the Almighty a similar plural form of expression. The repetition of the word Holy (Isaiah vi. 3) is doubtless simply emphatic; and may be equivalent to the superlative *most holy*.—Comp. Jer. xxii. 29, "O earth, earth, earth, hear the word of Jehovah:" also Ezek. xxi. 27; Rev. viii. 13. So Num. vi. 23-26.

† Gen. xviii. 1-21.

‡ The conception of the sacred writer surely is that Jehovah was accompanied by two attendants.

§ B. L., pp. 52-56.

inadmissible, assumption that there is no legendary element in these narratives of the early Hebrew history, let us notice the inquiries which Dr. Liddon founds upon them. Do not these remarkable apparitions, he asks, " suggest, as their natural climax and explanation, some personal self-unveiling of God before the eyes of His creatures? Would not God appear to have been training His people, by this long and mysterious series of communications, at length to recognise and to worship Him when hidden under, and indissolubly one with a created nature? .... Is there any other account of them so much in harmony with the general scope of Holy Scripture, as that they were successive lessons addressed to the eye and to the ear of ancient piety, in anticipation of a coming Incarnation of God?"*

Such is the very hypothetical conclusion. The difficulty in admitting it is obvious and, surely it is insuperable,—although, strangely enough, it remains unnoticed by its eloquent expounder. This training of the ancient generations of the patriarchs, two thousand years or more before Christ,—how could it prepare the people of his far distant age, who had not themselves experienced it, to receive the doctrine of the incarnation of a divine person of the Godhead in Jesus of Nazareth? And if such were its purpose, did it not entirely *fail?*—for did not the great mass of the Jewish people, including their rulers and leading men, reject Jesus Christ, deny that he was the Messiah, and put him to death? What then was the utility of the Theophanies, in the sense alleged, and how could they have served as "successive lessons addressed to the eye and to the ear of ancient piety," in preparation for that which they so entirely failed to produce?

Similar remarks must be made on what Dr. Liddon next advances respecting the personification of Wisdom in the Book of Proverbs; respecting the Sapiential Books, the Logos of Philo,

* B. L., pp. 58, 59.

and the anticipations of Messianic glory scattered throughout the Prophets. So far as these were designed, as we are told they were, to prepare the Jewish people for the incarnation of the second person of the Trinity in Jesus of Nazareth, they manifestly did not attain their object. The only alternative to this will be to say that, while so failing in regard to the Jews, they have succeeded as regards the Christians. But is even this correct? If it were so, it would scarcely have been necessary for Dr. Liddon to have constructed the elaborate argument contained in this volume, or to have tasked his ingenuity and his learning, to say nothing about the patience of his readers, as he has found it necessary to do, in order to remove the objections and difficulties to which his leading proposition is open; nor should we, with many others, have found ourselves, as earnest inquirers, so unable to assent to his conclusions,—impeded or repelled, as we are, by something doubtful, or wrongly presented, on almost every page of his book. This position of the question is undeniable; and forms, in itself, a conclusive answer and refutation to this part of the case, ingeniously reasoned as it is.

Before leaving the subject, we may briefly notice, from another point of view, the extreme difficulty of believing that these peculiar forms of expression can have had the preparatory purpose attributed to them.

We have seen that, during many centuries, the Hebrew nation was extremely prone to very gross "backsliding;" to apostasy, that is to say, from their faith in Jehovah—and that rulers and people alike were from time to time guilty of this devotion to strange gods, to Baal, Moloch, Chiun, the "queen of heaven," Gad and Meni.* Is it not incredible that it should have been sought or intended to exercise upon such a people, by these refinements of phraseology, the enlightening, elevating influence

* Jer. ii. 19; vii. 17; Isaiah lxv. 11; Amos v. 26.

which is supposed? They were unable to maintain a firm grasp even of the simple doctrine of the Divine Unity, as inculcated in their own law, by their own prophets and legislators. Yet we are asked to believe that, in the midst of their gross idolatries, they were being trained for the reception of Trinity in Unity! We are asked to believe that by the plural form of a word for God, by the threefold rhythm of a Psalm, by the utterance, as many times repeated, of a priestly blessing, or of the word Holy, in the little known writings of a prophet, that, by such impalpable means as these, such a people were being led on to think of a mysterious plurality in the nature of the Godhead! We are asked to believe that such a people were being prepared, centuries in advance, by such delicate refinements of expression, for the future reception of doctrines, on the right understanding of which the salvation of the world, a thousand years afterwards, more or less, was mainly to depend!

The climax of the argument is not reached, until we remember that we are asked to believe all this, in the face of the fact that the alleged preparation proved in the end a manifest *failure*, and never had the effect among the Hebrews which is attributed to it.*

* This failure is sometimes very fully and candidly admitted. Thus the present Bishop of Lincoln has said—"It cannot be denied that the Jews *ought* to have deduced the doctrine of the Messiah's divinity [deity] from their own Scriptures, especially from such texts as Psalm xlv. 6, 7. . . . . . But the question is not, whether the Jews *might not and ought not* to have inferred the Divine Sonship of the Messiah from their own Scriptures, but whether for the most part they really *did* deduce that doctrine from those Scriptures? They ought doubtless to have been prepared by those Scriptures for a *suffering* Messiah; but this we know was *not* the case; and the cross of Christ was to them a stumbling-block (1 Cor. i. 23); and one of the strongest objections which they raised against the Christians was that they worshiped a man who died a death which is declared to be an accursed one in the law of Moses, which was delivered by God Himself."—Bishop Wordsworth, article *Son of God*, in Dr. W. Smith's Dictionary of the Bible. In reference to the last sentence of the above passage, it may be observed that there is no evidence whatever in the New Testament of any objection having been brought against the disciples on the ground that they *worshiped* their departed Master. See *infra*, Chapter on the Worship of Christ.

Truly the faith is very great, very enviable, at least very wonderful, which can really attribute weight to this argument from plural forms.

CHAPTER XI.

JESUS OF NAZARETH—THE CHARGE ON WHICH HE WAS PUT TO DEATH.

IN approaching the subject now before us, we are reminded both of its difficulty and of its importance, by the controversies to which it has given rise, in ancient and in modern times;—in the former case, among the Christians of the third and fourth centuries; in the latter, between Socinian and Unitarian writers on the one side, and orthodox, that is to say Trinitarian, and also Arian, writers on the other. And yet it is, in truth, a subject to the settlement of which a few considerations, and those of a simple and even obvious character, would appear to go a very great way. If it were only possible that old and accepted doctrines could be freely held; if, that is, they could be detached not merely from the prepossessions of education, but also from manifold interests of a more tangible kind which are now legally bound up with their maintenance, in this country and in others,—there can be no doubt that a rational and really Scriptural form of belief in regard to the person and work of Christ would speedily win its way throughout the churches,—or would, at least, have a far better chance of doing so than it has at present.

The question before us is briefly this: WHO, or rather WHAT, was Jesus of Nazareth?—more definitely still, Was he the ALMIGHTY BEING in a human form?—he who was born of a human mother, and lived as an infant, a child, a youth, in his parental home; who perhaps, according to the ancient tradition, followed his father's trade of a carpenter; who lived thus a man among the people of his time, ate and drank, talked and slept, was hungry, thirsty and weary, and worshiped and prayed, and went about as they did, finally ending his brief career by an ignominious death at the hands of Roman soldiers;—was the person who thus lived and died under the name of Jesus of Nazareth, the Almighty Being Himself, and was this familiarly known to many around him, and by them openly acknowledged and acted upon? Truly it is a proposition hard to receive, and one that should have clear and cogent evidence, to carry conviction of its truth to the thoughtful, reasonable mind.

Let us, with the view of answering our question, take one of the most prominent scenes in the life of Christ,—that of his accusation before the authorities who condemned him to death. As this occurs near the close of his career, any peculiar claim of his to be a Divine person incarnate must have been made, and well known to those among whom he lived, previous to the enactment of this scene. It is, therefore, a scene in which such a claim may reasonably be expected to appear, either by express statement or by implication, in the account of what took place.

It is hardly necessary to observe that the only original sources of knowledge on this subject are the evangelical narratives; such slight and incidental notices of the origin of Christianity as are found in one or two of the Latin historians being wholly insufficient for our information. The Gospels are not, indeed, the oldest part of the New Testament, a distinction which belongs, as we have seen, to St. Paul's Epistles. But then it is equally true, that the latter would not at all adequately afford us the details which we need. That Apostle did not know our Lord personally, had never seen him in "the flesh." The allusions which his writings contain to the events of the life of Jesus, or to his teachings, are therefore both rare and slight. The whole interest of the Apostle seems to have been fixed upon the risen Christ, his present exaltation, his future coming in his glory.* He does not even allude to the miraculous birth, suitable as this would have been to illustrate some of Paul's own statements respecting the Messianic character and dignity of Jesus—provided only it had been the reality which is commonly supposed.

And this remark is even more strikingly true, as we may here notice, in connection with the opening chapter of the fourth Gospel, where nothing could have been more appropriate, in speaking of the incarnate Word, than to have at least alluded to the mode or medium by which the incarnation had taken place. But neither here nor anywhere else in the New Testament, except in the two introductions of Matthew and Luke, is there any use made of the miraculous conception and birth of Jesus; nor can any reference to it, even the slightest, be anywhere found. Those two introductions stand wholly unsupported, in all their inconsistency or contradiction to one another. They are indeed most probably to be regarded as non-authentic additions to the original form of the two Gospels—although it is, nevertheless, true that they are found in all existing manuscripts and versions of those Gospels. For this negative conclusion, it is well known to the learned, there is not wanting very important and independent evidence, on which, however, it does not concern us to dwell minutely in the present connection.†

It is evident, then, to return to our principal argument, that the writings of St. Paul afford little information, either as to the

---

* Rom. i. 3, 4; 1 Cor. xv. 20-28.

† See Norton, *Genuineness of the Gospels*, 2nd ed., I. pp. 204-210. Comp. *Schleiermacher on Luke*, pp. 44-52, in the English translation of this work made by the present Bishop of St. David's, when (as he has explained) he was "a young law student."

birth or any other recorded event in the life of Christ. We are thus necessarily thrown back upon the historical portions of the New Testament, and more especially upon the three Synoptical Gospels, which in point of time come nearer than the Fourth to the actual generation in which Jesus lived. It may, however, be observed that all the four Evangelists agree substantially with one another, as regards leading facts, in their respective accounts of the trial of Jesus, and of the charge brought against him. Hence it will be sufficient for our present purpose to take their statements much as they lie before us in the four Gospels.

The first Evangelist speaks of the accusation in the following terms :—" Now the chief priests, and elders, and all the council, sought false witness against Jesus, to put him to death; but found none; yea, though many false witnesses came, yet found they none. At the last came two, and said, This man said, I am able to destroy the temple of God, and to build it in three days. And the high-priest arose, and said unto him, Answerest thou nothing? What is it that these witness against thee? But Jesus held his peace. And the high-priest answered and said unto him, I adjure thee by the living God, that thou tell us whether thou be the Christ, the Son of God. Jesus saith unto him, Thou hast said : nevertheless I say unto you, Hereafter shall ye see the Son of Man sitting on the right hand of power and coming in the clouds of heaven. Then the high-priest rent his clothes, saying, He hath spoken blasphemy; what further need have we of witnesses? Behold now ye have heard his blasphemy. What think ye? They answered and said, He is guilty of death."*

Mark gives the same account; while Luke and John omit to notice the charge respecting the temple, and confine themselves

---

* Matt. xxvi. 59-66 ; Mark xiv. 55-64 ; Luke xxii. 66 71 : John xviii. 19-23 and 28-40.

more especially to the allegation that Jesus had claimed to be the Christ—the latter Evangelist, moreover, saying little of the accusation as brought before the high-priest, and speaking mainly of what took place before the Roman tribunal.

When Jesus is brought before Pilate, a similar charge is made against him, but it is necessarily a little altered in the terms, so as to be more comprehensible to the Roman. He is now accused of having made himself a king, "perverting the nation, and forbidding to give tribute to Cæsar." So the Evangelist Luke. The other Evangelists substantially agree, as we learn from the question of Pilate to Jesus, recorded in each, "Art thou the king of the Jews?"* Thus it is clear that, while before the Jewish Sanhedrim the religious aspect of the charge is made prominent, before the Roman procurator it is the political; but the crime imputed is essentially the same in the two cases.

In the accusation thus brought there was certainly a degree of truth. Jesus *had* said that he was Christ, and had spoken of the kingdom upon which he was to enter. The "kingdom of God," and the "kingdom of heaven," were no uncommon expressions on his lips; but we have no reason to think that he used them in any political or temporal sense; while he expressly declared to Pilate himself, "My kingdom is not of this world."† Nor was it true that he had forbidden to pay tribute to Cæsar. This could only be a false inference from his claim to be "the Christ," as the latter was understood, or misunderstood, by those around him. It was a false inference; and doubtless many of those who now urged it knew it to be false, for Jesus had really said in public, "Render unto Cæsar the things that are Cæsar's, and unto God the things that are God's."

There was a mixture, therefore, of truth and falsehood in the

---

* Luke xxiii. 2; Matt. xxvii. 11; Mark xv. 2; John xviii. 33.
† Matt. xvi. 16; Mark iv. 11, *seq.*; Luke xii. 31; xiii. 28, 29; John xviii. 36.

charge brought against him by his adversaries. And the falsehood predominated, in so much that these unscrupulous men would not have hesitated, we may be sure, to lay hold of any plausible means of securing the death of the accused man. This being the case, we cannot but be struck with one thing, which is that *they do not accuse him of having claimed to be God!* Supposing it to be true, as now usually alleged, that Jesus had made himself known among his followers as being the Almighty in a human form, how is it that his enemies, or his judges, Jewish or Roman, make no allusion to this? They had difficulty, it would appear, before the Sanhedrim, in finding a sufficient accusation, until they found two witnesses who charged him with speaking against the temple. How then was it that no witness came forward to speak of that far greater blasphemy, his pretending not only to be able to destroy and rebuild the temple in three days, but even to be God Himself?

It is impossible that such a claim should have escaped the keen eyes and ears of Jewish accusers. We have seen with what reverence the Israelites were accustomed to regard the name of Jehovah, and that they would not even permit themselves to pronounce the word; as also it is a chief commandment of their Law to make no image or likeness of God, in any visible form. Hence, to give that sacred name to any other, to attribute the Divine nature to a human being,—even to say that he was God Himself in the visible form of a man,—would have been looked upon as blasphemous in the highest degree. Yet here, we are told, was Jesus of Nazareth, brought up before the Jewish and the heathen tribunal, on a charge partly political and partly religious; here was he who had gone about among his disciples and his countrymen in Galilee and in Jerusalem, arrogating to himself the very name and glory of the invisible Jehovah; saying that he and the Almighty Father were, in the now popular orthodox sense, One

God; here is he standing before enemies who, obviously, could not have admitted these claims, who were eager for his destruction, and ready to say everything in their power to prove the object of their ill-will worthy of death—and yet they leave out of sight that greatest presumption and blasphemy of all, that he, being a man, had made himself God.

Such an omission, on such an occasion, affords a conclusive reply to the allegation that Jesus was accustomed to represent himself as the Almighty Being, the second member of a divine Trinity of Persons in the Godhead. Had he done so, the fact could not have failed to make its appearance on his trial, and must have been urged with all the vehemence of angry and determined opponents, to the greater injury and condemnation of their innocent victim.

This difficulty in the way of the popular doctrine of the deity of Christ has not escaped orthodox writers—although, we are bound to add, we have not met with anything in what they have said which avails to remove it out of their way—indeed, we have scarcely met with an instance in which it is fairly looked in the face. Dr. Liddon, with all his versatility and eloquence, makes no direct attempt to meet it—all that he says in allusion to it amounting only to one or two assumptions which are really surprising.

Nothing is more certain, he tells us, than that the Sanhedrim condemned Jesus, "because he claimed Divinity"—that is, because he claimed Deity. Nothing is more certain, we reply, from the Evangelical narratives, nothing is more certain from the words of all the four Gospels relating to the trial, than that Jesus was condemned because he claimed to be the Christ, or Messiah, or Son of God, in the Messianic sense of this last expression. "Tell us," the high-priest said, "whether thou be the Christ, the Son of God. Jesus saith unto him, Thou hast said." That is, Jesus answered affirmatively, or assented. And "then the high-priest rent his clothes, saying, He hath spoken blasphemy."*

It is admitted by Dr. Liddon that the Jews were looking "for a political chief, victorious but human, in their expected Messiah." But hence, he adds, the claim of Jesus to that character would not of itself " have shocked the Jews; they would have discussed it on its merits." † It might have been so, perhaps, had the outward circumstances of the claimant corresponded, in their estimation, to the greatness of his pretensions, and if Jesus had stood, at the moment, before friends, not before enemies. But he was one of lowly condition, and destitute of political power ; they were unscrupulous men, eager for his death. Their course was plain ; namely, at once to construe as blasphemous the reply of their victim. This, according to the Evangelical record, they did, and this was amply sufficient for their purpose. But it nowhere appears that he was accused of making the incomparably greater claim alleged by orthodox writers; nor did the possibility of bringing such a charge enter into the mind of any one concerned, so far as can be gathered from the account of the transaction.‡

The exposition on which we are commenting goes yet a step further. It expressly holds that " the blasphemy did not consist either in the assumption of the title Son of Man, or in the claim to be the Messiah. . . . . It was the further claim to be the Son of God, not in any moral or theocratic, but in the natural sense, at which the high-priest and his coadjutors professed to be so deeply shocked." § The question is obvious, How does Dr.

---

* Matt. xxvi. 63–65, and parallels. † B. L., p. 187.

‡ Bishop Wordsworth meets the difficulty, by telling us that Jesus claimed to be "the Messiah *and* Son of God." This improvement upon the sacred narrative is one which the Bishop will hardly expect us to receive, even on episcopal authority. Article *Son of God*, Dict. of the Bible. So apparently Archbishop Thomson, article *Jesus Christ*, in the same work, I. p. 1068.

§ B. L., p. 191.—Archbishop Thomson also observes, "The question was really twofold, 'Art thou the Christ, and in that name dost thou also call thyself the Son

Liddon know this? Where is it *said* that Jesus was condemned because he claimed to be the Son of God "in the natural sense"? And what is meant by the words, "in the natural sense"?

For it is, in truth, one of the very plainest things in the New Testament that the expression Son of God, as used among the Jews and Christians in the New Testament times, simply denoted and meant the Christ,—or, in other words, was a usual appellation of the expected Messiah. The two expressions appear to have been perfectly equivalent. Thus Nathanael says to Jesus, "Thou art the Son of God, the King of Israel." He could not, obviously, have used the former words in any "natural," mysterious, or metaphysical sense,—just converted, as he was, from a state of ignorance or disbelief as to the Messiahship of Jesus. The devil says, "If thou be the Son of God," evidently meaning, If thou be the Messiah.* "Tell us," the high-priest exclaimed, "whether thou be the Christ, the Son of God." Martha exclaims, "Yea, Lord; I believe that thou art the Christ, the Son of God." And the Evangelist declares, "These things are written that ye might believe that Jesus is the Christ, the Son of God."† In 1 John v. 1, we read, "Whosoever believeth that Jesus is *the Christ* is born of God." In the same chapter, v. 5, we read, "Who is he that overcometh the world but he that believeth that Jesus is the *Son of God?*" Thus the two phrases are manifestly, in the New Testament usage, of identical import, or rather, we should say, the words Son of God are used simply as a well understood appellation of the expected Messiah.

Yet there are instances, it may be freely admitted, in which the fourth Evangelist, writing in accordance with his peculiar concep-

---

of God?' There was no blasphemy in claiming the former name, but there was in assuming the latter." Art. *Jesus Christ: ibid.*

* John i. 49; Matt. iv. 3.
† Matt. xxvi. 63; John xx. 31; compare John vi. 69; xi. 27.

tion of the Logos in Jesus, attributes to the latter the use of the words Son, and Son of God, in a sense corresponding to that conception, and going beyond that of the " theocratic sonship,"*— the relation borne by kings and saints of old, and thought to exist in an especial degree between Jehovah and the Messiah. This point will engage our attention hereafter. But meantime we may observe, the mode of representation now referred to will not be found in the Synoptical Gospels, hardly, we believe, anywhere in the New Testament, except in St. John and the introduction to the Epistle to the Hebrews. In the Synoptics, indeed, Jesus is rarely designated as the Son, or the Son of God,† but only as " Son of Man." This expression occurs also in St. John, and is an appellation of the Messiah derived most probably from its use in the Book of Daniel.‡ Accordingly, this phrase, " Son of Man,"

---

* John v. 19-23 ;—there are various other instances, although, even in John, the words "Son of God" are often used simply as equivalent to Messiah, e.g., i. 49 ; ix. 22, 35 ; x. 24, 36.

† In the Synoptics he is addressed as "Son of God" in a few cases by others : that is to say, they address him as the Messiah. It is impossible, in some of these instances, to think that the speakers regarded him as the Divine Being, and *therefore* termed him Son of God: e.g., Matt. xxvii. 54, where the words are used by the Roman centurion in command of the soldiers at the cross. See Matt. iv. 3, 6 ; viii. 29 ; xiv. 33 ; also xxvii. 40, 42, 43—in this latter passage the words "King of Israel," are clearly parallel to the words "Son of God," exactly as in John i. 49,—both phrases, again, designating the Messiah. In Mark i. 1, the words "Son of God" are doubtful, and are rejected by Tischendorf. The rest of this Gospel, and the Gospel of Luke, are in close agreement with the first Gospel on this particular point. In one instance only in two of the Synoptics is there a deviation from their ordinary usage, and an approximation to what we may term the Johannine form of expression respecting the Son and his relation to the Father. In Matt. xi. 27, we read, "All things are delivered to me of my Father ; and no man knoweth the Son but the Father ; neither knoweth any man the Father, save the Son, and he to whomsoever the Son will reveal him." The words are reproduced in Luke x. 22, with a slight variation. The verse in both Evangelists interrupts the strain of the Gospel, and looks strangely out of place, though it would have been perfectly suitable to John. Whatever interpretation any one may put upon the words, they cannot be held to be intended to contradict the uniform tenor of the first three Gospels. See *infra*, Chapters XIV. to XVII.

‡ Dan. vii. 13.

does not require or justify the explanation sometimes met with,—to the effect that Jesus by his constant use of it intended, in the conception of the Evangelists, to designate himself as the model of a perfect human character, or even to refer to his own humble and despised condition. It is used, in all probability, as simply equivalent, in the ideas of the time, to the title of Messiah.*

There are a few passages which might at first appear to indicate that "Christ" and "Son of God" are not simply equivalent and convertible expressions. On examination, however, the contrary clearly appears. Thus, for example, Acts viii. 37, "I believe that Jesus Christ† is the Son of God." This verse is altogether omitted, on sufficient critical evidence by Tischendorf, and by Dean Alford. Similarly in Acts ix. 20, "He preached Christ in the synagogues that he is the Son of God." The critical authorities tell us here to read "Jesus," instead of "Christ." It is evident that what St. Paul preached in the synagogues was what, in common with the unbelieving Jews, he had previously denied, viz., that Jesus of Nazareth was the Christ. Here and elsewhere we read of their having denied that Jesus was Christ; we never read of their having denied that he was GOD. The same thing is evident, again, from Acts ix. 22, where we are told, he "confounded the Jews that dwelt at Damascus, proving that this is very Christ"—or, more simply rendered, "proving that this [man] is Christ." What he is said to have preached in the one case (in the synagogues) and

---

* The title Son of God may have originated from Ps. ii. 7, as applied to the Messiah. (Comp. Acts xiii. 33; Heb. i. 5.) Being thus of Hebrew origin, it coincided, however (accidentally), with one of the appellations given, as we shall see, to the Logos, though in a very different sense. From both points of view, therefore, the Hebrew and the Greek, Jesus would be the Son. Comp. *infra*, Chapters XV. XVI. In Ps. ii. 12, the words, "kiss the Son," should be rendered, "kiss sincerely," *i.e.* render homage to the exalted personage spoken of (probably Solomon), by humbly kissing the hem of his garment.

† "Jesus Christ" early became a personal name. The above verse, therefore, means, "I believe that the person called Jesus Christ is the Messiah." A similar remark applies to Mark i. 1, if the words "Son of God" be authentic.

proved in the other (at Damascus), is evidently the same thing, viz., that Jesus was the Son of God, in other words, that Jesus was the Christ.

The alleged blasphemy, then, it may be repeated, consisted in the claim to be the Christ, the Messiah, *or* Son of God, and this latter in no mysterious, incomprehensible " natural sense," but in the theocratic, and also the moral sense, in which the Messiah was usually conceived of as being pre-eminently a Son of God. Before Pilate the same charge was differently expressed, as seen in the words of the accusers, to the effect that Jesus had said that he was "Christ, a king;" and as seen also in Pilate's question, "Art thou the king of the Jews?" But neither before the Sanhedrim, nor before Pilate, does the accusation, or anything else, indicate that Jesus had made the claim to be GOD :—a claim which the Jews could not but have held to be blasphemous in the highest degree, and which the narrative of the trial and condemnation could not have failed to disclose. Such a claim, therefore, as we shall further and abundantly see, our Lord did not make; nor is it ever attributed to him by any New Testament writer. If the case be otherwise, let the passage be produced, and let it speak for itself.*

CHAPTER XII.

JESUS OF NAZARETH, AS HE APPEARED TO HIS OWN CONTEMPORARIES—THE TRUE IMPORT OF THE TITLES CHRIST AND SON OF GOD.

THE impression as to his own character and claims which Jesus really made upon those among whom he lived may be learnt

---

* John x. 30, "I and my Father are one," will not answer the purpose, for it is explained by Jesus himself, in verses 35, 36, as meaning simply "I am the Son of God."

from many places of the Gospel narratives. For example, we read: "Now Herod the Tetrarch heard of all that was done by him; and he was perplexed because it was said of some that John was risen from the dead; and of some that Elias had appeared; and of others that one of the old prophets was risen again."* It would not have lessened Herod's perplexity, if he had been told that it was the Divine Being Himself that was going about among the people in the person of Jesus. But among all the things that were said, as they have been recorded for us, there is no trace of this,—the one thing above all others that could not have failed to be said, had there been any real ground for saying it.

Later in the same chapter, we read that Jesus asked his disciples, "saying, WHOM say the people that I am? They answering said, John the Baptist, but some say Elias; and others say that one of the old prophets is risen again. He said unto them, But whom say ye that I am? Peter answering said, the Christ of God." In these replies we see the ideas that were aroused in the popular mind by the life and deeds of Jesus Christ. He had gone about doing many wonderful things among them; he had spoken with a wisdom and power which made them exclaim, "Never man spake like this man." In these and other ways, he had awakened the attention and interest of the people, and they followed him in crowds, and when they saw his wonderful works they "marvelled and glorified GOD who had given such power unto men"—they glorified the invisible God who had *given* to Jesus his power to do such deeds. But do they ever say, Lo, here is God, Jehovah Himself, come down from heaven in the likeness of men, as happened to Paul and Barnabas at Lystra? Did the people who knew Jesus personally, and saw his deeds, ever say this, or anything equivalent to this? Did his own more intimate disciples ever say this? So far as appears in the Gospels, or in the New Testament,

* Luke ix. 7, 8.

they never did so; but simply that God had given power to his chosen servant,* his well-beloved Son, and enabled him to do the mighty works which were done in their sight. Such is clearly the conception of the New Testament, and here was explanation enough for the people of Christ's own day, though not, it would seem, for those of ours.

They thought, indeed, some of them, that perhaps one of their ancient prophets had been restored to life. But still the Jewish people, with few exceptions, did not admit that he whom they saw among them, gifted with such powers, was to be accepted even as the Christ. Some of them even said that he acted by the power of Beelzebub. And "could there any good thing come out of Nazareth?" Such was the feeling and the doubt of the many, when they remembered the origin of Jesus, and saw his lowly condition, and his deficiency in the power of this world. The true Messiah, they expected, would not be such as he: and hence neither his wonderful works, nor the eloquence with which he spoke, nor the purity and devoutness of his life, could lead them to receive him in that exalted character, but only as perhaps a forerunner of the Christ, or one of the prophets come back from the dead.

But some of the apostles, the immediate companions and friends of Jesus, had evidently learnt better. In reply to his question, "But whom say ye that I am?" they were able to answer, "The Christ of God."† In the first Gospel the same incident is related somewhat differently. Jesus asks, "Whom say ye that I am? And Simon Peter answered and said, Thou art the Christ, the Son of the living God. And he answered and said unto him, Blessed art thou, Simon Bar-jona, for flesh and

---

* Jesus is termed the "servant" of God, Acts iii. 2, 26; iv. 27, 30 (not *Son* or *child*, as in the English N. T.); Matt. xii. 18.

† Luke ix. 20.

blood hath not revealed it unto thee, but my Father which is in heaven."* That is to say, Peter was led by divine illumination so far to triumph over the prejudices of his people, that he could recognise the true character of Jesus, in spite of the outward circumstances in his condition which made it so difficult for the common people to see in him the exalted personage for whom they were looking. And we observe that, while in the one Gospel the answer simply is, "the Christ of God," in the other it is, "the Christ, the Son of the living God." The phrases, we have seen, are of equivalent value; only the one is somewhat fuller than the other. And, at any rate, we see that Peter does not confess that his Master was God! He says simply that he was "the Christ," repeating this acknowledgment, and rendering it more emphatic, in the added words, "the Son of the living God."

In this case, the Apostle Peter shews himself more enlightened and open to conviction than the fellow-townsmen and neighbours of Jesus, of whom we read in the Gospel that "they were offended in him."† Thus we see, again, how far these persons were from believing even that Jesus was Christ; much less could it have entered into their thoughts that he was God. For what does Jesus say in reply to their objections? He said to them, "A prophet is not without honour, save in his own country, and in his own house." The Messiah he was and claimed to be; a prophet he also called himself; and again the Christ, the Son of God, the highly-favoured, highly-gifted and well-beloved of the Almighty Father. But God Himself he nowhere says that he is; nor do any of his immediate friends and disciples say it for him; nor do we really meet with such a statement until we reach a time some generations after his death,—when, as before

---

* Matt. xvi. 16, 17, comp. *ibid.* v. 20.
† Matt. xiii. 54, *seq.* Comp. xxi. 11, 46; Luke vii. 16; xxiv. 19.

observed, certain Gentile converts and writers, looking back upon the wonderful life of Jesus, and the mighty results which had sprung from it, thought they could best account for the whole by saying not only that God was in him and with him, not only that he was the brightest manifestation upon earth of the Heavenly Father's glory, but even that he was God Himself.*

In the New Testament, the conception entertained by the Evangelists of the relation between the Lord Jesus Christ and Almighty God, comes out into view at many points in the history. Jesus prays to God;—nay, even, as we read, he goes apart into a mountain or a desert place, to pray alone. Here, there is directly revealed to us the very same relation which exists between ourselves and God, and which is repeatedly recognised by Jesus in express terms—as where he teaches his disciples when they pray to say, "Our Father which art in heaven;" and when he sends word to his "brethren" after his resurrection, "I ascend unto my Father and your Father, and to my God and your God."† In the moment of his great trial, when he saw the near approach of a terrible death, although with natural human feeling he did not wish to die, and shrank from the dread moment, yet with words of perfect submission he resigned himself to the divine will—"O my Father, if it be possible, let this cup pass from me; nevertheless, not as I will, but as thou wilt;" and at the last moment of all he still com-

---

* We again refer to Réville, *Histoire*, &c., for a concise but ample justification of these statements. See also Donaldson, *History of Christian Literature and Doctrine*, Vol. II. i. iii. 12. The latter writer observes in regard to Justin :—"Justin had simply to apply Philo's method, Christianised, or, in other words, the Christian method; and all he has done is to apply that method most fully and minutely. The result is, that an *unquestionably new mode of speaking of Christ is introduced*. He is now for the first time recognised fully and clearly as God; not merely the Son of God, but God."—Donaldson, II. p. 181.

† Matt. vi. 5, 6, 9; John xx. 17. In one instance, he speaks to his disciples of God as "the only God;"— a fact which is concealed from the English reader by a misrendering, "the honour that cometh from God only:" John v. 44.

mended himself to God: "Father, into thy hands I commend my spirit."* Thus, the relation between Christ and God comes distinctly into view at many points, and is seen to be exactly the same as that in which we, of ordinary human kind, ourselves stand.

In one instance, noticed by Dr. Liddon, our Lord draws the very strongest distinction which it is possible to draw between himself and God. When the young man comes to him and addresses him as "Good Master," Jesus replies, "Why callest thou me good? None is good but one, that is God."† Here the distinction suggested between Jesus and the Heavenly Father is one not merely of power, wisdom, greatness; it is a *moral* distinction. The expression is such as we should anticipate from the humility and piety of the speaker; but if he were himself consciously God as he uttered such words, how are we to understand them? Did he intend to mislead that young man, and others who heard him, by declining for himself the epithet "good," and ascribing it to God alone?

The force of this difficulty Dr. Liddon seeks to evade, in one of the most singular of his expositions. He thus represents the reply of Jesus, "Why callest *thou* me good?—as though it were the "unreal and conventional manner" in which the epithet was addressed to him to which he objects.‡ But the inaptness of this explanation is evident, when it is observed that the pronoun *thou*, thus emphasized, does not exist as a separate word in the original. It is as little prominent or emphatic as is possible in a Greek sentence, being simply included or implied in the form of the verb. The whole emphasis is clearly on the two words "me" and "good;" especially on the former, because of its position in

* Matt. xxvi. 39; Luke xxiii. 46.
† Luke xviii. 18, 19, and the parallel passages. The peculiar reading which Tischendorf gives in Matthew only can hardly be the original form.
‡ Liddon, B. L., p. 193.

the sentence. The epithet *good*, accordingly, Jesus absolutely disclaims for himself, pointing out that it is applicable to One alone, and that He is God.*

If, again, we consider the principal names or titles by which Jesus is designated, the same relationship between him and God comes clearly into view.

He is the CHRIST. This world literally means "the anointed," and the idea conveyed by it is derived from the ancient ceremony of consecrating a king to his kingly office. In connection with Jesus it is clearly a figurative term, involving, however, the idea that he who bore it had been called and appointed to his office; intimating, therefore, the existence of a higher power which had chosen him. Hence Peter terms him "the Christ of God"— God's Christ, that is, one anointed of God, or appointed by Him to be what he was.†

This word, we need scarcely remind the reader, is the same in meaning as the Hebrew word "Messiah," and the same explanation holds good of both. We learn the true value and import of the latter, when we find that it is applied, in the Old Testament, to a heathen king, one who is made the instrument of executing a particular purpose of Jehovah. Cyrus, the king of Persia, was the means of putting an end to the captivity of the Jews. Hence the later Isaiah says of him, "Thus saith Jehovah to his *anointed*, to Cyrus."‡ Literally this might be rendered "to his Messiah," the same word which in Christian times is applied to Jesus under the Greek form of Christ.

Jesus, indeed, was Christ pre-eminently and permanently. He is also now, according to the Christian conception, the risen and spiritual Christ, by our faith in whom we are Christians. Thus

---

* Comp. *note* on John v. 44; *supra*, p. 118.
† Comp. 1 Cor. iii. 23; xi. 3, "the head of Christ is God."
‡ Isaiah xlv. 1.

the term which was applied to Cyrus only incidentally and because of a particular purpose, is used of Jesus as his usual and abiding designation; and he is, therefore, Jesus the Christ,* an appellation which soon passed into a personal name, and became Jesus Christ. But this fact does not alter the relation between him and the Creator which the word denotes. That was the same, in truth, as for the time existed between the Almighty Being and His chosen instrument the king of Persia. The one was the Anointer and the other the anointed; the one the Sender and the other the sent; the one was the Creator and the Source of power, the other the creature and the recipient of any authority or power which it pleased the Father to confer upon him.†

The term SON leads us to the same conclusion. According to our usual ideas and experience of human relationships, a *son* is, indeed, of the same nature with his father. The same or like mental and bodily powers belong to both; and therefore it might be inferred, in the case of Jesus, that he, being said to be the Son of God, is in all respects of the same essential nature as the Being of whom he is so often termed the Son. And this is constantly either expressly affirmed, or tacitly assumed, by orthodox writers. But even granting this, there is at least one important point in which the word necessarily implies *inferiority*, according to all ordinary ideas and the usual force of human language—except, indeed, among persons who are satisfied to set human language at defiance, and speak of "Eternal Sonship," and pledge their ministers at ordination to believe in it.‡ A son, at all events, is *younger* than his father, so that to speak of eternal sonship is something like speaking of an eternal fifty years. Hence, then, if any one would insist with strictness on this term as denoting

---

* Matt. xvi. 20. † Comp. Ephes. i. 20–22; Coloss. i. 19.
‡ See Grindrod's *Laws and Regulations of Wesleyan Methodism*, pp. 14, 15 (5th ed.).

a perfect sameness of nature in Christ and in God, he must, to be consistent, admit that it also indicates the inferiority of the former in regard to one of the essential attributes of Deity, that of eternity.

But, in truth, it is well understood that the words Father and Son are used in Scripture with far more latitude than with ourselves at the present day. In Job, for example, we read that " the morning stars sang together, and all the sons of God shouted for joy"—the latter words probably denoting the angels. " Son of peace," " son of perdition," " sons of the stranger," and similar forms, are common Hebrew idioms, familiar to all readers of the Scriptures. The prophet Ezekiel is repeatedly addressed as " son of man" in the book which bears his name. " I will be to him a father, and he shall be my son," Jehovah says to David by the prophet Nathan, in reference to David's successor upon the throne.*

Such expressions, as used in Scripture, imply sometimes creation and dependence, sometimes favour and protection bestowed, approval or love manifested, on the one side, and the same received on the other. Hence the Messiah, the Christ, as being pre-eminently the appointed, the protected and inspired of God, is also pre-eminently the Son of God;—while yet it is to be observed, that the title is not limited to Jesus, for Christians in general are also, according to the same idiom, called " sons of God."†

It is true, however, that the title is applied to Jesus far more frequently and emphatically than to any one else. He is the "beloved Son," "the only begotten Son" (the latter only in St. John), terms of high endearment applicable to him as the Christ; for in this character he was conceived to be the most gifted, the most highly favoured and approved, of all the servants of God.

* 2 Sam. vii. 14. † Gal. iv. 6; Rom. viii. 14, 15.

But still the use of such terms does not at all imply that he was looked upon, by those who applied them to him, either as God Himself or as equal to God, or of the same nature as God. There is nothing in the well-known Scriptural use of such words which can justify us, on their account, in exalting Jesus, the " meek and lowly," to that high eminence. He, we may be sure, would have shrunk from the idea of being made equal to God, as, indeed, he did shrink from it; for when the Jews in their malice brought against him the accusation that he, "being a man, made himself God," he immediately disclaims such an intention, and puts himself in his right position by explaining that he meant only to say, " I am the Son of God."*

Yet, clear as this is, the constant tendency of Protestant theology, as popularly taught, has been to forget the position thus so emphatically assumed by Christ. It has been almost uniformly to exalt and glorify him, by putting him in the very place of the Heavenly Father, while at the same time leaving strangely out of sight the Fatherly love and mercy. In the, Roman Catholic communion the same tendency has gone even further; for there the Virgin Mary has been raised to the highest honours, and all but made a member of the Godhead—a final result which it is not unreasonable now to anticipate, as a fitting sequel to the new dogma of the personal infallibility of the Pope. Among Protestants, it is true, the Virgin mother is scarcely heard of,—as in Scripture she is hardly mentioned, except in immediate connection with the birth of her son. Nevertheless, the Protestant sects, especially the more popular of them, seem to delight in attributing to the son of Mary an absolute equality with God. This they do, in formal creeds and formal acts of worship paid to Jesus Christ, manifestly without warrant or precedent in the Bible,

---

* John x. 33-36.

and simply on the strength of their own inferential and disputable reasonings from its language.

In thus proceeding, the religious bodies referred to certainly cannot allege that they are acting faithfully on their own avowed principle of deference to the Scriptures alone. For these clearly tell us, in express terms, of "one God the Father," and represent everything as dependent solely on His supreme will. It is He who "sent" Jesus Christ into the world; who "for His great love wherewith he loved us," raised up Jesus and exalted him " to be a Prince and a Saviour:" it is He who did this of His own "grace;" for "it is the gift of God," that men may become "the children of God by faith in Christ Jesus."* Such is the primitive and genuine sentiment of Christianity in relation to God and Christ. The latter is everywhere in the New Testament the creature, the servant, the beloved son, endowed with power and wisdom from on high, exalted by the Divine choice to the office which he held and holds, as "head over all things to his church."†

And this relationship to God all the words and acts of Jesus most simply and naturally accept or imply. He prays to God in private, as in public; he instructs his disciples to do the same, while he *never* tells them to pray to himself.‡ He said to his adversaries that it was God's power in him that enabled him to do his "works," as, indeed, in all things he devoutly referred to Him whom he expressly termed "my Father and your Father," "my God and your God;" declaring that the very words which he spake were not his own, but the Father's who sent him.§

If, then, a man will be contented to accept the plainest statements of the Scriptures—if he will follow the precepts and the

---

* Acts v. 30, 31; Ephes. ii. 4–9; Gal. iii. 26.
† Acts ii. 22; Ephes. i. 22.
‡ He rather tells them the *contrary*, John xvi. 23.   § John xiv. 24; xx. 17.

example of Christ; if, in other words, he will manifest a true faith in Christ by obeying him, and following his teaching rather than later doctrines of human devising, it is evident to Whom he will look, to Whom he will pray, Whom he will worship as the "One God and Father of all." It is evident that, however highly he may "honour the Son" as the founder of our Christian faith, and the Spiritual Head of the Christian Church, to whom is given "a name that is above every name,"—every other human name,—he will yet do this "to the glory of God the Father,"* reserving still his highest reverence and honour for Him who is and shall be "all in all."

CHAPTER XIII.

MR. GLADSTONE'S TESTIMONY TO THE HUMANITARIAN CHARACTER OF THE EVANGELICAL NARRATIVES—"ECCE HOMO."

THE representation of the two preceding Chapters is mainly, though not entirely, founded upon the statements of the Synoptical Gospels, with some corroboration from other parts of the New Testament. The peculiar portraiture of Jesus contained in the fourth Gospel stands so much alone, that it must of necessity be considered by itself. That this course is dictated by the nature of the case will be abundantly seen in the sequel.

So far, however, as regards the information we have drawn chiefly from the Synoptics respecting the person and the teaching of Christ, although this speaks sufficiently for itself, and needs no illustration from without, yet it may be well to take the opportunity of citing in its behalf a witness who will generally be considered unexceptionable, as he is certainly not in any way prepossessed in favour of the views expressed in these pages.

* Ephes. iv. 6; Philip. ii. 9–11.

He is one, therefore, whose testimony should serve all the more to corroborate what has just been said as to the silence of the three Evangelists respecting the supposed deity of Jesus Christ. We allude to what Mr. Gladstone has written in his volume on Ecce Homo.*

In this work the distinguished statesman comes forward in vindication of the course taken by the author of the book just named, in confining his narrative almost exclusively to the "human side" of our Lord's life and character. It is well known that author and book were severely criticised and blamed in certain quarters on this account.† The book professes, indeed, to be " a Survey of the Life and Work of Christ." But what, it is asked, are the life and work of Jesus Christ, with his Deity left out? And yet, replies Mr. Gladstone in substance, the author of this book, in his treatment of his subject, has only done very much what our Lord himself and the Synoptists have done. "Undoubtedly," he observes, the book " exhibits the character of our Lord on the human side. It purports to shew, and actually shews Him as man : and it leaves us to see, through the fair curtain of His manhood, what we may. The objection taken to this mode of treatment, in substance, perhaps amounts to this: that our Saviour is not a mere man, but is God made man; and that He ought not to be exhibited in any Christian work as a man only, but as God and man. And justice compels us to add, that those who challenge the author of 'Ecce Homo' on this ground are not always persons whose judgment can be summarily put aside on the score of bigotry and blindness."‡

Such is the substance of the charge against which Mr. Gladstone undertakes to defend the writer of Ecce Homo, as we may

* "*Ecce Homo*," by the Right Hon. W. E. Gladstone. 1868.
† By Lord Shaftesbury, for example, who characterized it even as "diabolical," or worse.
‡ "*Ecce Homo*," pp. 8, 9.

see again, in a later passage: "He is principally charged with this, that he has not put into his foreground the full splendour and majesty of the Redeemer about whom he writes." But Mr. Gladstone immediately adds: "If this be true of him, it is true also thus far of the Gospels."*

The words "thus far" refer to the picture of the life of Christ drawn by the Evangelical writers. In contradistinction to that picture, Mr. Gladstone goes on to speak more especially of the method which Christ himself followed in his teaching. "If we pass on," he says, "from the great events of our Lord's personal history to his teachings, as recorded in his discourses and sayings by the Synoptic writers, we shall find that they, too, are remarkable for the general absence of direct reference to His Divinity, and indeed to the dignity of his person altogether."† In another place Mr. Gladstone writes: "It appears, then, on the whole, as respects the Person of our Lord, that its ordinary exhibition to ordinary hearers and spectators was that of a Man engaged in the best, and holiest, and tenderest ministries, among all the saddest of human miseries and trials; of One teaching in word, too, the best, and holiest, and tenderest lessons; and claiming, unequivocally and without appeal, a paramount authority for what He said and did; but, beyond this, asserting respecting Himself nothing, and leaving Himself to be freely judged by the character of His words and deeds."‡

Again, Mr. Gladstone writes:—"If the reader has patiently followed the argument to this point, it is now time to release him by proceeding to apply it to the case of 'Ecce Homo.' Supposing, then, that the author of that work has approached his subject on the human side, has dealt with our Lord as with a man, has exhibited to us what purport to be a human form and lineaments, is he therefore at once to be condemned? Certainly

---

* "*Ecce Homo*," p. 52.   † *Ibid.*, pp. 61, 62.   ‡ *Ibid.*, p. 103.

not at once, if it be true, as it seems to be true, that in this respect he has only done what our Lord himself, by his ordinary and usual exhibition of himself, both did and encouraged the common hearer of his addresses and beholder of his deeds to do."*

How perfectly true these statements are, we will take the liberty of illustrating in a way which has not occurred to the able and candid writer of the quoted words. Let us for this purpose refer to another of the great scenes in the history of Christ, as set forth in the Gospel narratives, including the fourth as well as the synoptical writers. Let any one read the accounts of the crucifixion, and observe how entirely wanting is each narrative in the smallest allusion to the most astonishing and marvellous circumstance of all—if it were only *real*—the circumstance that in that crucified Jesus, who is there nailed to the cross, and there bows his head and dies, just like one of the malefactors beside him, that in his person, thus lifted up and crucified, it is not simply a human being that we look upon, but even God Himself! The writers of these narratives well knew this, it is alleged, but they say *nothing* about it, make no allusion to it whatever; and throughout the whole of their account, from beginning to end, there is the same extraordinary silence; no word occurs about that greatest fact of all, compared with which everything else sinks into utter insignificance.†

---

* "*Ecce Homo*," p. 108.—The reader may compare these remarkable admissions with the very different tenor of Dr. Liddon's representation in his fourth Lecture. He repeatedly declares that our Lord "revealed his divinity [deity] to his disciples, to the Jewish people, and to his embittered opponents, the chief priests and Pharisees." B. L., p. 177. See also the headings of Dr. L.'s pages, from p. 177 to p. 179, which run thus:—"Our Lord reveals His Godhead explicitly:"—"Christ reveals His Godhead to the Apostles:"—"Christ reveals His Godhead to the Jewish people."

† How differently modern writers proceed may be illustrated by a single instance. M. de Pressensé, in a recent work, speaking of the siege of Jerusalem, observes of that terrible time, that "Josephus knew not that Jerusalem was expiating a yet darker crime, and that its soil, once sacred, had been stained by the *blood of God*"!
—*The Early Years of Christianity* (1869), p. 364.

Mr. Gladstone, as we have seen, fully admits, strongly maintains, that there is silence, reserve, limitation, in the teaching of Christ himself in regard to his own person. He takes care, however, to point out that there were good reasons for this, in the unprepared state of the Gentile world, and of the people who witnessed our Lord's ministry. But now, granting that, during his own life, there was every reason why Jesus should not have spoken of his deity, yet how does such a consideration apply to narratives that were written thirty, forty, fifty years after his death—to writers who must surely have been desirous to exhibit to the world the full glory of the great subject of their narrative? *They* need not have continued the reserve from any of the motives which are said to have influenced *him;* but, on the contrary, they owed it to the world to set forth the simple truth, the marvellous truth.

Thus, in effect, the popular theory of the Godhead of Christ receives no support, but rather a decided injury, from the argument of the eminent man who has come forward so remarkably in its defence—or rather, we should say, in defence of what may be termed the humanitarianism of Ecce Homo.

In one respect, however, Mr. Gladstone has brought into view what might seem to be a new consideration. He thinks that the reticence of our Lord in speaking of himself in the Gospels, is not quite so great as might at first be thought. In some of his parables, he at least implies that he is a personage of great importance. He is the central figure of a new dispensation; he is the Sower of the seed; the Owner of the vineyard; the Householder in whose field of wheat the enemy had intermixed the tares; he is the Lord of the unforgiving servant; the Nobleman who went into a far country; and, lastly, he is the Bridegroom among the wise and foolish virgins. In all these instances, Mr. Gladstone urges, our Lord "appears in the attitude of kingship.

K

He rules, directs, and furnishes all; he punishes and rewards." These instances, he adds, "must be considered, surely, as very nearly akin, if they are not more than nearly akin, to declarations of His Deity."*

Now, accepting all these instances as fairly put, it will nevertheless be much nearer the truth, to regard them as declarations, express or implied, *not* of his Deity, but of his *Messiahship*. It was in his character of Messiah that he did, or assumed to do, all the actions attributed to him. This fact is constantly overlooked, or lost sight of, by popular preachers and writers; and it has here escaped even so good an eye as Mr. Gladstone's. The Messiahship of Jesus is everywhere the most characteristic feature throughout the New Testament; and has never been questioned as the great fact of primitive Christian history, except, indeed, by the unbelieving Jews. Can the same be said of his alleged Deity? Has not this been denied and controverted from the first; and does not Mr. Gladstone himself admit that it cannot be said to make its appearance, except perhaps in obscure implications, even in the synoptical Gospels—the most detailed and literally historical records of his life?

Jesus, then, as the CHRIST, is undoubtedly sometimes spoken of in terms which could not be applied to ordinary men. It does not follow that he is *God;* and as such the Evangelists never represent him. It follows, simply, that he is the Christ; and we know how he himself said, and how every statement of the New Testament on the subject declares, that whatever he was, and whatever he had, he was and he possessed by the giving of the Father who "sent" him.†

Hence, therefore, again, Mr. Gladstone in writing as he does on this subject, has too readily fallen into a very common and popular error; he has lost sight of the distinction between the

* "*Ecce Homo*," p. 83. † John v. 19; vii. 16; xiv. 10, 24.

Messianic character, unquestionably attributed by the Evangelists to Jesus of Nazareth, and the unapproachable supremacy of the One Almighty Jehovah, which is never attributed to him. It may, indeed, be perfectly true, as Mr. Gladstone and Dr. Liddon respectively insist, that Jesus speaks with great dignity and authority; that he exercised powers which could not belong to any ordinary man; that "his recorded teaching is penetrated by his self-assertion;" that, as spiritual lawgiver and king, he claims the unreserved obedience and self-surrender of his followers; nay, that he thus not only asserts his right to "rule the whole soul of man" in this life, but also "literally and deliberately puts himself forward as judge of all the world," in the life to come.* All this may be perfectly true, as well as the further statement that Jesus said he was Lord of the sabbath, that he had a right to do his works on that day, and that even as the Father worked, so he, the Son, had authority to work also. But yet all this does not establish the Deity of him who thus spoke, taught and acted. What it proves is, in the language of the New Testament, simply this—namely, that Jesus Christ was "a man approved of God by miracles and wonders and signs, which God did by him;" that the Heavenly Father had "anointed Jesus of Nazareth with the Holy Spirit and with power;"† *giving* him authority and power to be and to do all that is spoken of him. Dr. Liddon himself observes, "Certainly our Lord insists very carefully upon the truth that the power which he wielded was derived originally from the Father."‡ The New Testament writers tell us exactly how it was that Christ was what he was: "God had given such power unto men." Jesus himself declares the same thing: "If I by the finger of Beelzebub cast out demons, by whom do your children cast them out?"—meaning obviously by this question that it was by the "finger of God" that he acted. The state-

---

* Liddon, B. L., p. 174. † Acts ii. 22; x. 38. ‡ B. L., p. 81.

ments even of the fourth Evangelist are to the same effect. The incarnate Logos there tells us, "The Son can do nothing of himself;" and of the Father he says that as He "hath life in himself, so he hath given to the Son to have life in himself."*

Similarly, too, St. Paul on Mars' Hill, when he alluded to the future judgment of the world, spoke of a day in which God will "judge the world in righteousness by that man whom he hath *ordained;*" and, both in this place and elsewhere, the same Apostle directly attributes to God the raising of Jesus from the dead: "Yea, and we are found false witnesses of God, because we have testified of God that he raised up Christ; whom he raised not up if so be that the dead rise not."†

The possession of miraculous powers could not imply, as Dr. Liddon would represent, the deity of the possessor; for, according to the Acts of the Apostles, miracles were wrought by St. Paul and by others. In short, it is clear from the usual tone and tenor, as well as the express statements, of the Evangelical history, that Jesus Christ was never thought of by the writers as possessed of power and wisdom independently, or in himself, but only by the giving of One greater than he. It is plain, therefore, as before, that he was not regarded as himself the original source of divine gifts, but simply as the receiver, the instrument, the faithful servant of God, whose "meat" it was, as he said of himself, "to do the will of Him that sent him, and to finish his work."

CHAPTER XIV.

THE CHRIST OF THE FIRST THREE GOSPELS AND OF THE FOURTH—DIFFERENCES.

WE read in the Book of Acts that the Apostle Peter addressed an assembled body of his countrymen on the day of Pentecost.

* John v. 19, 26. † 1 Cor. xv. 15.

Speaking of his departed Master, he describes him in the following terms: "Jesus of Nazareth, a man approved of God among you by miracles and wonders and signs which God did by him in the midst of you, as ye yourselves also know."* This description given by an Apostle, a companion and friend of Jesus, so shortly after the crucifixion, probably represents the earliest idea of his person and work left to us in the New Testament. At least, it may be taken faithfully to preserve, in several important respects, the impression of himself which the subject of it had made upon his immediate disciples. And this remark is confirmed by what we are told respecting our Lord in the first three Gospels. Both in the details given, and in the resulting impression arising from them, their representation, as we have already seen, agrees in a remarkable manner with that early description of Peter.

One who goes with us to this extent will probably have no difficulty in seeing, that in the synoptic Gospels we have what may properly be regarded as the most original and literally faithful picture of the life and character of Christ anywhere to be found. This may be said without any conscious desire to depreciate the fourth Gospel, or the peculiar idea of Christ which it gives us, and solely with the intention of expressing the simple facts of the case.

There are several considerations by which this statement may be illustrated, and its correctness very conclusively shewn.

In the first place, in the three Gospels we have a three-fold exhibition of the life of Christ, and one which undoubtedly comes down to us from the remotest period of Christian antiquity to which we can ascend for the details given. We have, therefore, the authority of three witnesses for what is there reported, and for the particular form and manner in which it is reported. This remark applies more especially to all matters in which there is a

* Acts ii. 14-22.

substantial agreement between the three Evangelists. We always ascribe a preponderating weight to a decided majority of testimonies, even in the case of persons who may, in other respects, be perfectly equal to each other.

In the second place, the character or quality of what is reported tends to the same result. The three Gospels agree very completely with each other in regard to the substance, as well as the form, of our Lord's teaching, and in regard to what is, perhaps, of less essential importance, the principal incidents of his career. In these Gospels he often speaks, for example, in short parables; many parables occur in each of them, and they are among the most simple and effective of his modes of teaching.

But, moreover, the three synoptists also preserve for us many longer, as well as shorter, discourses and sayings of Christ. These are usually of a very practical kind, setting forth various moral and religious duties or principles, in application mostly to the men and circumstances of that day. Throughout the three Gospels a very graphic picture is presented to us, both of the actions and of the teaching of Christ—shewing us how he went about among the people, speaking to them constantly as occasion arose, healing diseases, casting out demons, everywhere taking the opportunity of uttering some little practical lesson of moral or religious value; or else teaching the same things, even more impressively, by his own example.

Now, while the synoptics agree so constantly with one another in these respects, such features are, to a great degree, absent from the fourth Gospel. In this, for example, there are no parables whatever, nor a single instance of the casting out of demons; the miraculous birth of Christ is never alluded to, not even in the opening chapter, which speaks of the incarnation of the Word; nor the temptation of Christ; nothing like the Sermon on the

Mount occurs, nothing like it either in manner or matter; neither does the institution of the Lord's Supper; nor the agony in the garden of Gethsemane. There are other important omissions of a similar kind—shewing us, at least, that the respective Evangelists were, for some reason, led to take and to give a radically different view of the life and teaching of the great subject of their narratives.

But it is not only that we find such omissions in John, as compared with the other Gospels. What does occur in the former is to a large extent different in its kind and in the manner of its expression, from what occurs in them. Doubtless there are some resemblances, for how was it possible that there should not be?—while yet it is true that it requires careful attention to find them; and of these resemblances, such as they are, it will be seen that Dr. Liddon has made the most. But still the statement is correct, that the fourth Evangelist differs extremely from the others not only in what he omits, but in what he records.

For example, the teachings of our Lord are here often delivered in discussions with hostile Jews. In the other Gospels they occur more in intercourse with his own friends and disciples. In John, he appears everywhere anxious, above all things, to assert and vindicate his own divine origin and dignity as the Messiah. So it is in the interview with Nicodemus; in that with the woman of Samaria; in the case of the Samaritans in the same chapter; in that of the Jews who seek to kill him; of those to whom he said he was the "bread of life;" of those who took up stones to stone him;* and in other instances. On the contrary, in the synoptics, he repeatedly enjoins upon those who are with him not to tell any one of his wonderful character and deeds.† Various passages occur in John which are, more or less, difficult to follow

---

* John iii.; iv.; v. 18; vi. 28, *seq.*; x. 24, *seq.*
† Matt. xvi. 20; xvii. 9; Mark viii. 30; Luke ix. 21, 22.

and understand, the great end of which seems to be, not, as in the earlier Gospels, the moral and religious instruction of his auditors, so much as the assertion of the speaker's own authority, of his descent from the Father, and his intimate communion with Him.*

Moreover, all this is presented in very peculiar language. If we compare the Gospel with the first Epistle of John, we find that the style is the same; and that the Evangelist has represented our Lord too as speaking in the same style in which he has written his own Epistle. The same characteristic words and phrases occur in Gospel and Epistle, shewing us that the writer of the former cannot have put down the exact words of Christ; or, at least, that if *he* has done so, the three synoptists have *not*, and that the utmost which can with any probability be alleged is, that the former has embodied in his own form of words the *substance* of the ideas uttered by Jesus.

In the first three Gospels, however, it cannot be questioned that we have actual words of Christ. Strauss † long ago compared his sayings to fragments of granite, which, though they may sometimes have been detached and carried away from their original position, yet could not be dissolved by the flood of oral tradition, but still retain their native coherence and force. So, for example, we must believe it is in the case of the Lord's Prayer. Have we not here the very words of Jesus Christ?—allowing, of course, for the change from the language which he used to the Greek form in which we now have them, and allowing also for the circumstance that the prayer, in its separate sentences, may not be, strictly speaking, original. But this prayer is not found in St. John, nor anything at all resembling it. So, again, it must be with the parable of the Good Samaritan; with that of the

---

* E.g., v. 32–47; viii. 52–59; xv. 1–8; xvi. 28–31; xvii.
† Life of Jesus, § 76.

Prodigal Son; that of the Talents, and many others; with the words used at the institution of the Lord's Supper,* an incident which, important as it is, does not occur at all in the fourth Gospel.

The differences which we have now pointed out between the three and the one are such as cannot be denied; nor does Dr. Liddon attempt to deny them. He seeks, however, to lessen their amount and significance, and is anxious to shew, differences notwithstanding, that the "divine Christ of St. John is identical with the Christ of the synoptists."† How far this is so the reader will judge for himself; and the matter may safely be left to the intelligent verdict of any candid person who will take the trouble duly to weigh the facts of the case.

On two points only, in Dr. Liddon's discussion of the subject, would we here, before proceeding further, offer a brief comment. He lays great stress on the "history of the nativity" in Matthew, and on the "Evangelical Canticles" in Luke,‡ as containing expressions in substantial harmony with the introductory statements of St. John's Gospel, inasmuch as they *point* to the "entrance of a superhuman being into this our human world." § The question inevitably presents itself whether the learned writer really receives the "history of the nativity," with the poetical utterances of Mary and Elizabeth, and the announcement of the angel Gabriel, as truly historical, and with the feeling that he is treading on solid ground in his reliance upon such details—details to which he appeals as guarding the Evangelical narratives "against the inroads of Humanitarian interpreters." Such questions he would doubtless answer in the affirmative; for he accepts without question all the statements that occur respecting the "annunciation," the "miraculous conception," "the virgin mother."

---

* Matt. xxvi. 26-28; Luke xxii. 17-20.   † B. L., pp. 244, 245.
‡ Matt. i. ii.; Luke i.   § B. L., p. 249.

We can only express our admiration, even our amazement, at a faith so undiscriminating and comprehensive; while we do not doubt, nevertheless, that the judgment of all free and instructed minds will sooner or later pronounce very differently on this, as on other material points in this inquiry.

Dr. Liddon further observes that the agreement between the synoptists and John is also seen in their accounts of the teaching of our Lord, " and in the pictures which they set before us of his life and work."* How exceedingly different this is from the facts, we need not further attempt to illustrate. But in connection with one point in Dr. Liddon's representation, we must notice the incorrectness of his statement. The synoptists, he says, often present Jesus to us as "the Son," and in this title he naturally sees, not merely a usual Jewish designation of the Messiah, as especially and before all others the protected and beloved of God, but also an allusion (even in the synoptics) to an " original nature," in which of necessity ordinary men have no share. " Accordingly," he observes, Jesus " never calls the Father *our* Father, as if he shared his Sonship with his followers. He always speaks of *my* Father."†

In reply to this statement, it may be asked, did not our Lord teach his disciples when they prayed to say, " Our Father which art in heaven " ?—and, although he is not himself said to have joined with them in the use of his prayer, are we to suppose that he intended them to employ the word " Father " in some special and limited sense, which was not applicable to himself? When, as so often occurs, in addressing his disciples, he uses the words " your Father," apparently in the most direct, simple and natural manner, are we to suppose that he consciously meant to employ those words with a certain reserve, or, as we may almost say, with a kind of double meaning, and that his hearers too were aware of this, although there is no statement to such an effect throughout

---

* B. L., p. 249. † *Ibid.*, p. 250.

the New Testament? For, even in John, where, as already admitted, the "Sonship" has most probably at times a metaphysical sense, not elsewhere found, does not Jesus say, "I ascend unto my Father and your Father, and unto my God and your God"? Here, again, is it possible to think that he uses the word "Father" within the space of this short verse in two different senses?—that God was, in his own conception, God and Father to those whom he was addressing, quite otherwise than he was to the speaker himself?

Such questions must surely be answered in the negative by one who has any regard to the truthfulness and sincerity of Jesus Christ; and that answer is virtually the confutation of the assertion that Christ never spake "as if he shared his Sonship with his followers." In one sense, indeed, this assertion might be true, but it is not the sense intended by Dr. Liddon. Jesus could not share his *Messiahship* with his followers; and so far as this is involved in the Sonship, or identical with it, the latter may be regarded as necessarily limited to Jesus alone. But it is quite evident that he often speaks of and to the Heavenly Father in no such artificial sense. "O my Father, if it be possible, let this cup pass from me." Was this an outburst of true natural feeling, such as any human being might utter before the ever-present Spirit, or was it only a kind of official address to Him, whether implying the metaphysical "Sonship," or only the relationship of Messiah? The general strain of the New Testament ought surely to be sufficient to answer this question for us; for example, those words of Paul to the Galatians, " God has sent forth the spirit of his Son into your hearts, crying, Abba, Father,"—making them too sons (the Apostle means), even like Christ himself, as also the New Testament repeatedly declares.*

---

* Gal. iii. 26 ; iv. 7. Comp. John viii. 41, 42 ; Matt. v. 48 ; Mark xi. 25, 26; Luke vi. 36.

It is clear that the use by Jesus of the form "*your* Father," arose mainly from the fact that his teachings consisted so largely of direct and familiar conversations with those around him. He naturally addressed them in the second person—and used pronouns suitable to that form of address.

Returning, however, to the principal subject of the present Chapter, we have next to inquire, how are the remarkable differences, above described, between the one Gospel and the three, to be accounted for? Most probably the explanation lies in the circumstance that in the latter we have the simple facts, incidents, sayings and discourses of Christ's ministry very much as they actually occurred; as they were preserved and cherished for long years by faithful friends and disciples, until finally written down from the oral traditions, much in the form in which we now have them. The Gospel of John, on the other hand, was written considerably later, as the ancient authorities agree in telling us, and as modern investigators mostly allow. It was written also, not in Palestine, by one intimately familiar with Jewish scenes and usages at the moment of writing, but most probably in the distant city of Ephesus, and by one who, even if by birth a Jew and a native of Palestine, must have been long separated from his early home, and unfamiliar with the associations of his younger days. Few, probably, can read what has been said on this point by Bretschneider and others after him, without being convinced of this, although they may not go to the length of saying that the Apostle John, the beloved disciple and friend of Jesus, could not have been the author of the Gospel.

If this Evangelist, again, were acquainted with the three older Gospels as works of Apostolical authority, or with one of them, he would seem to have carefully avoided going over the same ground; while yet it is remarkable that he should not have intimated in any way that he had done so, or intended to do so.

So far as any express statement is concerned, he leaves us in ignorance as to his plan in writing, for he merely intimates, in one place, his desire to shew that Jesus was the Christ, the Son of God.*

Having this object in view, it would seem that he pursued it in his own manner, without regard to the accounts given by the Evangelists who had preceded him, even if he were acquainted with them, of which we cannot be certain. And not only was this the case, but the fourth Evangelist evidently wrote with a certain freedom; that is to say, in his own style and words simply. Hence the sameness of manner observable in the Gospel and the first Epistle; and this too even in words, or discourses attributed to Christ;—although we can hardly suppose that our Lord expressed himself in the peculiar style of the Epistles of John, especially when this is so different from what is reported of his words in the synoptics.

It will illustrate and account for this peculiarity in the language of John, if we remember that it was the custom with ancient historians to ascribe to the personages of their histories such speeches as they thought suitable to their particular characters and circumstances. Writers, we know, who were probably the contemporaries of the fourth Evangelist, and doubtless subject to the same literary rules and influences, have followed this method of composition. The fact alluded to is familiar to all who have the slightest knowledge of the ancient historians. †

The question, then, is inevitable, Did the author of the fourth Gospel follow the same plan, and is *this* the cause of the remarkable difference between the words of Christ as found in that Gospel, and as found in the others? That is to say, have we in

---

* John xx. 31.

† We need only mention here the names of Dionysius of Halicarnassus, Tacitus, Josephus, abundantly to justify the statement in the text. ! The last of these authors attributes speeches of his own composition to various biblical persons.

the three Gospels the genuine words, or nearly so, much as they fell from the lips of the Teacher, treasured in the memory of devoted and affectionate followers, until at length committed to writing and left as we now read them; and in the fourth Gospel have we only the *substance* of what Jesus said, recalled by the Evangelist after the lapse of many years, and clothed not at all in the original words of the speaker, which were long ago forgotten, but in such language as occurred to the writer, and seemed to him fitted to embody the ideas which he wished to make known to his readers, of the teaching and the actions of Christ?

Into this important question it is not necessary that we should here enter further, except only to express the conviction that it ought to be answered affirmatively, even on the supposition that the fourth Evangelist was the Apostle John. Those who are unable to admit the identity of the Apostle and the Evangelist will the more readily assent to it; and if it be the truth, it will abundantly explain the fact that the Gospel of John is so different from the other three;—different in its facts, in its style, in the actions attributed to Christ, and in the very subject-matter of the thoughts reported to have been expressed by him.

But leaving this point, we are brought back to our former position, and may see, even more clearly than before, that it is to the Gospels of Matthew, Mark and Luke, that we must look for the most original and faithful picture of our Lord's life and character; while St. John's Gospel, on the other hand, is a composition of later date, and of such a character that its testimony can only be received so far as it is in substantial agreement with that of the other Gospels.

The relation subsisting between Christ and God which is set forth or implied in the synoptical accounts, is the point which now claims our attention. What that relation is, is sufficiently declared, and has already in fact been described. The Almighty Being, it is throughout implied, or expressly stated, is the original Source of the divine gifts possessed by Jesus. He is everywhere represented as a distinct personality; one living consciousness and will; a Being of unspeakable might and holiness; our Father in heaven. And this great Parent Spirit it is who gives to Jesus the wisdom and the power which he manifests. "If I by the power of Beelzebub cast out demons, by whom do your children cast them out?"—thus Jesus asked on one occasion. It was *not* by the help of Beelzebub, he meant to assert, but by a greater and better power that he acted, even by the power which he had from God. And so, on another occasion, as noted before, the people, on witnessing the cure of the palsied man, are said to have "marvelled and glorified GOD which had given such power unto men."

The relation, then, subsisting between Christ and God is clearly revealed to us in such expressions. Christ is the recipient, and God is the Source and the Giver. How this intercommunion took place we are not informed; but that it was thus conceived of by these Evangelists is more or less distinctly declared throughout their three Gospels. The invisible Deity is, in all this, revealed to us as a definite personal existence, as much as Jesus himself; and from Him it is that our Lord, amidst the changing scenes of his human life, derives the power, the eloquence and the wisdom which attract to him the crowds of his countrymen, and make them exclaim, "Never man spake like this man."

Much of what has just been said has been noted before; but the reader will forgive the repetition, as it is necessary here to bring out the contrast between the synoptics and the fourth Gospel. On turning to the latter, we find that Jesus is all that he is represented in the others, but apparently also he is something more. He is, in particular, the personal incarnation of the Divine Word, or Logos:—"In the beginning was the Logos, and the Logos was with God, and the Logos was God;"—"And the Logos was made flesh and dwelt among us."* Such, in few words, is this Evangelist's statement; a statement which recurs several times, at least by implication, in the course of the Gospel.

The question then arises, What is the probable meaning of this language; and does the Evangelist John really place before us a view of the person of Jesus, and of his relation to God, essentially *different* from that which we have found in the other Gospels, and in the speech of Peter on the day of Pentecost?

It is a well-known statement of Clement of Alexandria, repeated by others in succession after him, that this Gospel was written as a kind of supplement to the other three. John, he relates, observing that the things concerning the bodily or human life of Christ had been recorded, determined, at the instigation of friends, to compose a spiritual Gospel. This view of the matter is greatly approved by Dr. Liddon, while yet he remarks with some truth, that the Gospel "is rather a treatise illustrated by history than a history written with a theological purpose."† He would, probably, have been still nearer the truth if he had said, that it is substantially a "treatise" written with a distinct "theological purpose." It is easy, in fact, to gather from the Gospel itself, as will hereafter be sufficiently seen, that the Evangelist has gone upon the simple plan of giving mainly such details and discourses as might serve to confirm and illustrate his doctrine of the Logos in Jesus, and that he has probably omitted from his narrative whatever may have seemed to him unnecessary to that doctrine, or inconsistent with it.

At all events, the Supplement theory is not borne out by the

---

* John i. 1-18—"became flesh" is the more literal rendering.
† B. L., pp. 219, 220.

facts of the case. The Gospel does not, in truth, supplement the other Gospels. It simply differs from them, and that to such a degree that it has always been felt to be one of the most difficult of problems to harmonize the two forms of representation; to shew that they are not absolutely exclusive the one of the other. Nor is the ancient idea borne out, but strongly discountenanced, by the particular statement before referred to, of the Evangelist himself, who tells us expressly for what purpose he wrote his Gospel:—"Many other signs truly did Jesus in the presence of his disciples, which are not written in this book; but these are written, that ye might believe that Jesus is the Christ, the Son of God; and that believing ye might have life through his name."*

And yet the object thus declared is manifestly the same object which the other Evangelists had in view. To shew that Jesus was the Christ, the Son of God, was indeed the great aim of all the teaching and preaching of the primitive Church. To bring men to believe this, Paul too toiled and suffered; so that the primary design of John's Gospel, as stated by the writer of it himself, was the common aim and endeavour of the first Christian disciples, to "bring all men, everywhere, to the knowledge of the truth," that "the promise which was made unto the fathers God had fulfilled the same," "in that he had raised up Jesus again."†

Such, then, being the agreement between the first three Gospels and the Fourth, in regard to the leading purpose for which they were severally composed, the presumption arises, that the apparent divergence of John from the others, which in the first instance so much strikes the reader, is not in reality expressive of any substantial difference of belief in the respective writers in regard to the person of Christ or the relation between Christ and God, but

---

* John xx. 30. The Evangelist doubtless intended his readers to understand that Jesus was the Christ by the indwelling of the Logos. Comp. *infra*, Chapter XVI.
† Acts xiii. 32.

only a variation in the mode in which the later Evangelist has been led to express himself; and that a due attention to the subject will shew that these seemingly disagreeing forms of representation in reality set forth one and the same essential truth. To test the correctness of this presumption will be the purpose of the next two Chapters.

CHAPTER XV.

THE DOCTRINE OF THE LOGOS — PHILO — JUSTIN MARTYR — EARLIER TENDENCIES AMONG THE JEWS.

THE inquiry before us is, in substance, this—whether there is an essential harmony between St. John and the Synoptics, in the accounts which they respectively give of the relation between Jesus Christ and God. To answer the question it is necessary to ascertain in what sense the former have employed the term Word (Logos), which he introduces so conspicuously at the beginning of his narrative. The use of this expression constitutes the great peculiarity of this Gospel. It is not found in any other, and hardly occurs anywhere else in the New Testament, with the exception of the first Epistle of John. The idea of the Logos is, indeed, introduced at the beginning of the Epistle to the Hebrews, but the word itself is not there used.* We do not, therefore, find any material assistance in the New Testament, in the inquiry as to what exactly may have been meant by this expression. It is evident, however, that, employing the term, as he does, in the very first sentence of his Gospel, the Evangelist must have taken it for granted that his readers were already familiar with it. He

---

* Comp. also Heb. iv. 12. It has been supposed that St. Paul introduces the Logos idea at the commencement of the Epistles to the Ephesians and Colossians. On this point, see *infra*, Chapter XIX.

gives no explanation of it, but introduces it at once, as though it were well known to those for whom he was writing.

And such, there is no reason to doubt, was the case. For, let us observe, this Evangelist, although the only New Testament writer who makes so prominent an object of the Logos, is by no means the originator of the term, or of the peculiar mode of representation of which it is a part. On the contrary, he only adopts a well-known, long used expression of his time—a term, with its connected ideas, widely employed in the age and region in which the Evangelist lived; and one, therefore, which he might properly regard as sufficiently familiar to all who were likely to read his Gospel, without any explanation from him.*

To understand, then, what this term may have meant, as used by the Evangelist, we have to look beyond the New Testament, to any contemporary sources of information left to us; and these may be found principally in the writings of the Jewish author, Philo of Alexandria. In his works abundant materials are met with for illustrating the use of the term in question. Philo was probably about sixty years of age at the time of the death of Christ. His chief works, it is well ascertained, were composed not later than that event—a fact from which it is easy to infer that Philo cannot have borrowed from the Christian teachers, much less from the Gospel of John, which could not have been in existence for several decades after he wrote. He was, however, an elder contemporary of the reputed author of that Gospel; and we may consequently expect that, if the two are found to use the

* This statement may be illustrated by the following passage from a learned Bampton Lecturer of a past generation:—"One of these Æons was termed Logos; and we may say with truth that between the genuine followers of Plato and the corrupters of his doctrine, the Gnostics, the whole learned world at the time of our Saviour's death, from Athens to Alexandria, and from Rome to Asia Minor, was beset with philosophical systems in every one of which the term Logos held a conspicuous place."—Dr. E. Burton, *Bampton Lectures*, 1829, p. 215.

same words and expressions in connection with a given subject, they will throw light upon each other.

The same remarks are in some respects applicable to Justin Martyr, a Gentile philosopher converted to Christianity, who suffered martyrdom at Rome about the year 165. His writings also contain much that throws light on the subject of the Logos; but it is a later phase of the subject than that presented by Philo. Justin wrote at a time when some progress had certainly been made by the doctrine of the deity of Christ. Moreover, the period of his literary activity lies at some interval after that of the Evangelist, while between Justin and Philo the space is still longer, and is probably not less than a century, or even more. In the works of the latter writer, therefore, the doctrine of the Logos may be found still unaffected by later Christian influences; and as the writer of the Gospel cannot have drawn anything from the works of Justin, while it is possible, if not probable, that he was acquainted with those of Philo, it is to our purpose to seek the information and illustration we need from the earlier author, rather than from the later.*

It is necessary to commence with the fact that the idea of the Logos was intimately connected with the peculiar mode of conceiving of God which was widely prevalent in the period to which Philo's life belongs. In the philosophical systems of the time, derived partly from Plato and partly from oriental sources, the Deity was conceived of as having existed from eternity, the absolute fulness and perfection of being, withdrawn and apart by Himself, and incomprehensible to man. He stands out of and above the sphere of matter. Being, in His essence, an absolutely perfect and immaterial Spirit, He could not have any immediate contact with that grosser world which is accessible to human sense. But how, then, is He to be the Creator and Lord of the

* For the sources of information here used, see Appendix to this Chapter.

universe? In this essential disconnection or antagonism between the Self-existent Mind and things material, how are these to be acted upon and reduced to obey the will of the Supreme?

It was by means of His δυνάμεις, or powers, and by the Logos most especially among these, that this was conceived to be effected, and the connection maintained between the hidden and far-off God and the visible world. Without attempting to enter into the obscurities of the subject, or to trace the idea of the Logos to its origin in Platonism, it is necessary to state that the term has a double meaning, namely, thought and speech,—denoting, in other words, that which exists in us first as thought, and also goes forth from us as words spoken. Again, after this human analogy, a distinction was made between the Logos, as in God, and with God,—the Divine reason, intellect, thought, also the Divine idea according to which the visible world was created,—and the Logos, as it came forth from God to be the instrument of His supreme will. Thus, from the one point of view, it is the thought or idea in the Divine Mind, or it is even the Divine Mind itself; from the other, it is the same thought or idea manifesting and realizing itself outwardly,—seen, for example, in what we usually speak of as *design*, in the works of nature,— coming forth from Him whom it thus revealed, and embodying itself in the life, order, beauty and grandeur of the material universe.

According to this latter conception, the Logos is, properly, the self-revealing and creative activity of God. It is the manifestation of the One God, but is not itself a personal being, although, as we shall see, the strong tendency was to regard it in the latter character. It comes forth from God, just as a word uttered issues, as it were, from the mind within, and produces its effect. So, for illustration, when God *said*, "Let there be light," the word came forth, the instrument, and was followed by its effect,—

"there was light." In this conception of the Logos coming forth from the otherwise invisible and unknown Source of all, was comprehended not only creation, but every active relation of God to the world, every manifestation of Him in outward things. There is a great deal that is obscure and fluctuating in the conception; but this is clear and constant, namely, that the Logos holds an intermediate place between God and the world, as the active and efficient instrument of the Divine power. It is, therefore, in effect, the true mediator, or medium of communication between God and man, and not only between God and man, but between Him and everything that is external to His own Divine nature.

The step was not a great one, nor difficult to take, to the personification of this medium of the Divine activity. That step is already virtually taken by Philo. His idea of the Logos, in truth, varies between that of a person and that of a mere attribute of the Infinite Mind, or manifestation of God's hidden energy. Nevertheless, the language in which he speaks of it as a distinct personal being is at times so strong, that it is difficult to think that he did not in reality look upon the Logos in that light. Accordingly, some authors of high authority have decided that Philo did conceive of the Logos, not merely as an imaginary being, a manifestation of divine power, poetically clothed with personal qualities, but as a real person.*

As examples of the varieties of expression which have caused doubt on this point, the following may be mentioned. As just noticed, the Logos bears the same relation to the Supreme Mind that speech does to the human; or it is only the idea or purpose of the Creator, after the pattern of which the external world was

* Speaking of the Logos of Philo, Professor Jowett observes that with that writer "the idea of the λόγος just ends with a person, or rather leaves us at last in doubt whether it is not a quality only or mode of operation in the Divine Being."—*Epistles of St. Paul*, I. .414.

formed. It is the Divine power or energy in the world; maintaining all things together in harmony, and being their bond of law and order. It is the pervading providence which rules and controls among nations; the giver of good gifts to men. It is spoken of as law; as the moral sense in man; as the indwelling reason: wisdom and goodness especially are its gifts; and sometimes it appears to be identical with wisdom, this term being used for it. In one remarkable passage, in which Philo allegorizes the six cities of refuge, the Logos clearly appears as one among other attributes of the Almighty.

In several of these particulars the idea would seem to be nearly the same with the ancient Hebrew conception of the Holy Spirit. Elsewhere, however, the Logos is spoken of in very different terms. It is the agent or instrument by which God created the world. Philo names it the first begotten Son of God;* the image of the Divine perfections; the mediator between God and men.

---

* Here, in connection with the Alexandrine philosophy, we come to an expression "Son of God," employed also in the New Testament to designate the Hebrew Messiah, and derived, as we have seen, in the latter case, from Old Testament sources. (Comp. *supra*, Chapters XI. XII.) This coincidence, in the application of the epithet Son of God to the Christ on the one hand and to the Logos on the other, would no doubt facilitate the transference of the latter term to Jesus, with all that it involves. In what sense the application was made in the first instance (*i.e.*, in the fourth Gospel), will be considered in the next Chapter. The tendency, in Philo and subsequently, was constantly to personify and hypostatize the Logos; and this later import and acceptation of the latter term speedily displaced and prevailed over the old Hebraic meaning of the words Son of God. A step or two further, and, in the Fathers, Jesus is the Son in the new sense of being God; or, as Mr. Donaldson has expressed the same thing, Jesus "is now for the first time recognized fully and clearly as God; not merely the Son of God, but God." (*Ubi supra*, p. 117.)

It is evident that the phrase Son of God was used of the Logos long before the latter term was applied to Jesus. The same phrase is also constantly applied to our Lord by the Apostle Paul, who does not, however, make use of the term Logos. All the Evangelical narratives clearly presuppose and assume that the phrase was in use in connection with Jesus as the Christ, during his own lifetime; and this we take to be the most probable conclusion from the evidence relating to the point.

He regards it as a substitute and ambassador for God; a δεύτερος θεὸς, or second God; a God to those imperfect creatures that are incapable of the knowledge of the Supreme. The same being, he also tells us, in various phrase, was the source of the inspiration of the prophets; and in all the theophanies of the Old Testament, it was not Jehovah Himself that appeared. For it would have been impossible to Him, and beneath Him, to come into any such close contact with gross matter and sinful men. It was, therefore, the Logos that was thus manifested, the second or representative God, taken by ignorant men for the Highest Being. He it was who not only formed the world out of matter, but also spoke with Moses in the bush, was present in the pillar of cloud, and conducted the Israelites from Egypt to the promised land.

In such expressions as these the distinct personality of the Logos would seem to be clearly conveyed; and hence the conclusion that Philo did really believe in it as a kind of inferior God, who stood between the incomprehensible Parent Mind, and formed the medium of communication between Him, and the visible world.

But, on the other hand, Philo was a Jew, and must have shared the strict belief of his people in the absolute oneness and sole deity of Jehovah. Is it possible, then, that he can really have regarded the Logos as a separate personality, a second God? Justin and later Fathers doubtless did so; but they were men of different birth and education, and belonged to a very different class as regards religious belief and feeling. If, under certain philosophical and semi-pagan influences, they could without difficulty forget their monotheistic faith, and go to the verge or into the depths of ditheism and tritheism, there appears to be no necessity to suppose that Philo could do the same. The latter was most probably nothing more than inconsistent and self-contradictory, and this perhaps only on the surface, or in his forms of expression.*

One thing appears to be quite certain, and that is, that he did not intend to recognise a second, co-equal God. The Logos, even in the personal conception of it, was, at all events, regarded by him as subject and inferior to the Supreme Being; as His representative or substitute, indeed, in the government of the world, and in communication with men, but as being so only by a kind of delegation or appointment, not by any natural, independent right or power. And even when he calls it a God, he could do so in full accordance with ancient Hebrew usage; for, as before noticed, in the Old Testament the word Elohim is applied even to kings and judges, simply, perhaps, because they were representatives of Jehovah. This character, and others equally divine, were borne by the Logos, which indeed, it must be evident, stood in a relation to God far more intimate than could be conceived to belong to any mundane existence, however mighty, however exalted.

Such, then, is a rapid outline of the doctrine of the Logos, as it was held long before the fourth Gospel was written, and before Christ himself was born. As to the immediate influences which might lead a Jewish mind to follow this mode of speech respecting God and His revelation of Himself in the world, it is not necessary here to speak at any length. The following points, however, may be noticed.

We know that the Jews had long refrained from pronouncing

* The question whether the Logos in Philo is "a personal being," or only "a pure abstraction," is somewhat doubtfully decided by Dr. Liddon, in the latter sense. He observes, however, that a study of certain passages will "convince any unprejudiced reader that Philo did not know his own mind; that his Logos was sometimes impersonal and sometimes not, or that he sometimes *thought* of a personal Logos, and never *believed* in one."—B. L., pp. 66, 67.

the sacred Name. In the Targums, or paraphrases of the Old Testament in Chaldee, made about the time of the birth of Christ, or within the century following, they have omitted the word Jehovah altogether, and have substituted for it the phrase "Memra of Jah," or Word of Jah. This expression coincided in a remarkable way with both the meaning and the use of the term Logos; of which, as we have seen, the radical idea was, that it served as the outward representative of God, and preserved Him, as it were, from contact with gross matter. Similarly the Memra would conceal and protect the divine Name. Again, Jews scattered throughout the East, those living in Alexandria in particular, necessarily came under the immediate influence of the Gentile philosophy—that peculiar compound of oriental and Platonic mysticism in which the Logos doctrine held so prominent a place. Thus in a large degree Hellenized, they were ready and anxious to prove that their own sacred Scriptures were also in harmony with true philosophy, or might rather, indeed, be considered as the primary fountains of it. Hence their painful efforts, by means of allegorical interpretations, to spiritualize the ancient Mosaic history, and to shew that its representations of the Divine Being and His intercourse with men, as related in the Old Testament, were such as even a votary of the high philosophy of the day need not despise.*

In the Hebrew Scriptures themselves various passages may be pointed out which would directly favour both the allegorizing tendencies of the later Jews, and their disposition to adopt the new way of speaking of God and His manifestation of Himself in the world. For example, in Psalm xxxiii. 6,—"By the Word of Jehovah were the heavens made, and all the host of them by the breath of his mouth." Yet this alludes, it need

* See the remarks of Professor Jowett on this subject, in his dissertation before referred to. *Supra*, p. 150, note.

scarcely be observed, not to the Logos, but only to the account of the creation, at the beginning of Genesis. In the Book of Proverbs, again, chapter viii., the Divine Wisdom is spoken of poetically as a person. It is with God at the creation of the world, perhaps as his darling child* brought up beside Him, and playing before Him. A similar personification of Folly† occurs in the following chapter of the same book. Dr. Liddon is very careful to point out that Wisdom in the former passage "is personal." Doubtless it is so, exactly as Folly is; and, in both instances, by the poetical licence so natural to an oriental imagination. Had it suited Dr. Liddon's purpose, he might have informed his readers that Wisdom in this place is not only "personal," but also of the feminine gender, and in one instance‡ even plural in form;—a piece of information, however, which would scarcely have recommended his singular suggestion that the personification of this Divine attribute in the Book of Proverbs was an anticipation of "our Lord's Divinity." Similar personifications of wisdom were very familiar to the later Jewish writers.§

In the Apocryphal book of the Wisdom of Solomon, we have the Divine word itself personified in a remarkable manner; and perhaps here it is the Greek doctrine of the Logos that was in the writers' mind:—"Thine almighty Word leaped down from heaven out of thy royal throne, as a fierce man of war......and standing up filled all things with death; and it touched the heaven, but it stood upon the earth." 'In the same book we have the following: "O God of my fathers......who hast made all things with thy word,......give me wisdom that sitteth by thy throne." ‖

Various other expressions to the same effect might be cited

---

* Prov. viii. 22-30.   † Prov. ix. 13.
‡ Prov. ix. 1.   § Wis. Sol. vi. 12-16; vii. 11, 12; x.
‖ Wis. Sol. xviii. 15, 16; ix. 1-4.

from the Apocryphal books. They concur in shewing us that, some generations before the birth of Christ, this peculiar way of speaking of God and His attributes, and of conceiving of Him as acting upon the world by powers going forth from Him and often conceived of as personal beings, was beginning to prevail even among the Jews. In some cases, these forms of thought and speech may have been followed independently of the influence of the Greek philosophy. The ancient Hebrew belief in Angels, as servants and instruments of Jehovah, was evidently related to them; as was also the later idea of emanations and æons, so widely accepted throughout the East, in the centuries immediately before and after the birth of Christ.

The point, therefore, at which we have arrived is briefly this: at the time when the Evangelist wrote his Gospel, and long previously, it was a common and well understood mode of expression, to speak of the Deity as manifesting Himself in the world, putting forth His creative and inspiring energy, not by His own immediate presence and action, but by His Logos. By this term, however, was not meant an independent substantive being, much less a separate or second God. The essential idea conveyed by it was simply this—that the Logos was the manifestation of God; in other words, that it served as the medium of communication between Him on the one hand, and man and the world on the other.

Thus, as before, the Logos was simply a name for the thought and volition of God Himself in action.* It was indeed called the Son of God, the eldest and first begotten Son; but even this probably denoted, at first, an imaginary or figurative personality —just as we also know that the thoughts and determinations of men were sometimes, in a similar way, personified and spoken of as their children.

* This, as we shall see, is clearly admitted by Dr. Liddon, B. L., p. 228.

APPENDIX TO CHAPTER XV.
SOURCES OF INFORMATION RESPECTING THE LOGOS DOCTRINE.

THE account of this doctrine above given is founded chiefly upon the collection of the principal passages from Philo relating to the subject, published by the late Dr. Pye Smith, in his *Scripture Testimony to the Messiah* (Book ii. Chap. vii.), with some addition from the sections of Gfrörer on the same subject (*Philo und die Alexandrinische Theosophie,* Capp. 7, 8). We have thought it expedient, in the present work, to take the evidence bearing on this subject principally from a writer at once so learned and so orthodox as the author of the Scripture Testimony. No objection, probably, will be made by any one to his summary of Philo's doctrine of the Logos as given in the following passage,—in which, however, the term "Logos" should be substituted for "Word," the latter being evidently an inadequate representative of the former:

"To this object he [Philo] gives the epithets of the Son of God, the First-begotten Son, the Eldest Son, the Word, the Divine Word, the Eternal Word, the Eldest Word, the Most Sacred Word, the First-begotten Word, the Offspring of God, as a stream from the fountain, the Beginning, the Name of God, the Shadow of God, the Image ($εἰκών$) of God, the Eternal Image, the Copied Image ($ἀπεικόνισμα$), the Express Image ($χαρακτήρ$) of the seal of God, the Branch or Rising Light ($ἀνατολή$), the Angel, the Eldest Angel, the Archangel of many titles, the Inspector of Israel, the Interpreter of God, a Representative God, a Second God, a God to those creatures whose capacities or attainments are not adequate to the contemplation of the Supreme Father.

"This Word is described as presiding over all things; superior to the whole universe; the eldest of all objects that the mind can perceive, but not comparable to any object perceptible by sense, nor capable of being presented in a visible form; next to the Self-existent.

"To this Word are ascribed intelligence, design, and active powers; he is declared to have been the Instrument of the Deity in the creation, disposition and government of the universe, and in holding all its component parts in their proper order and functions, clothing himself with the universe as with a garment: he is the instrument and medium of divine communications, the High Priest and Mediator for the honour of God and the benefit of man, the Messenger of the Father, perfectly sinless himself, the Beginning and Fountain of virtue to men, their Guide in the path of obedience, the Protector and Supporter of the virtuous, and the Punisher of the wicked.

"Yet, the WORD is also represented as being the same to the Supreme Intellect, that speech is to the human; and as being the conception, idea, or purpose, of the Creator, existing in the Divine mind previously to the actual formation of his works."—*Scripture Testimony*, I. pp. 566, 567.

With this summary the reader may compare what Prof. Jowett has written on the same subject in his "St. Paul and Philo."—*Epistles of St. Paul*, I. p. 363, *seq.*

CHAPTER XVI.

ST. JOHN'S DOCTRINE OF THE LOGOS—ITS MEANING AND PERMANENT VALUE.

ON turning to the words of the last Evangelist, the first and inevitable inference from the facts just recounted is, that his doctrine or statement respecting the Logos is not offered to us as a revelation of *new* truth. The Evangelist's doctrine of the Logos cannot justly be regarded in the light of a divine revelation, as Dr. Liddon regards it, because it was already in the world long before St. John wrote his Gospel; and absolutely nothing is said by the former concerning the origin, the nature, the action, or even the personality, of the Logos, which had not already been said by others before him.

One thing, however, is peculiar to John, and had never been said by any one, so far as is now known, before he said it; and that is, that "the Logos became flesh and dwelt among us," and that it did so in Jesus Christ.*

And in saying this we may now perceive, this Evangelist states in substance what the Synoptics also give us clearly to understand, though in different terms; namely, that there was a manifestation of the invisible Being to the world in Jesus Christ: that is to say, the wonderful powers of Jesus, his wisdom, and the holy spirit which he possessed, were from God. The infinite and incomprehensible Father revealed Himself among men in Jesus Christ. "The Logos became flesh," became man, in him; the Logos which was in the beginning with God and was God, being indeed, as we have seen, the Divine thought itself, by which all things were conceived and called into being, in which was the life and the light of men,—this revealer and instrument of the great Parent Mind was manifested among men in a human form in Jesus Christ.

Here, then, is unquestionably a doctrine of incarnation; but how different it is from the ecclesiastical doctrine of the Creeds, as commonly received, it is unnecessary to point out.† And yet the objection may be raised, that the words of the Evangelist, καὶ ὁ λόγος σὰρξ ἐγένετο (and the Word became flesh), are too express and definite to allow us to think that he intended only to convey the idea of a mere indwelling of God, by the Logos, in the

---

* John i. 14.

† The reader may compare Dr. L. Alexander's Tract on the *Incarnation*, 1871; in which will be found an elaborate defence of a doctrine usually said to be the most express and essential doctrine of the Christian revelation, based, not on direct Scriptural evidence, but on patristic theology and inferential reasonings!

person of Jesus; for that these words, in truth, go far beyond the statement that Jesus was a man specially inspired and "approved of God," through whom divine powers and qualities were manifested among men. But, in reply to this, it may reasonably be urged that the words in question ought not to be understood too literally. They cannot really mean what they appear to convey, namely, that the Logos, the exalted spiritual conception so called, was actually converted into "flesh." Nothing so grossly material as this can reasonably be attributed to the writer. He cannot then mean anything more than that the being or power called Logos was the animating, inspiring presence in the man Jesus; and that this being or power was in him in some special and extraordinary manner.

The idea of incarnation, in very material forms, was indeed a familiar one in the days of the Evangelist. But this was not among either Jewish or Christian writers. It was among those who had been brought up to believe, or to despise, the Greek and Roman mythology. We cannot for a moment suppose that any Christian Evangelist has intended us to believe that the Logos "was made flesh," became man, in that heathen sense, much less in the still grosser sense which the words of St. John might seem at first to convey—the literal conversion of the spiritual essence of the Logos into palpable flesh and blood.

Thus, so far as we have gone, the doctrine of the Evangelist may be fairly understood to mean simply this, that the Spirit or energy of the One Incomprehensible God was specially manifested among men in a human being, in the man Jesus Christ. But here the question may be asked, If the Evangelist represents the Logos as incarnate even in this sense, is not this in fact equivalent to saying that Jesus Christ was God? This question, in its turn, may be answered by another. When it is said that the Holy Spirit was given to an Apostle or a Christian convert, or was in some way manifested in or by a human being,* does the writer mean to represent that Apostle, or convert, or holy man of old, as God incarnate? Considering always what was meant by the term Logos, the cases appear to be strictly parallel; and consequently it cannot be maintained that the representation of the presence or incarnation of the Logos in Jesus Christ can have been intended to lead us to look upon the latter as the Divine Being Himself in a human form. This idea is, in truth, unwelcome or even revolting, not only to the coldest reason, but also to our natural sentiments of reverence towards God. These prompt the thoughtful mind to shrink from every attempt to conceive of Him under a material form; and such sentiments, it may well be believed, nothing but a long training from early years, and the constant repetition of established creeds and forms, could avail to overcome, or expel from the mind.

It would therefore appear that the fourth Evangelist, in speaking of the Logos as incarnate in Jesus Christ, tells us in effect what is equivalent, in the older Hebrew phraseology, to the statement that the Holy Spirit was possessed by him; that the Spirit was given to him without measure; or, in the language of Peter at the Pentecost, before cited, that "Jesus of Nazareth" was "a man approved of God," by miracles and wonders and signs, "which God did by him."

But why, it may next be asked, should this Evangelist employ so uncommon a mode of stating so simple a fact, when he might have used the same form of expression as other speakers and writers of the New Testament? The answer will, of course, be found, partly in the consideration that the Evangelist had now himself been led to abandon the older Hebrew mode of thought on these subjects; partly in that of the regard which he would naturally have to the persons for whom, and amidst whom, he

---

* Acts ii. 17, 22; iv. 31; ix. 17; x. 44–47; xix. 2, 6; 2 Pet. i. 21.

composed his Gospel. In Ephesus, where the Gospel, according to ancient testimony, was most probably composed, and, indeed, throughout all the Hellenized East, the peculiar philosophy and modes of expression respecting God and His relation to the world, before spoken of, were well known and prevalent among cultivated persons. One, therefore, who wished to convey to readers familiar with such conceptions and forms of expression his own idea, that the power and wisdom of Jesus were from God, would naturally do so in the language most readily and clearly declaring this fact to them.

A reader of the present time cannot, perhaps, fully enter into the case, for such forms of thought and expression are essentially remote from our own. The latter are founded largely upon the more usual tenor of the Scriptures, which teach us to think and speak of God as of a personal Existence, as One who is not far removed from the world, but, on the contrary, ever near us, and without whom not a hair of our heads can fall to the ground. It is probable, however, that had it been stated to one imbued with the spirit of the ancient philosophy now alluded to, that the Invisible Being was in immediate contact and communion with Jesus of Nazareth, as represented and implied by the first three Evangelists, such a person would have regarded the statement as simply an absurdity, and the alleged fact as an impossibility; whereas were it stated that the Divine Logos was in him, this would have appeared to be in harmony with the nature of things, easily possible and comprehensible.

To this, however, it may seem to be an objection that St. John constantly speaks of Jesus as in intimate union with the Father: the Father is said to dwell in him, and the works which he does, as well as the words which he speaks, are the Father's. In all probability we ought to understand such expressions in subordination to the declaration at the beginning of the Gospel, that "the

Logos was God." It was God Himself all the time, for that expression was but a name for the self-revealing activity of the One Supreme. In such expressions, therefore, as those just referred to, it is everywhere implied, though it was unnecessary to be constantly repeating it, that it was by the medium of the Logos that the Father was in Jesus, and did the works and spake the words which Jesus ascribes to Him.

We may, indeed, even believe that the venerable writer of the Gospel, in so frequently referring to the intimate union between Jesus and the Father, was really desirous to guard himself against being supposed to intend to represent the Logos as a separate being from God, a "second God," although he adopted the current phraseology respecting it. The Evangelist, accordingly, says repeatedly that it was, in truth, the Almighty Father that was with Jesus and in him, enabling him, as He did, to manifest the power and presence of God among his fellow-men. Hence our Lord could even say, "He that hath seen me hath seen the Father;"— while yet the Evangelist declares also, "No man hath seen God at any time, the only begotten Son which is in the bosom of the Father he hath declared him."* The sense in which men could "see the Father" in Christ cannot be doubtful. It was in no material, literal sense; but in his power, in his gracious and merciful spirit, in the love towards men which he manifested. It was especially in those Divine moral attributes and qualities of which the Christian mind usually rejoices to consider Jesus Christ as the personal embodiment, and as, in regard to these, the "beloved Son," in whom the Heavenly Father was "well pleased." It was, and is, in these that Jesus Christ may be thought of as the true moral image and representative of God to man, and in him we see the Father.† Certainly it is not in any grosser sense that he is so, or that the Evangelist can have intended us to believe that he is so.

* John xiv. 9 ; i. 18.   † Comp. Heb. i. 3 ; Coloss. i. 15.

What has just been said may be expressed in different words. The strong monotheistic faith of the Evangelist would necessarily lead him, notwithstanding the introduction of the Logos idea, still from time to time to refer all that Christ was and did to the Father who sent him. If this be true, it leads at once to the further conclusion, that the real, permanent, underlying belief of the Evangelist's mind, upon which he raised, as it were, the superstructure of his Gospel narrative, was a belief in the simple humanity of Jesus Christ; and that the whole representation amounts to this, that the man Jesus was the human medium through which the Almighty Being revealed Himself to the world. And this simple view of the subject certainly harmonizes in a remarkable manner the claims of Reason and the statements of Scripture, while it fully accounts for the origin and growth of the orthodox doctrine of the deity of Christ.

And yet the question must now be more definitely asked, Does the Evangelist, in his first verse, represent the Logos as GOD, or does he, after the manner of Philo, speak of it as "*a* God"? The same question may be expressed in a different way, thus: Does the Evangelist, even in the first verse of his Gospel, so positively assign a separate personality to the Logos, that he there speaks of it as "a God," as Philo does?—or does he only say that the Logos is not different from God, but that it *is* God, although he also personifies it, and speaks of it, and makes Jesus speak, as if it were a distinct personal being, present in him?

The tenor of the foregoing remarks would lead us to adopt the latter supposition as the true one. We have seen the doubt which attaches to the representation of Philo, the doubt whether or not he really regarded the Logos as a distinct personal being, a second and subordinate God. If, on account of his Jewish monotheism, that writer cannot be supposed to have done this, there is manifestly the same reason for thinking that an Evangelist of Jewish birth cannot have done so. Hence, if this be true, when the latter says, "the Logos was God," he simply intends us to understand that, although, in accommodation to prevailing modes of thought, he wrote of the manifestation of God in Christ in accordance with the Logos doctrine, he yet did not mean that the Logos was a separate being from the One God, but only the medium, or manifestation, of the Divine activity; for that, in truth, "the Logos was God."

According to this interpretation of the Evangelist's meaning, the word God, θεός, in the final clause of his first verse, is exactly equivalent to the same word as it is used immediately before. There is, however, this difference: in the one case we have the article, and in the other it is absent. The difference is not without importance, for it was noted by Origen and Eusebius that the absence of the article before θεός, in the second clause of the verse, indicates that this word may be used here in a secondary sense; and that the Logos accordingly is not represented as Supreme God.* But this, again, is not absolutely certain, although, according to the testimony of these Fathers, it is perfectly admissible. The word θεός, being in the predicate of the sentence, would grammatically stand without the article, and may, therefore, be simply equivalent to the preceding τὸν θεόν.

In the presence of this doubt, we can only have recourse to expressions which occur later in the Gospel, and allow them, if they will, to throw light on the point in question. And it must be admitted that various passages occur which tend strongly to show that the Evangelist did, at least occasionally, give himself up to the conception of the Logos as a real personal existence, separate from God, and become flesh in Jesus Christ; that he did so quite

---

* Passages to this effect from the two Fathers are given by Tischendorf, crit. note, John i. 1. (N. T., 8th ed.) Philo has a similar remark as to the subordinate force of θεός without the article. Comp. Meyer on the words θεός ἦν ὁ λόγος.

as decidedly as Philo might have done; and that he, therefore, in his first verse intended only to say, "the Logos was a God."

For example, the following passages: "No man hath ascended up to heaven, but he that came down from heaven;" "I came down from heaven not to do mine own will, but the will of him that sent me;" "Jesus said unto them, Verily, verily, I say unto you, Before Abraham was, I am;" "Now, O Father, glorify thou me . . . . . . with the glory which I had with thee before the world was;" the exclamation of Thomas, "My Lord and my God."* It may be observed that this last passage is the only instance in the Gospel in which the term "God" is addressed, or applied in any way, to Jesus personally,—if it be so here. But, indeed, the words in question may be only a general exclamation of astonishment. As, however, the conception of the Evangelist is that the Logos was in Jesus, the application of the words Lord and God to him in this instance is accounted for. "My Lord," might even be considered as addressed to the human person; "My God," to the Divine power present in him; for this, being essentially God's power, or even God, might appear to warrant such an application of the term.

Such expressions, then, and some others which occur, would appear to indicate that the Evangelist at times conceived of the Logos, not as a mere power or manifestation, but as a personal being, present in Jesus; and that he also represents the latter as speaking in accordance with this conception, as he would naturally do.

Those readers who take this view of the subject, and who also consider this Evangelist's representation as that which they ought to receive, rather than that of the Apostle Peter and the other Evangelists, will adopt in substance the Arian doctrine of the person of Christ and his relation to God—according to which he was the incarnation upon earth of a great pre-existent spirit, of angelic

---

* John iii. 13; vi. 38; viii. 58; xvii. 5; xx. 28. Comp. viii. 42; xiii. 3; xvi. 27. John iii. 13 may be a parenthesis, added by the Evangelist.

or divine nature, the first of all created existences, and the instrument of the Almighty power in the creation of the universe.

One thing, at all events, is very clear. There is no evidence in the fourth Gospel, when read, as it ought to be, in the light of those local and contemporary considerations before referred to,—there is no evidence in this Gospel for the popular view of the person of Christ;—according to which he is not the Son of God, but "God the Son," an expression never found in the Bible; —according to which, again, he is co-eternal with the Father, in all respects His equal, one God with Him, in a sort of incomprehensible co-partnership of Deity, while yet in some inexplicable sense distinct from Him, and from the Holy Spirit—as much so, according to the comparison of Bishop Sherlock, as three human beings, Peter, James and John, are separate and distinct from one another. Explain it away, as some may seek to do, such appears to be the Athanasian doctrine of the Trinity as set forth by the Church of England and understood by ordinary people, in accordance with the obvious meaning of the words employed. In St. John's Gospel, there is clearly nothing to justify such a doctrine as this; for everywhere throughout this Gospel, the Father is the One Supreme, and the Son, or divine Logos in Jesus, is the subordinate, whose very words are not his own, and who can do nothing of himself.

There is, however, another conclusion, which perhaps brings us more nearly to the truth. We have seen that the idea of the Logos was by no means a constant quantity, but variable, and sometimes almost self-contradictory. This is without doubt the case in the various expressions of Philo, according to whom it is sometimes a power, an inspiration, and sometimes a person, a second God. Is there not something of the same indefiniteness and variableness of conception in the Evangelist's statement also? May he not, in short, while usually conceiving of the

Logos as simply the Divine power and wisdom in Jesus, yet at times also allow himself to speak of it as a substantive being, living and acting among men in the human personality of the man Jesus?

If such be the case, we should still observe that this latter mode of conception is only exceptional and temporary; and that the Evangelist constantly recurs to the true and natural relation subsisting between God and Christ,*—agreeing in substance with the synoptics in representing the Father as the original Source and Sender, and Jesus the Christ as the recipient and the sent.

But here it is necessary to acknowledge, more distinctly than we have yet done, the difference which there is, in some important respects, between the Jewish Philo and the Christian Apostle, notwithstanding the nature and extent of the agreement of which we have spoken. Some amount of difference, more or less decided, was clearly to be expected, considering the character and the circumstances of the two writers. What we refer to has been recently pointed out by M. Pressensé, as it is by Dr. Liddon, by each in terms which will be found a little stronger than strict accuracy would warrant.† But difference, nevertheless, there is. While Philo is so purely metaphysical and allegorical, the Evangelist is far more practical and moral. Above all, he sets forth the possibility of man's communion with the unseen God, and the possibility also of the direct action and influence of the Divine Spirit upon our human life. This he does in a manner with which the Alexandrine philosopher would have had little sympathy.‡ Nevertheless, in regard to the subject of the Logos, the sameness of the representation in the Evangelist

---

* See, for example, the narrative of the interview with the Samaritan woman; that of the restoration to sight of the blind man, and that of the raising of Lazarus. John iv. ix. xi.

† Pressensé, *Jesus Christ*, Book i. Chapters iii. iv. Liddon, B. L., pp. 68, 229.

‡ See John x. 38; xiv. 9, 10, 23; xvi. 3; xvii. 3, 21.

and in Philo is not to be denied. Everything that is said by St. John in his proem had already been said by Philo, and a great deal more. What he does *not* say, we have duly pointed out, namely, that the Logos became flesh in Jesus of Nazareth; and the exact meaning and purpose of this language we have endeavoured to ascertain. And here, as before, and indeed at every point in the discussion, we are forcibly reminded that the doctrine of the Logos was not introduced, but only *adopted*, by the Evangelist, as a convenient medium of expression. An old doctrine of the Græco-oriental philosophy cannot with any reason be regarded as a Divine revelation, being, in truth, the mere product of human speculation,—and, shall we not add, of human error?

We may now briefly recapitulate what has been said in this and the two or three preceding Chapters. It is evident that at an early period—that is to say, towards the close of the first century, and probably for long afterwards—the relation between God and Christ was contemplated under two very different aspects, according to the education and the habits of thought of the disciple. One of these aspects we find in the three Gospels of Matthew, Mark and Luke, in the Acts of the Apostles, and in most of the Epistles.* It is also represented by what Peter said of his departed Master on the day of Pentecost, as before pointed out. It is the more literal and simple view of the case, closely corresponding to the facts. It shews us clearly all that Jesus was in his human life, and gives us the first fresh impression which he left on his immediate friends and disciples. It is also in true harmony with the natural or Christian mode of thought and speech respecting God, that, namely, which is exemplified by Christ himself; according to which the Infinite is not a Being that

---

* It has been elsewhere noticed that the doctrine of the Logos does not occur in St. Paul's Epistles: *infra*, Chapter XX.

dwells far apart from the children of men, bearing no direct relation to them. the fundamental idea of the Logos philosophy—but One who is near to us when we call upon Him, who is merciful and gracious, and not only Creator and God, but also the Heavenly Father and Friend of man.

The other aspect is that which we find in the fourth Gospel most conspicuously; though it is not confined to that, but most probably appears in the first Epistle of John, and also in the introduction to the Epistle to the Hebrews. This second form of belief arose long after Jesus had passed away from the earth. It does not represent so directly and freshly the impression of what Christ was, as left by him on his immediate companions. It is the product rather of those obscure philosophical ideas, respecting the nature of God, and his manifestations of Himself, which so widely prevailed both before and after the commencement of the Christian era, and which gave origin to much that is still retained in the popular theological systems of the present day. For it is, in truth, to the same source that the world owes the doctrine of the Trinity,—of which, as already shewn, there is no real trace in the New Testament, not even in connection with the doctrine of the Logos.

From special causes, again, this view of the subject was adopted by the fourth Evangelist. Yet this came to pass in so purely accidental a way, that the new doctrine can only be regarded as an extraneous element, introduced into the primitive Christianity. It will therefore of necessity be dropped again, as the progress of knowledge brings men back to simpler and truer ideas of the historical Christ, and of the relation between him and God, and between God and the world. In all probability, however, the same element materially assisted the early diffusion of Christianity, rendering it possible for the Hellenized world of the first and following centuries after Christ to admit the divinity of his mission, without contradicting the established principles of human knowledge.

Still, the doctrine referred to is not in itself a permanent expression of divine truth. It stands in the same relation to us as the ancient belief in the stability of the earth and the motion of the sun. This belief and similar things (for example, diabolical possessions), are also found in the Bible, assumed and implied in the Christian teaching, mere relics of the imperfect natural philosophy of early times. But we can now separate such ideas from what is truer and more permanent, and lay them aside in our estimates of the character and value of Christianity. And so we should endeavour to do, in regard to that peculiar mode of expressing the relation of Jesus to God on which we have been dwelling. We must allow for that also as a human and non-essential product of the times. And when we have done so, the substantial residue of truth that remains is this, that Jesus of Nazareth was one " approved of God," in the estimation of those who were the eye-witnesses of his life, by the possession of special gifts and graces; that the Holy Spirit was poured without measure upon him; that Jesus has " shewn us the Father." There is still left to us, indeed, all that is necessary to form the basis of Christianity, regarded as a revelation of the Divine will, and of the paternal love and mercy of the invisible Creator, through and in the life and mind of Jesus Christ.

A final consideration remains. It relates to the more special practical value for our later times of the doctrine of the Word made flesh in Christ. This doctrine has still a great and an abiding value. For it bears witness to the extraordinary moral and spiritual pre-eminence of Jesus Christ. It shews us how lofty and holy a person the actual living Saviour must have appeared to those who knew him, and to the generations which came immediately after him; and what an impression, notwithstanding his brief career and his premature death, his life must have left upon the people who witnessed it.

This is clearly seen when we recall what is implied in the statement that the Logos became flesh in Jesus; that this exalted being, the image and glory of the invisible God, the life and light of the world, was incarnate upon the earth in Jesus. Granted, indeed, that this mode of speaking has no actual foundation in the nature of things; that the Infinite Spirit exists and manifests Himself to the human soul quite otherwise than was thought by the early philosophizing converts to Christianity; and that the representation of the fourth Evangelist is altogether remote from the simpler and more literal account of the Synoptics. Nevertheless, that the Evangelist has made such a representation, while it certainly does not shew that he looked upon Jesus as personally God, implies, of necessity, the extraordinary character of his life, his moral and spiritual greatness, his divine wisdom and wonderful works.

Such being the estimate of the personal life and character of Jesus Christ, known to have been entertained by minds like those of the fourth Evangelist and the writer of the Epistle to the Hebrews, and received so readily as it was by many other good and truthful men of the second century, we easily see how improbable it is that Jesus could have been any ordinary person of the time—whether a Jewish Rabbi of eminent wisdom and knowledge, as some would suggest, or only a sweet-tempered Galilean peasant, according to the romantic version of the sacred story with which the world has recently been favoured by the inventive genius of M. Renan.

Such, in few words, is the practical lesson derivable from the doctrine of the Word made flesh. It helps to shew us the more distinctly and impressively, even as the history of the world ever since he lived may shew us, that Jesus of Nazareth was God's highly distinguished minister to sinful men; that we, therefore, should give "the more earnest heed" to what he has said on many points: respecting our Father in heaven; His providence over us; His divine will that we men should make the cultivated sense of Duty the supreme law of our lives, living together as His children, and therefore as brethren, ready to help and benefit one another in all good works; His merciful design to lead us on, even by the trials and conflicts and sorrows of this life, to a better life in heaven; that we should give the more earnest heed to all that Christ has thus taught us and shewn us,—for that he spake " as one having authority," not only to those who immediately heard him, but to us also of these later generations.

CHAPTER XVII.

REMARKS ON DR. LIDDON'S EXPOSITION OF THE DOCTRINE OF THE LOGOS.

THE exposition above given of the meaning and use of the word Logos, and of the ideas connected with it, will be sufficient to shew how futile the attempt must be to construct the ordinary ecclesiastical doctrine of the deity of Christ upon the representations of the fourth Gospel. It is, nevertheless, to be noticed that, in Dr. Liddon's judgment, this Gospel is the great stronghold of that doctrine. " It is undeniable," he says, " that the most numerous and direct claims to Divinity [deity] on the part of our Lord are to be found in the Gospel of St. John;" and again, "St. John's Gospel is the most conspicuous written attestation to the Godhead" of Christ.* Doubtless it is so—to this extent, namely,

* Liddon, B. L., pp. 207, 208.

that if the deity of Jesus Christ cannot be conclusively established from the fourth Gospel, it will be in vain to attempt to prove it out of any other book of the New Testament.

With the evidence, therefore, which has been laid before the reader, shewing that this Gospel is not really to be cited as a witness for the orthodox side of this great argument, we might now leave this part of the subject. There are, however, a few passages of the Gospel which have not yet come specially before us, and to which Dr. Liddon attaches great importance. It will, therefore, be desirable briefly to notice these in the light of the preceding exposition, as well as in connection with Dr. Liddon's own account of the Logos, and thus endeavour to ascertain how far the preceding statements help us to their adequate interpretation.

On the question of the authenticity of this Gospel, it is not necessary here to express any decided opinion. Dr. Liddon gives a rapid summary of the evidence which tends to attribute the work to the pen of the Apostle John. He brings forward, it will be seen, such evidence as belongs to the positive side of the question. The very grave difficulties which attach to some of that evidence, and the very strong case which may be presented on the other side, he does not at all adequately notice. It would be much out of place to enter minutely into the question in these pages. It is sufficient for our purpose to observe, that there can be no reasonable doubt as to the *existence* of the Gospel in the first quarter of the second century. There is no direct evidence, however, to shew that it was at that time spoken of, or known, as a work of the Apostle John.[*] Nevertheless, it is evidently a document which comes down to us from the heart of Christian antiquity. It is a witness, therefore, of the greatest weight to the belief of the Christian community in the latter part of the first century and in the century following. The question as to the actual person of

[*] See J. J. Tayler on the Fourth Gospel, 2nd ed., 1870, §§ vii. and xi.

the author is one, perhaps, of only secondary importance; inasmuch as the real value of the Gospel must depend largely upon its internal character, and the possibility of reconciling its statements with those of the Synoptics.

And this reconciliation can evidently be effected in the way which has been pointed out. The two modes of representation may be harmonized, by accepting the narrative of the fourth Gospel as substantially equivalent to the statements of the Synoptics—to the effect that Jesus was the possessor of special gifts conferred upon him from on high; that it was God's power and wisdom in him,—in other words, that it was "God in Christ," that enabled him to be what he was, and to do what he did. But the representation of the fourth Evangelist cannot be truly harmonized with the earlier Gospels, if the Logos doctrine be taken, as it is by orthodox theologians, to be anything more than a peculiar mode of conceiving of the same relation between God and Christ which the synoptical writers exhibit. The two forms of statement cannot be truly harmonized, if the conception of the Logos as a distinct personality be admitted to correspond to anything that is real in the nature or mode of the Divine existence; if, that is to say, the Gospel be supposed to represent the incarnate Logos not merely as the manifestation of the "Only true God," but as a second Divine person, virtually, in other words, as a "second God." There is nothing that corresponds to this in the Synoptics, but much that is strongly opposed to it. Moreover, in the latter case, the Christian world would evidently owe the revelation of the Divine nature, *not* to Christianity at all, but to Philo and Greek philosophy—a consideration which ought to be a fatal objection to the ordinary view of this subject with all who receive Christianity as a divine revelation. In the presence, too, of so strong a disharmony between John and the Synoptics, it would be very safe to say that the fourth Evangelist must, sooner or later, be looked upon as the less credible witness, in the inquiry as to the person and work of Christ.

In accordance, however, with the foregoing exposition, this Evangelist's evidence as to the character and influence of Christ is of equal weight and compass with that of the three earlier Gospels. It follows also that the various expressions in which St. John's idea of the relation between Christ and God is conveyed should receive careful consideration, and should have due importance attached to them. A few of these, not as yet adequately noticed, will now come before us.

In the first place, let us observe that the account above given of the philosophical conception of the Logos is in essential harmony with that of Dr. Liddon, although the conclusions here drawn are so different from his. This will be seen from the following passage, which, although in one or two points scarcely intelligible, contains probably as good a description of the Logos idea as it is possible to give in so few words: "St. John's doctrine of the Logos has from the first been scrutinized anxiously by the mind of Christendom. It could not but be felt that the term Logos denotes at the very least something intimately and everlastingly present with God, something as internal to the Being of God as thought is to the soul of man. In truth, the Divine Logos is God reflected in His own eternal Thought; in the Logos, God is His own Object. This Infinite Thought, the reflection and counterpart of God, subsisting in God as a Being or Hypostasis, and having a tendency to self-communication—such is the Logos. *The Logos is the Thought of God*, not intermittent and precarious like human thought, but subsisting with the intensity of a personal form. The very expression seems to court the argument of Athenagoras, that since God could never have been $ἄλογος$, the Logos must have been, not created, but eternal. It suggests the further inference, that since reason is man's noblest faculty, the

Uncreated Logos must be at least equal with God. . . . . . But was the Logos then an independent being, existing externally to the One God? *To conceive of an independent being, anterior to creation, would be an error at issue with the first truth of monotheism;* and therefore Θεὸς ἦν ὁ Λόγος. The Word is not merely a Divine Being, but He is in the absolute sense God."*

Now these statements are doubtless substantially correct; and they clearly amount to the Evangelist's proposition that the Logos was God. The Logos, as we have formerly seen, and as Dr. Liddon here expressly says, is "the thought of God;" but "subsisting in God," he adds, "as a Being or Hypostasis." What is meant by these extraordinary words? What can they mean, except that the Logos, being simply "the thought of God," was yet speculatively *conceived of* and represented as "a being or hypostasis?" Dr. Liddon cannot surely intend literally to speak of the Divine mind as containing "a being or hypostasis"?—or to affirm that the Divine "thought" was something "subsisting with the intensity of a personal form," otherwise than by a kind of poetical licence of conception? His words, therefore, so far as they have a definite sense, mean that the Logos was no other than the thought of the Divine mind; and this, within the limits formerly pointed out, is doubtless a true account of it. It plainly follows, that the Logos was eternal,—in accordance with the self-evident proposition quoted by Dr. Liddon, that "God could never have been ἄλογος." It follows also that "the uncreated Logos must be at least equal with God." It could not well be more. The simple truth is better stated in the Evangelist's own words, καὶ Θεὸς ἦν ὁ Λόγος:—the Logos was really God Himself, in His outward manifestation by the words and deeds of the human Christ.

---

* Liddon, B. L., pp. 228, 229. We have emphasised the more important admissions in this passage.

In another passage Dr. Liddon speaks of the terms Word and Son as "metaphors."* This, it is clear, they are essentially; but, as he thinks, they counterbalance and correct each other. "Each metaphor reinforces, supplements, and protects the other."† It may, however, be asked, Can any combination of two "metaphors" make up a "personal subsistence distinct from that of the Father," such as Dr. Liddon claims for the "Son-Word"? And how can that which the Word, according to Dr. Liddon himself, really denotes, namely, the "Eternal Thought or Reason," be taken, in any rational sense whatever, as a separate "personal subsistence," so as to be conceived of and worshiped as a distinct being under a different name, as a second and co-equal God? For if the eternal Thought or Reason be thus taken, as it were, from the Father, and regarded as a separate being, what is there left to the Divine mind itself? This most weighty question is not duly considered by Dr. Liddon. The statement of it is, in effect, a virtual refutation of this part of the orthodox scheme, according to Dr. Liddon's exposition of it; and, until a satisfactory reply can be furnished, truly it will be best to adhere very closely to the words of the Christian Master, and to remember still that with him, as with Moses of old, the "first of all the commandments" includes the proposition that "the Lord our God is One Lord."

We have formerly seen that the Evangelist, by his mode of speaking, probably guards against the possibility of being supposed to imperil his monotheistic faith. "The Father" is everywhere supreme, the true original source of power and thought even to the incarnate Logos. "The words which ye hear are not

---

* B. L., p. 234. It will not be forgotten that Dr. Liddon has formerly urged that Jesus Christ is the Son in a "natural sense." Here he tells us, "Son" is a metaphor. The latter is essentially the truth, but how far is the one statement consistent with the other?

† Liddon, B. L., p. 235.

mine, but the Father's which sent me:" and the works which Christ does are equally by the power of the Father. "My Father is greater than I"—Logos incarnate though he was; and we know that the Evangelist depicts him, in solemn and private prayer, as addressing the Heavenly Father as "the Only True God." In reference to such expressions, Dr. Liddon justly observes that it would have been something strange and monstrous to represent a mere man as saying of the Infinite, "My Father is greater than I." Most readers will fully assent to the remark. Nor does the Evangelist say this of any ordinary man. He says it of one whom, for the moment, he conceives of as the Christ, by virtue of the indwelling of the divine Logos. He, therefore, in effect, gives us to understand, that even the Logos, conceived of as come forth from God and present in Christ, is less than the Father, subordinate to the Father, from whom he is come.

In this way of speaking, it may be urged, is there not some degree of inconsistency on the part of the Evangelist, especially if he says, in the first verse of his Gospel, that the Logos is God Himself? For in that case, does he not, in one sentence, represent the Logos as no other than God—therefore, it is to be understood, equal with God, and to be honoured as God; and in another, does he not speak of it as if it were a separate existence present in the person of Jesus, and inferior to the Father; the latter, again, being in another passage the "only true God," whom the true worshipers are to worship "in spirit and in truth"? Such questions may without doubt be asked; for difficulties of this kind appear to be inherent in the subject; and they are certainly not relieved by "hypostatizing" the Logos into a divine person, the second and co-equal member of a triple Godhead.

In the next place, it is observable that Dr. Liddon fails to distinguish sufficiently between the Logos, conceived to be in Jesus, and the person of the latter. He says, for example: "Taking the prologue of St. John's Gospel in connection with the verses which immediately succeed it, let us observe that St. John attaches to our Lord's Person two names which together yield a complete revelation of His Divine glory. Our Lord is called the 'Word' and the 'Only-begotten Son.'"*

Now this statement, we apprehend, is far from correct. The Evangelist evidently does not attach to "our Lord's *person*" the name "Word;" what he says is that the "Word became flesh," that is, *in* Jesus Christ. The Word, he also says, was God (or, a God); but he nowhere says that Jesus Christ was personally God; nor does he anywhere even term Jesus the Word, that is to say, apply the term Word to him in place of his own proper name. Even in the exclamation of Thomas, "My Lord and my God," we may, as before noticed, understand the appellation "Lord" to be addressed to the human Jesus (who is often termed Lord in the New Testament), and the appellation "God" to the Logos, present in him—such being the Evangelist's conception.

The same oversight occurs more than once on the part of Dr. Liddon. Thus he asks, "How can we account for St. John's conduct in representing him as God, if he was in truth only man?"—and he afterwards speaks of the exaggeration which it would have been, on the part of the Evangelist, to transform " a human friend into the Almighty and Everlasting God."† The reply is, that St. John does not do so. He nowhere represents Jesus Christ as personally God; or gives us to think that he designed to transform "a human friend" into Almighty God. This is what Dr. Liddon, in obedience to orthodox necessities, does for him. What the Evangelist says is this, that the Logos was God (or a God), and "became flesh" *in* Jesus of Nazareth,

* B. L., p. 226. † *Ibid.*, pp. 268, 269.

speaking and acting in and through him,—even as St. Paul also, in one instance, says that "God was in Christ,"—and as again, the Holy Spirit itself is elsewhere said to be in human agents, and to act and speak in and through them. And yet no one ever conceives that these human agents are represented, by any New Testament writer, as transformed into Almighty God, by virtue of that presence in them of the Divine power.

As we have before seen, Dr. Liddon attaches great importance to the expressions "Son," and "only-begotten Son," as applied to Christ; and he remarks that, in virtue of his "Sonship," the bearer of that title is "a partaker of that incommunicable and imperishable Essence which is sundered from all created life by an impassable chasm." We have in substance admitted that such a statement may be true of the Logos, *conceived of* as a personal being. Clearly it might be thus described, by one who was willing to attribute personality to it, even by way of "metaphor" only; and it was also "only-begotten"—there was only one divine Logos—although the term *logos*, it is true, is not withheld from certain other powers or attributes of the Divine Being, regarded as outward manifestations of God. Hence, again, the epithet, which it would appear that even orthodox translators are unwilling to repeat in an English version, the epithet "only-begotten GOD," which is the reading of the Sinaitic and Vatican manuscripts, and a few others, in John i. 18.* The Nicene Fathers, and the copyists of their century, were evidently less fastidious, or more uncompromisingly orthodox, than modern theologians.

The word "only-begotten," as used of the Logos, doubtless implied the peculiar and intimate relation to God of which Dr. Liddon speaks. But when either the term Son, or the phrase

---

* Dean Alford (English N. T., *in loco*) adheres to the old rendering. Compare Liddon, B. L., p. 234. Tischendorf also prefers "Son."

"beloved Son," is used of Jesus Christ in the Synoptics, it designates him simply, as we have formerly seen, in his character of Messiah, regarded as pre-eminently the beloved, the chosen and favoured instrument, of the Almighty Father.* The idea of participation in the "incommunicable Essence" of the Divine nature, is an idea which most probably never occurred to the first three Evangelists, in connection with Jesus of Nazareth. At least, Dr. Liddon will render a service to this discussion, if he can produce any passage from their narratives in which it appears really to have done so.† The word "only-begotten" is used in reference to Jesus (or rather the Logos) in John alone of the four Gospels,—a fact which is not without significance, as shewing us that the peculiar conceptions of the fourth Evangelist are altogether alien to the others.‡

The reader may again be reminded that the term Son, in its relation to God, is not applied to Jesus only, for that Christian disciples also are designated by the same term.§ Sonship, therefore, when affirmed of him, cannot necessarily of itself denote participation in the "incommunicable Essence" of which Dr. Liddon speaks. The latter, indeed, himself acknowledges it to be probable that many of our Lord's contemporaries applied the title of Son to him only as an official designation of the Messiah.‖ Manifestly they did so, as formerly pointed out. The metaphysical use of that title by Christians belongs to a later generation; and the admission just alluded to virtually concedes the question of

---

* Comp. Matt. iii. 17; xii. 18; xvii. 5; Mark i. 11; ix. 7; Luke iii. 22; ix. 35.

† We have before referred to Matt. xi. 27 (Luke x. 22)—a singular verse which looks as if by some chance it had been transferred from the fourth Gospel. Its difference in style and sentiment from the synoptics is very evident. Comp. *supra*, p. 112.

‡ The Synoptics have the term "only-begotten," but not in connection with Jesus. It usually expresses the sense of strongly, dearly-beloved, as an only child: Luke vii. 12; viii. 42; ix. 38: Heb. xi. 17 of Isaac.

§ Matt. v. 45; Gal. iv. 5-7; 1 John iii. 10.   ‖ Liddon, B. L., p. 247.

meaning—excepting always as regards the fourth Gospel. It shews too, as plainly as need be, that no conclusive argument for the deity of Christ can be founded upon the application to him of the word Son.

In harmony with the Johannine idea of Sonship as belonging to the Logos, the fourth Evangelist introduces several expressions, which orthodox writers usually consider of great importance as denoting the equality of Jesus Christ with the Divine Father. "All men shall honour the Son even as they honour the Father."* This could evidently be said in reference to the Son (and even to Jesus himself) in his character as the Logos, the manifestation and instrument of God Himself. In one instance, however, the reason assigned by the Evangelist is a very significant one. It is that "the Father has *committed* all judgment unto the Son." Thus the obligation to honour the Son, in the Evangelist's idea, follows upon the representative character which the Father has given to him.

And this is in harmony with what is found in other places. "My Father worketh hitherto, and I work:" this is said of the miracle which had just been done on the sabbath day. The speaker justifies the deed, not merely as one of his own working, but by referring it to the Almighty power by which he had performed it. The expression shews, again, that the Evangelist conceived of the power of Christ not as something independently in him, but as derived from One that was greater than he— here again excluding the idea of a co-equal participation in Divine attributes, such as Dr. Liddon and the Creeds ascribe to him.

When, on the same occasion, in consequence of what he had just said, the Jews impute to him the intention of "making himself equal with God," he replies in language which strongly

* Liddon, B. L., p. 182. See John v. 10-23.

disclaims the assumption, and affirms that his power is given to him: "The Son can do nothing of himself."* So, in a later verse, the life of the Son is given to him by the Father,—given to him, that is, by virtue of the Divine power conceived to be in him. He adds (v. 30), "I can of mine own self do nothing." Whether it be the human agent that here speaks, or the Logos in him, it is clear that he could only act through the power given him by the indwelling energy of the Supreme God.

In this exposition, it may indeed be said, there is too much shifting of the personality; the human Jesus, apparently, sometimes speaking, and sometimes the Logos. This is not to be denied; and whatever objection it may form to the Evangelist's narrative, or however incompatible it may seem with clearness of ideas, it serves, at all events, to shew us that there is a certain unreality in the whole representation,—that it is a mode of conception only, not literally corresponding to anything in the relation between Christ and God. In other words, as Dr. Liddon admits, the whole idea of the Logos is a kind of "metaphor." For the peculiarity referred to, the modern expositor is in no way responsible. He can only read and interpret the Evangelist's language as it is.

In one passage of the Gospel the following words occur: "This is life eternal, that they might know thee, the only true God, and Jesus Christ whom thou hast sent." † On this it has been observed, "The knowledge of God and a creature could not be eternal life." So Dean Alford, quoted approvingly by Dr. Liddon. But, in the first place, the Logos in Jesus is not a *creature*; and in the second place, if it be answered that it is not here the Logos that speaks, but "Jesus Christ whom thou hast sent;" still it is evident that the knowledge of Jesus Christ was,

---

* John v. 19, 26 ; comp. vi. 39, 40 ; viii. 28, 29.
† John xvii. 3 ; B. L., p. 237.

in this mode of conception, the same thing as the knowledge of the divine Logos in him; and moreover that knowledge, whether it were of the logos or of the human Jesus in his teaching and works, is "life eternal" by the gift and appointment of God. "What creature," again, it is asked, "could stand before his Creator and say, Glorify me that I may glorify Thee"? It would certainly be presumptuous in any ordinary creature to say this; unless, as represented by the Evangelist, the Almighty had so appointed that it should be; and Jesus declares, in John, as in the Synoptics, that all his power and wisdom, and the words which he spake, are given to him from above. What might be arrogantly presumptuous in a creature, who should speak in his own name and without authority, might be perfectly allowable, in the view of the Evangelist, when all was done by the express appointment of the Almighty Being himself.*

In conformity with the foregoing remarks, we can follow Dr. Liddon with full assent in nearly the whole of the following statement: "The Word incarnate is ever conscious of His sublime relationship to the Father. He knows whence He is. He refers not unfrequently to His pre-existent Life. He sees into the deepest purposes of the human hearts around Him. He has a perfect knowledge of all that concerns God. His works are simply the works of God. To believe in the Father is to believe in Him. To have seen Him is to have seen the Father. To reject and hate Him is to reject and hate the Father. He demands at the hands of men the same tribute of affection and submission as that which they owe to the Person of the Father."†

All this occurs, it need not be added, in the fourth Gospel *only;* all is in harmony with the conception upon which that

---

* John xi. 21, 22; xvii. 6-9; Matt. ix. 8; xxviii. 18; Luke xxii. 42, 43.
† Liddon, B. L., p. 236.

Gospel is composed, or is even demanded by it. But while this is admitted, it is also true that all such statements as these partake of the essential non-reality, and of the metaphorical character, which attaches to the Logos conception;—which attaches to it, as being in truth only an accidental and temporary mode of expressing the relation between God and Christ, and between God and the world.

Dr. Liddon insists upon the importance of the expression of our Lord, "I and my Father are one."* But the Logos could speak thus with peculiar force and truth; although it may well be that what is expressed is simply the idea of oneness of design, co-operation and affection, on the part of the human Jesus. The unbelieving Jews, indeed, as we read in the same place, "took up stones to stone him," on account of this declaration of his oneness with God. They chose to consider it blasphemous, and alleged again that he, being a man, made himself God. But he immediately shews them that this was an unfounded accusation. He, the man Jesus, had *not* intended to make himself God, even though he may have meant to imply that the divine Logos in him was one with God. All that he claimed for himself was the character of one to whom the word of God came: "If he called them gods," he says, "unto whom the word of God came" ...... say ye of me that I blaspheme when I called myself,—not God, but simply—the Son of God?†

It is observed by Dr. Liddon, that "if our Lord had been, in reality, only man, he might have been fairly expected to say so." But, plainly, to the Evangelist's idea he could not have been "only man," and could not be expected to say so. He constantly speaks, according to this Evangelist's representa-

---

* John x. 31. See a similar expression in 1 Cor. iii. 8.
† John x. 34-36. Comp. Psalm lxxxii. 1, 6, and similar O. T. expressions.

tion, not only for himself, but for the Logos in him; or rather he had so to speak as to reconcile the claims of both; and this the Evangelist represents him as doing. Any difficulty or inconsistency involved in the mode in which this is done is not of the reader's making. It is inherent in the nature of the subject, in the original plan according to which this Gospel is constructed.

Once more, Dr. Liddon cites the passage in which our Lord appears to speak of himself as "in heaven," even while present upon earth, and refers to it as an illustration of the two spheres of existence which belonged to him as "both God and man." That he speaks of himself as having come down from heaven appears to be certain.* Such expressions are found exclusively in John, and are in harmony, as before, with the leading idea of the Gospel. The Logos, for which Jesus so often speaks, or which, as we may also say, so often speaks through him, had come down from heaven; "became flesh" in him. But the words expressing that he was in heaven "while yet speaking" to Nicodemus, are well known to be, in one sense, of a doubtful character. Are they not parenthetical? The fourth Evangelist is fond of parentheses.† The words, "the Son of man, which is in heaven," or perhaps even the entire verse, may therefore be a parenthetical addition, affirming the existence of the risen Christ in heaven, not when Jesus was speaking to Nicodemus, but when the Evangelist was writing. Certainly it comes too near to pure paradox, and puts too great a strain upon Christian faith, to represent our Lord as saying that he was in heaven while he was conversing with Nicodemus. If this were the meaning, the latter must be admitted to have received the announcement very calmly; while yet we are told that he had only learnt to consider Jesus as "a teacher come from God," for that no man

---

* John vi. 33, 38.   † For example, iii. 23, 24; iv. 2, 8; vii. 39; ix. 7.

could do the miracles which he had done, "unless God were with him." *

Before closing the present Chapter, we may briefly notice an expression in the Book of Acts, to which Dr. Liddon attributes a surprising degree of importance. It is the verse in which God is said to have purchased the Church "with his own blood." † It should, however, be noted, that the manuscript authority for this expression is certainly doubtful, or rather, insufficient; and that some of the best manuscripts read "church of the Lord," that is to say, of Jesus Christ.‡ It is indeed true that the two reputed to be the oldest, the Sinaitic and the Vatican, read "church of God;" but, on the other hand, those documents are stated by the highest critical authority to come down from the fourth century, a period of intense controversy respecting the person of Christ, and one in which it was decreed by a council that he is "God of God." The "blood" of "God" may have been a bearable expression to the Bishops and Fathers who assembled at Nicæa. It is most probable that the nineteenth century will increasingly revolt from it, and come at last to see that even the authority of the two oldest manuscripts is insufficient to justify its acceptance. It is not to be forgotten that the Alexandrine, and other excellent manuscripts of the fifth and later centuries, which have the reading "Lord," must have copied this word from documents still older than themselves. There can be no doubt as to the tendency of the fourth century to substitute the more orthodox term. §

* John iii. 2.   † Acts xx. 23. B. L., p. 325.
‡ So Tischendorf, in his 8th ed.
§ The Vatican and the Sinaitic MSS. are also the chief MSS. which read "only begotten God" in John i. 18. A similar influence, we may conjecture, prevailed in their preference of this expression: comp. *infra*, Chapter XIX.

CHAPTER XVIII.

JESUS THE SPIRITUAL CHRIST—CHRISTIAN FAITH—JUSTIFICATION BY FAITH.

ACCORDING to various statements of the Evangelical history, Jesus accepted the title of the Christ, given to him by his followers.* It is clear, however, that he did not assume the character implied in it in the popular acceptation,—that, namely, of a temporal or political leader of his people. It is reasonable, indeed, to suppose that what he said on this subject, as on some others, has not reached us entirely unaffected by the peculiar medium through which it has been transmitted to us. But if, as it is fair to do, we may judge from what appear to be the highest and most characteristic sayings of the Lord, it is easy to learn that he did not profess to be a temporal Messiah, that he did not wish to make himself a king, in the ordinary sense of this term; that the kingdom which he was founding was not of this world.† The same thing is evident from the general strain of his teaching and the religious spirit of his life.

Most probably, nevertheless, the early disciples looked upon their Master as Christ in their own sense, supposing that his lowly condition was only temporary, or assumed for special purposes; and that he would eventually claim for himself the anticipated glory and power of him that was to come.

Traces of this popular belief will be familiar to the attentive reader of the Gospels. But such hopes Jesus did not encourage. He in fact repressed them, so far as he could without actually repelling his adherents from him.‡ Yet he allowed them to regard him as the Christ, and on some occasions he claimed this

* Matt. xvi. 16, 17 ; Luke vii. 19-23 ; John iv. 25, 26.
† Matt. xx. 20-28 ; Luke xxii. 24-30 ; ix. 22, 44 ; John xviii. 36.
‡ Matt. xx. 17-28 ; Mark viii. 29-34 ; Luke xii. 13-21.

character, as at his trial. He knew and felt himself to be the Son of God by genuine ties of spiritual affinity, as well as by virtue of the Divine protection and favour; while yet he knew too that the radical difference between his own ideas on the subject and those of the people around him would eventually lead to his rejection and death. He did not, on that account, shrink from the task which he had undertaken, which was no less than to purify and spiritualize the ancient religion of his nation. Nor was it limited to this. He had an ulterior object of still greater magnitude. He sought to gather into his fold "other sheep" besides those of the race of Israel; and doubtless he contemplated the time when the whole world should be regenerated by the influence of his life and doctrine.*

And the moral and spiritual qualities of Jesus are worthy of the exalted character which he thus assumed,—worthy of it both in its relation to God, and in its relation to man. His humility, devoutness, submission and filial trust towards the Almighty Father are everywhere conspicuous; as are his untiring beneficence, the righteousness and purity of his spirit, his love and pity towards sinful men. Such qualities as these shine forth in all that he says and does; constituting him in truth, for all time to come, the Christ, the Anointed King in things spiritual, the Light and Saviour of mankind. For eighteen centuries past he has thus stood before the world; and for untold centuries to come, so shall he stand, the true Son of God and Son of man.

This lofty spiritual position of Jesus the Christ involves a further relationship to his followers of the highest importance. He is their Example. This is duly brought forward in the New Testament, especially by St. Paul, in several familiar instances.†

---

* Mark iv. 30-32; Matt. xiii. 31-33; xxii. 10; xxviii. 19; John xii. 24, 32.
† Rom. xiii. 14; Ephes. iv. 13; Coloss. iii. 13; Philip. ii. 5; 1 Pet. ii. 21.

Dr. Liddon too speaks very earnestly of certain commanding features of the moral character of Christ. He was sincere, he was humble, he was unselfish; and the question is asked, "What becomes of these integral features of his character ...... if we should go on to deny that he was God?"* But may it not be asked, in reply, What becomes of them, if we should affirm that he was God? Can God be humble? Can He be unselfish, in the sense of sacrificing Himself, or in any intelligible sense whatever? Is it not unworthy of Him, to speak of Him as even sincere, implying, as this does, the possibility of the contrary?

And when our Lord exemplified these and other excellent moral and human qualities, was he merely acting a part which had no reality in it? The example of Christ, be it remembered, is held up to his disciples in the New Testament, as something which is to sustain and comfort them, and which they are to strive to imitate. But what sustaining or comforting power could his career have for us, on the supposition of the truth of the popular view of his person? Would the example of a superhuman being have, in this sense, moral value for frail, suffering, tempted man? If in the person of Jesus there were hidden a Divine nature, the exhaustless energies of God, how should *we* be told to take courage from what we see in Him; to "follow his steps;" to forgive as he forgave; to be patient and endure, to be lowly and considerate for others, even because he did so and was so? The infinite power of God, present in the one case, is absent in the other; and how should a frail, sinful, ignorant creature like man, take courage from the sight of one who was neither frail, nor liable to sin, nor ignorant, nor tempted as we are? How should mortal man hope, or be expected, to do that to which even an Almighty being, as it would appear,† proved hardly equal?

* Liddon, B. L., p. 195.   † Matt. xxvi. 39 ; Luke xxii. 42, 43.

Thus, the example of a God enduring could scarcely help us, or encourage us to hope that we might stand fast. On the other hand, the example of one " at all points tempted like as we are and yet without sin,"* the example of one "like unto his brethren," in the essential strength or weakness of his nature, yet bravely, patiently, bearing and submitting—this would have a moral value for us, and might aid us to go and do likewise. From such a sight we might take courage, feeling assured that what one of our number was equal to, could not be beyond the reach, or imitation, of any faithful servant of God.

Surely therefore this part of Dr. Liddon's argument conspicuously fails; and just in the same degree in which he succeeds in proving that Jesus Christ was God incarnate, he destroys the value of his moral example, and takes away meaning and force from some of the most cogent and fruitful exhortations of the New Testament.

In accordance with the conclusion that Jesus claimed to be the spiritual Christ, and is now to be received in that character by his disciples, is the idea derivable from the New Testament as to the nature of Christian faith. This, in the primitive church, was indisputably faith in Jesus, not as God, but as Christ. There is no instance producible from the New Testament in which faith of the former kind can be plausibly held to have been meant by the language employed. The word Christian itself is at once evidence and illustration of this. " The disciples," we are told, " were called Christians, first at Antioch."† That is to say, they were called *Christ*-ians; they took their name from the circumstance that they received Jesus as Christ.

This is entirely in harmony with what we know of the early

---

* Heb. iv. 15. Comp. John xx. 17, where Jesus speaks of his disciples as his " brethren."

† Acts ix. 9.

position of the Gospel. The great controversy, between the Jews and the disciples of those times, turned upon the question whether or not Jesus of Nazareth was the expected Messiah. That he was so, Paul after his conversion zealously preached. Where is there any indication to be found, in all the recorded addresses of this Apostle, that he ever preached that Jesus was God? His conversion, in truth, regarded as an intellectual change, consisted simply in this—that, having been a denier of the Messiahship of Jesus, and a persecutor of those who asserted it, he had now himself become a believer in it.* To prove the same thing the fourth Gospel was written, as the Evangelist himself informs us at the close of his twentieth chapter; and the same proposition that Jesus was Christ,† but never that he was God, St. Paul frequently asserts or implies, throughout his Epistles, as the one foundation on which alone the Christian can rest.‡

By such faith, the Apostle further said, a man is "justified." The full meaning and controversial bearing of this expression will be seen more at length in a subsequent Chapter. For the present it will be enough to observe, that what the Apostle so earnestly writes respecting justification by faith alone was occasioned by the feelings of his countrymen in reference to the heathen world of his time, and finds its true interpretation only in connection with those feelings. In the judgment of Paul,§ no

---

* Acts ix. 22. The statement made above is true of the other instances of "conversion" in the New Testament. They are very different, therefore, from the so-called conversions of a Methodist chapel in our own day.

† The admission of Dr. Liddon has been already noted, to the effect that the Christ expected by the Jews was a "human" Christ. There is nothing to shew that Paul ever spoke to those whom he addressed of a *divine* Christ, in the now orthodox sense of these words. *Supra*, p. 110.

‡ For example, Rom. i. 3, 4; iii. 22; x. 9; xi. 20, 23; 1 Cor. iii. 11; Gal. ii. 16; Philip. i. 29; iii. 9.

§ Rom. ii. iii. See *infra*, Chapter XXVI.

living man could be accounted righteous. All men were "under sin" before God, "by nature children of wrath,"* and unfit to enter into the kingdom of His Son. This was true of the Jew as well as of the Gentile. But the Almighty Father was "rich in mercy." He would not punish the world as it lay in its sins; but, says the Scripture in various places, "he sent his Son," even allowed the "beloved Son" Jesus, the Christ though he was, to "empty himself" and be poor, to live a life of lowliness and shame, without the glories naturally attaching to the Messianic office,† allowed the beloved Son to stoop even to the pain and ignominy of the cross, that he might call men from their sins, and give them time for repentance before his second and final coming to judge the world. Those, then, who would profit by this respite, who now received him as Christ, or in other words who had Faith in him, and became his disciples and took his name upon them, and followed in his steps, they, notwithstanding past sins, would be treated *as if* they were righteous before the Law;—provided always that they would henceforth live in faithful allegiance to their spiritual king, waiting for the coming of "the day of the Lord."‡ To such persons, Jew and Gentile alike, God in His mercy would not impute past sins; but would ascribe to them the "righteousness of God," through faith; and such persons would be justified "without the deeds of the law," and in spite of its condemnation.§

Such statements, called forth, as will be seen, by the strong Jewish antipathy towards the Gentiles, applied primarily and solely to the world as it was in the days of the Apostle. They

---

* It has formerly been noticed that these words do not refer to any notion of an hereditary depravity which, in the Apostle's idea, made mankind liable to punishment, but simply to the positive transgressions of the Gentile (or natural) state by which the Ephesians had become guilty. *Supra*, p. 20, note on Ephes. ii. 3.

† 2 Cor. viii. 9 ; Philip. ii. 6-8.

‡ 1 Cor. i. 7; xv. 23, *seq.*; 1 Thess. iii. 13; iv. 15, *seq.* § Rom. iii. 20-31!

express, it is true, in one important point, a belief which has not been verified, and which, as time has shewn, required to be corrected by the lessons of experience.* But they shew us also what, in the Apostle's conception, was the Divine method of "justification by faith."

Yet even so, St. Paul's own Epistles exhibit another and a better way, and one which for all time to come was to prove the real and true way. The justification or righteousness attainable by the Christian disciple, apart from the controversies about the Law, and after the Law had ceased to be of importance, was, and is still, to be dependent, in the most essential degree, upon his own conduct. It is no matter of mere imputation. It is not another person's righteousness that God accounts as ours, or reckons in some way to our credit; but it is, in the Apostle's words, "patient continuance in well doing;" it is a Christ-like life of obedience to all that the Law of God, expressed in our highest sense of duty, requires from us; this faithful practical obedience it is which will be acceptable to God, and win for the disciple the "glory, honour and peace" of the "eternal life."†

Numerous expressions in the Pauline Epistles, including whole chapters towards the close of some of them,‡ justify and require this exposition of the faith which "worketh by love," the faith which is not in itself "the greatest," but is surpassed by Charity. Hence the Apostle might well ask, "Do we then make void the law through faith? . . . . . God forbid; yea, we establish the law;" because faith in the Christ, as he contemplated it, while it admitted to discipleship, and by God's mercy secured forgiveness of past sins to those of whom and to whom the Apostle was writing, yet in no way dispenses with future obedience; but requires the

---

* The allusion here is to the belief in the second coming of Christ, on which see more particularly, *infra*, Chapter XXVII.

† Rom. ii. 6, *seq.*

‡ Rom. xii.; 1 Cor. xiii.; Gal. iv. v. vi.; Philip. iv.; Coloss. iii.

Christian still, in the spirit of true discipleship, to follow Christ, and by seeking to present himself as a "living sacrifice" to God, to gain the Divine blessing both for this world and the next.

Thus, again, is learnt what sort of righteousness it is which a true faith in Christ will produce. "By their fruits ye shall know them," says the Master himself; and it is easy to understand how and why one who has this practical faith need not trouble himself about the righteousness which comes by "works," or "deeds of the law" of Moses; by ritualistic observances of any kind, by assent to human creeds, or submission to priestly authority. From all these "beggarly elements" the Christian is now released, or he may be so, if he will. Christ is the "end of the law for righteousness," the end and fulfilment of the law of mere form and ceremony, to every one that believes on him with a true faith of self-denial and practical obedience.

CHAPTER XIX.

THE HUMILIATION AND THE GLORY OF THE CHRIST IN THE PAULINE EPISTLES.

THE Messianic exaltation of Jesus took effect, in the contemplation of the New Testament writers, through and from his death; that is to say, it attached to him in the spiritual state to which the cross had been the way of admission. It is frequently alluded to, and usually in such a manner as to shew us that the sacred authors conceived of it as conferred upon him, in consequence of obedience and submission. This they sometimes express in terms which entirely forbid the idea that he who had received it was himself Supreme God. We see this distinctly even in the first Gospel. Immediately after his resurrection, Jesus commands his followers to go forth and teach the nations, and to baptize them into the name of the Father, and of the Son, and of the Holy Spirit. And he introduces this command by a reference to the authority by which he gave it: "All authority is *given* unto me in heaven and in earth; go ye, therefore, and teach all nations."*

Similarly, St. Paul, to whose representation we have now more especially to attend, says that Jesus was of the "seed of David according to the flesh." He was a Jew by natural birth; but he was declared to be the "Son of God," or Messiah, "by the resurrection from the dead."† The Apostle does not say, either here or elsewhere, that he was declared or shewn to be the Son of God by his miraculous birth, or that he was so by virtue of his pre-existent nature, or on account of his inherent deity, as the second person of a Divine Trinity. The Apostle nowhere says this, or anything like this; but simply that Jesus was "declared to be the Son of God by the resurrection from the dead:" he was thus shewn to be the true Messiah.

This statement throws light on what is found in another place, namely, that God "sent forth his Son born of a woman, born under the law."‡ The Messiah came, not an angel or a god, not a personage of exalted station and power, as had been expected by many, but a man of ordinary human birth, a Jew, under the law of his people. This was so, we elsewhere learn, in order that his ministry might, in the first instance, be addressed especially to those that were under the law; and that he might also, through his death and resurrection, become the spiritual Christ, as more fully pointed out in the preceding Chapter, and in Chapter XXVI.

The surpassing importance of the resurrection, in the mind of

---

* Matt. xxviii. 18, 19 : the word "therefore," in v. 19, is perhaps interpolated; but it is of ancient origin, and truly corresponds to the primitive idea of the derived character of the power of Christ. On the meaning of this verse, see Appendix to Chapter IX.

† Rom. i. 3, 4.   ‡ Gal. iv. 4 ; comp. Job xiv. 1; xxv. 4.

Paul, is further seen where he states that if Christ be not risen, faith in him is vain; and again, where he even identifies Christian faith with the belief in the resurrection. In both cases, he lets us clearly see that Jesus was raised up, not by his own power, but by the power of God.*

It was a wonderful thing, however, to the Apostle's mind, that the Messiah should have come in so humble a form. According to all previous expectation, he ought to have been greater and higher than any Roman emperor, or other earthly potentate; but this his proper Messianic greatness he had renounced. He "was poor," and "humbled himself," taking "the form of a slave," and being "found in fashion as a man."† But while this is said respecting him, there is nothing to shew that such expressions ought to be understood as alluding to a pre-existent participation in the "incommunicable essence" of God. The reference implied is simply to that exalted condition which, in Jewish estimation, naturally and of right belonged to the Messiah's office. Of this the Apostle conceives that our Lord had deprived and emptied himself to suffer and die; as it was necessary that he should do, in order that he might enter upon his proper Messianic exaltation by the resurrection from the dead. Even when the Apostle terms him the "Lord of glory" (or glorious Lord), and the "image of God,"‡ there is nothing to shew that he uses these words in any other sense than that of which we are now speaking, in reference, namely, to the risen and glorified state of the once lowly and despised Jesus.

It is clearly, then, unnecessary, to say the least, to construe the expressions in question, and others like them, as implying or relating to the Godhead of Christ.§ For how, it may be asked,

---

* Rom. x. 8, 9; 1 Cor. xv. 14–17; comp. Rom. v. 10; 2 Cor. iv. 14.
† 2 Cor. viii. 9 ("he was poor"); Philip. ii. 7, 8.
‡ 1 Cor. ii. 8; 2 Cor. iv. 4; Col. i. 15.
§ Comp. Liddon, B. L., p. 310, *seq.* Here it is asked, "From what did Christ

could he have emptied himself of his Godhead? And moreover, as must now be more particularly observed, there is no real instance in St. Paul's Epistles in which Jesus is termed *God*. In two cases in the English version he appears to be so. But they are both of such a character that no reliance whatever can be placed upon them, as evidence for the popular belief on the subject.

The first of the instances referred to occurs in Rom. ix. 5, of which the common English rendering is this:—"Whose are the fathers, and of whom as concerning the flesh Christ *came*, who is God over all, blessed for ever." But the value and aptness of these words, as evidence in the present discussion, depend entirely upon their punctuation. The reader will remember that the ancient manuscripts of the New Testament are without stops, and that it is not always clear what stop should be used, or whether any at all. Accordingly, this verse may be divided and rendered thus:—"Whose are the fathers, and of whom as concerning the flesh Christ *came*. God who is over all *is* blessed for ever." Such is the rendering of Professor Jowett,* and it is

---

condescend?" The answer is given above. It may be noted also that Christ is not usually said to "condescend," in the New Testament. He is more commonly spoken of as exalted and glorified, especially in the Pauline writings;—e.g., Ephes. i. 10, 20, 21; Philip. ii. 10.

* Epistles of St. Paul, *ad loc.* Among those who adopt the same punctuation are the eminent critical authorities, Lachmann and Tischendorf, in their respective editions of the N. T. De Wette and Bunsen translate in accordance with it. In the version of the latter, Prof. Holzmann, the writer and editor of this part of Bunsen's great "Bibelwerk," expressly observes, "These words are not to be referred to Christ, but to God, to whom the Apostle, after recounting the privileges of Israel, ascribes praise as their author and bestower." Similar doxologies occur, Rom. i. 25; 2 Cor. xi. 31; Gal. i. 5; 1 Tim. i. 17. The words of Rom. ix. 5 may be rendered, "God who is over all *be* blessed for ever."

The German commentator Meyer, perhaps the highest living authority on a point of this kind, while himself a believer in the deity of Christ, maintains that the doxology cannot be referred to Christ, but to God only. St. Paul, he reminds us, has never applied the term θεός to Christ, although, as Meyer holds, he might have done so, in accordance with his own belief. On the contrary, the line of distinction

hardly necessary to add that the authority of the Greek Professor at Oxford is not a light one in a question of this kind. It is in fact amply sufficient to satisfy the unlearned reader both as to the meaning of the words, and as to the admissibility of this mode of punctuation. The earnestness with which Dr. Liddon defends the common rendering is easily understood. But surely even he cannot hold it to be imperative thus to construe the words in question, in the face of the testimony to the contrary given by such witnesses as those mentioned in the note.

The Apostle, it will be observed, has just enumerated various privileges of the Israelites. To these, as Dr. Liddon notices, "he subjoins a climax." That climax is, that from them had sprung "the Christ" (ὁ χριστός). The greatest privilege of the nation consisted in having given birth to the Messiah—a fact so glorious that the recollection of it calls forth from the writer these words of praise to Him by whom this and all their other privileges had been conferred. This interpretation assigns to the

---

between the Father and the Son is so observed throughout the N. T. that the appellation GOD is everywhere applied only to the Father, except in two instances (duly considered in these pages), namely, John i. 1, xx. 28, both of which occur in immediate connection with the Logos idea. This learned commentator further notices that it was not until after the apostolical times that the distinction just alluded to disappeared, and that the words ὁ θεός, ὁ θεός ἡμῶν (God, our God), and similar expressions, were used of Christ.

The argument for the common rendering, so urgently repeated by Dr. Liddon, from the position in the sentence of the word εὐλογητός (blessed), has evidently no weight with the German theologian. Indeed, a natural emphasis belongs to the fact that the author of the enumerated privileges of the Israelites was the Almighty Being and no other. The words designating Him stand, therefore, first,—as occurs in a similar doxology, in the Septuagint rendering of Ps. lxviii. 19.

Again, it is perfectly clear that "the Christ" is classed and co-ordinated by St. Paul among and with the other well-known privileges of his people. These were, the adoption, the covenants, the law, the temple service, the promises, the fathers, the Christ, by his descent and birth. Over *all* is GOD, who is Blessed for ever. Thus, by taking the final words of v. 5 as if they also referred to Christ, and not to God, as Dr. Liddon does at the bidding of the orthodox creeds, the Apostle's meaning is singularly perverted, or destroyed altogether.

words a full and sufficient meaning. It is obviously, therefore, unnecessary to assume that the privilege and glory for Israel consisted in something else, namely, in this, that the person so sprung from them was "God over all." Dr. Liddon observes that "this is the natural sense of the passage." Possibly it would be so, if it were sufficiently consistent with the usual teaching of the New Testament respecting God and Christ. But such is not the case, and consequently the other division of the words, with the sense resulting, is just as "natural," or rather it is far more so.* Nor have the words, "according to the flesh," any recondite reference to a Divine nature. They simply declare that the Christ, by his descent, belonged to the race of Israel, the fact so referred to constituting their greatest religious privilege. If any antithesis be implied, it is doubtless the Messianic glory conferred upon Jesus, in Paul's estimation, by his resurrection from the dead.† By this he was shewn to be the true Christ. Nevertheless, "according to the flesh" he was a Jew, sprung from the race of Israel.

The other instance in which St. Paul appears to call Jesus "God," is equally unfortunate for the orthodox argument. It occurs in 1 Tim. iii. 16, which in the English version reads thus: "And without controversy great is the mystery of godliness: God was manifest in the flesh, justified in the spirit, seen of angels, preached unto the Gentiles, believed on in the world, received up into glory." The word "God" is the one with which we are here mainly concerned. Its authenticity is so doubtful

---

* Meyer, orthodox as he is, admits the "invincible difficulty" of supposing that Paul should here have called Christ not only *God*, but even "God over all." The supposition, he observes, is not to be reconciled either with the general tenor of the N. T. in regard to the dependence of the Son upon the Father, or with such Pauline passages, in particular, as 1 Cor. iii. 23; viii. 6; xi. 3; xv. 28. So little "natural," in truth, is the orthodox construction of this passage!

† The same words are used in v. 3, without any antithesis, expressed or understood—as they often are.

that Dr. Liddon himself places no reliance upon it. The best critical authorities reject it, and read either ὅς or ὅ (*who* or *which*). Dean Alford translates, " And confessedly great is the mystery of godliness, who was manifested in the flesh, justified in the Spirit," &c.* The words may be literally rendered thus: " And confessedly great is the mystery of godliness: he who was manifested in flesh, was justified in spirit," &c.†

While abandoning the argument from the word " God," Dr. Liddon relies upon the verb following it. " Our Lord's pre-existence," he observes, " lies in any case in the ἐφανερώθη " (was manifested); " and this cannot without violence be watered down into the sense of Christ's manifestation in the teaching and belief of the Church."‡ Here, then, be it noted, is an instance, one of many such, in which the stupendous doctrine of the deity of Christ, so far from being plainly affirmed, is dependent upon the particular shade of meaning assignable to a single obscure word. Nor should it be overlooked that the verse occurs in an Epistle of doubtful authenticity, to say the least.

Without, however, pursuing the thoughts which the latter fact might suggest, we have still the question, what is meant by the words, " was manifested in flesh " ? Do they really imply an allusion, however obscure, by way of antithesis, to the Godhead of the person spoken of? This question may be answered by referring to a similar expression found elsewhere. In the first Epistle of John § there is more than one allusion to an ancient form of false belief concerning Christ, according to which he was not really a human being. He was so, it was held, only in appear-

* N. T. revised version. The Dean justifies the reading "who" in these words: "So all the most ancient authorities, except one, which reads *which*, neuter gender." Bishop Ellicott, *Pastoral Epistles, in loc.*, closes his review of the evidence with the remark, "We unhesitatingly decide in favour of ὅς" (who). See Appendix, note C.

† There is no article before either "flesh" or "spirit." Comp. Matt. i. 20, for a similar instance of the omission before "Holy Spirit."

‡ B. L., p. 312, note. § 1 John iv. 2, 3. Comp. 1 John i. 1, 2.

ance. This early Docetic heresy is carefully condemned by St. John. "Every spirit," he writes, "that confesseth not that Jesus Christ is come in the flesh is not of God; and this is the *spirit* of antichrist . . . . even now already it is in the world." A similar expression is used, with most probably the same reference, by the writer to Timothy. Accordingly, it is quite unnecessary to understand him, as is usually done, to imply any such doctrine as that of the Godhead of the person spoken of. "The mystery" of the Gospel, the Apostolical writer tells us, was great; the Christ who was manifested in a true human body (though this was denied by some), was "justified in spirit." The meaning of these latter words is by no means clear, and the commentators are not agreed about them. It is unnecessary to dwell upon them here, except only to suggest that they may contain an allusion to the descent of the Spirit at the baptism, by which the human Jesus was proved to be the well-beloved Son.*

A consideration of much importance remains. It is impossible to avoid the suspicion that this verse, like some others bearing upon the Trinitarian controversy, has been altered by early copyists— altered in the orthodox sense. Such passages are not numerous, but they are of the highest importance. Among them may be included Luke viii. 40, where instead of the words, "they were all waiting for him" (said in reference to Jesus), the Sinaitic manuscript has, "they were all waiting for *God*." A similar case is found in the same manuscript, and some others, in John i. 18, where the reading, "only-begotten Son," has been changed into "only-begotten God." In Acts xx. 28, it may be considered doubtful, according to the documentary evidence, whether the reading should be, "Church of *God*, which he hath purchased with his own blood," or, "Church of *the Lord*." Dr. Liddon, we

---

* The words would thus mean, "was justified *by* the Spirit." This use of *is* to express the means *by which* is common; e.g., Rom. x. 5, 9.

have seen, maintains the former reading; but, on the other hand, remembering the evident tendency of the early copyists, we may reasonably hold "Church of the Lord" to be by far the more probable original, as recognized by Tischendorf, De Wette, Bunsen, and other excellent authorities.

Similar remarks apply to the most notable of all these corrupted passages, 1 John v. 7, 8, in which the hand of the orthodox corrector is now all but universally acknowledged.*

The words of 1 Tim. iii. 16, which have just been under notice, must stand side by side with these remarkable and glaring instances of interpolation. The likeness common to all the cases is not to be denied. They form a group of would-be witnesses in this controversy whose testimony cannot be received, and to which the upholder of the popular theology cannot appeal with either confidence or satisfaction. It follows clearly from what has been said on the last-named passage, and on Rom. ix. 5, that there is no instance whatever in the Pauline writings in which the highest of appellations is given to Christ—a conclusion to be expected from the plain and unvarying tenor, not only of the rest of the New Testament, but of the writings of St. Paul in particular.†

For it must not be forgotten that this Apostle sometimes speaks of the Almighty Being as "the GOD and Father of Jesus Christ;" or also as "the GOD of our Lord Jesus Christ." He even writes, "The head of every man is Christ . . . . . . and the head of Christ is GOD." ‡ There is no interpolation and no "watering down" in these plain and emphatic words of an Apostle; and how incredible it is that one who could thus write should really have regarded him of whom he uses such terms, either as himself "God over all," or as "God manifested in the flesh."

* Comp. Rev. i. 11, where the words, "I am Alpha and Omega, the first and the last," are also spurious.
† For alleged instances in Tit. ii. 3; 1 John v. 20, see Appendix, note D.
‡ 2 Cor. xi. 31; Ephes. i. 17; 1 Cor. xi. 3.

The nearest approach, perhaps, to the application of the epithet God to Christ by St. Paul occurs in the Epistle to the Philippians. "Let that mind be in you which was also in Christ Jesus; who being in the form of God thought not the being equal to God a thing to grasp at, but emptied himself, taking the form of a slave, and being in the likeness of men."* In this statement, it is not said that Jesus *was* God, but that he was "in the form of God." The phrase cannot be paralleled anywhere in the Scriptures; but had the writer meant us to understand that our Lord in a pre-existent state, or in his essential nature, was God, he would doubtless have said so in more express terms—for the statement would have been one of the very greatest importance, and the Apostle has not made it anywhere else. When, therefore, we recall the marked distinction between God and Christ which St. Paul usually observes in his language respecting them, it is reasonable to conclude that he cannot intend here, more than elsewhere, to identify Jesus Christ with the Almighty Being. His meaning, it is not, in this instance, difficult to discover. It has, indeed, been already alluded to in the present Chapter. Jesus, in his Messianic character, had been properly and of right entitled, in the estimation of every disciple, to the highest pre-eminence on earth. He was thus, even as God, "in the form of God;"† or again, and more probably, as there is no article, "of a God." But, nevertheless, he did not eagerly grasp at that exalted condition; on the contrary, he emptied or humbled himself, took the form of a slave, was in the likeness of ordinary men, and became obedient even to death.

---

* Philip. ii. 5–7 ; the rendering above given closely follows the original.

† Dean Alford (Gr. Test. *in loc.*) observes, "That the Divine nature of God is not here meant, is clear, for he did not with reference to *this* empty himself." The word μορφή (form) occurs only in one other place in the N. T., Mark xvi. 12, where it unquestionably refers to outward appearance, not to essential nature. See Appendix, note E.

This interpretation of the words is required by the following verses. In these we read that for the self-sacrifice and lowliness of Jesus, God has rewarded him, by giving him "the name which is above every name, that in the name * of Jesus every knee should bow," and every tongue should confess him to be Lord, "to the glory of God the Father"—words, truly, which have been wonderfully fulfilled in the subsequent history of the Christian world.

It is impossible to think that the writer of such words could have conceived of Jesus Christ as God, in the proper sense of this term; that he intended to say of one already possessed of original inherent Deity, that he was highly exalted by the Heavenly Father. Such a proposition, thus plainly expressed, surely amounts to something like a contradiction in terms;—one Infinite Being rewarded and exalted by another! Here, again, therefore, it appears that in immediate juxtaposition with expressions which, if alone, might seem to set forth the deity of Christ, other expressions of modifying or counteracting force are supplied by the sacred writer himself. And this will be found to occur in several other cases—as, for example, in the introductory verses of the Epistle to the Hebrews. The circumstance referred to could hardly have occurred, had the truth in these questions lain on the side of the popular theology.†

Reference has just been made to the Epistle to the Hebrews, and although this Epistle is not to be reckoned as a writing of St. Paul's, it will here be convenient briefly to notice the remarkable statements with which it commences. The character attributed to the Son (the Messiah) is one of the highest conceivable.

* Philip. ii. 10 ; "in the name," *not* "at the name."
† See Col. ii. 9, compared with Col. i. 19 ; Heb. i. 8, comp. v. 9 ; 1 John ii. 23, comp. *ibid.*, v. 22 ; 1 John v. 5, comp. *ibid.*, v. 1 ; John x. 30, comp. *ibid.* v. 35, 36 ; Matt. xxviii. 19, comp. *ibid.* v. 18 ; Luke xxii. 70, comp. xxiii. 2, 47 ; Rev. i. 11, 17, comp. *ibid.* v. 18.

The whole is in evident harmony with the Logos doctrine, and of that doctrine the passage is probably an expression. The Son is, accordingly, the image, representative, instrument of God;* himself, indeed, "appointed" to be what he is, just as the angels are; but yet he is "better" than they;—a strange thing to say of one that was essentially God, and the Creator of men and angels! He is even, in the words of a quoted Psalm, spoken of as "God;" but, doubtless, this appellation is used in a subordinate sense, as it is in the Psalm from which the words are taken, and which is a nuptial ode in celebration of the marriage of a Jewish prince. The writer to the Hebrews, applying the Psalm in a Messianic sense, speaks of the Son as God:—"Thy throne, O God, is for ever and ever." He thus represents the Almighty as addressing the Son; but he immediately adds the words, "Therefore God, thy God, hath anointed thee with the oil of gladness above thy fellows."†

The question is obvious, if the person thus addressed were truly Supreme God, in what sense could there be a God to him? And, again, how could the Infinite Being have "fellows"?—the last word evidently alluding to the angels previously mentioned.

The popular theology is not, however, without an answer to questions of this kind. It tells us that the expressions referred to, and others like them, relate to the subordination of Christ in his mediatorial capacity, and especially while he was incarnate upon the earth—to these assumed and temporary states and characters only. The reply to this assertion is simple: it is, that *the Scripture does not say so,*—nowhere says so. Such a

* The words, "by whom also he made the worlds," may be literally rendered, "through whom also he made the ages." The allusion may be, as in John i. 3, to the creation of all things by the Logos; or, if the rendering "ages" be adopted, the reference in this word will be to the Jewish and the Christian dispensations, elsewhere spoken of as "this world" (age or dispensation), and "the world (age) to come." Matt. xii. 32; comp. Ephes. i. 21.

† Heb. i. 4-9; Psalm xlv, 6.

limitation of the Scriptural language is unwarrantably introduced by dogmatic theologians, and is, in truth, merely an after-thought dictated by the necessities of the case. Nor does it really solve the difficulty; for, if Jesus Christ were Almighty God, how could he, even for the interval of his supposed incarnate manifestation on earth, become subordinate to any other being? How could he lay down his deity? How could there be a God that was *his* God, in any sense of the words that would not be delusive to our human understanding?—unless, indeed, there be two perfectly distinct beings, each of which is God, a supposition which at once lands us in an irrational and self-contradictory ditheism.

CHAPTER XX.

THE CREATION OF ALL THINGS THROUGH JESUS CHRIST.

THERE are several remarkable expressions in the Pauline Epistles, from which it might be inferred that Jesus Christ was conceived of by the writer as the Creator of the world. It is not to be doubted that this construction was put upon the words referred to in the early Christian times. They could not fail to be so accepted by those who had adopted and become accustomed to the doctrine of the Logos in Jesus. That doctrine would naturally lead to such an interpretation. It is not necessary, however, that the modern inquirer should always follow the guidance of the philosophizing Christians, to whom the world is indebted for the distinctive doctrines of the orthodox faith, and who, it is well ascertained, were in many cases ill-judging and superstitious men. It is the better course to inquire whether the New Testament does not itself throw sufficient light on this subject; and in truth a little inquiry will be found to correct the impression conveyed by the *primâ facie* import of the passages in question.

The introductory chapter of the Epistle to the Colossians is the most conspicuous instance in which the work of creation is apparently attributed to Christ. Several expressions closely related to this passage occur in the first and third chapters of the Epistle to the Ephesians;* and whatever may be the true interpretation of the former, most probably is so of the latter also. In speaking of these two Epistles, we may accept them both as St. Paul's, although their authorship is by no means free from doubt. It cannot be questioned, however, that they both represent a very ancient conception of the character and work of Christ.

Of these the Colossians speak in the following terms:—" Who [Christ] is the image of the invisible God, the first-born of all creation. Because in him were all things created *that are* in heaven and *that are* on earth, visible and invisible, whether *they be* thrones, or dominions, or principalities, or powers; all things have been created through him and for him."†

It has been thought that we have here the conception of Christ as the divine Logos, much as it occurs in the proem of the fourth Gospel; and that here, too, the material creation is attributed to him in that character.‡ If this be the meaning, the interpretation of the passage will necessarily follow that of the proem. It is, however, doubtful, or more than doubtful, whether the Logos idea is to be found in any writing of St. Paul's. The term itself he nowhere employs in its philosophical sense. The words,

* In Ephes. iii. 9, the words "by Jesus Christ," are an interpolation, and are omitted by Tischendorf, Dean Alford, and other critics.

† Col. i. 15, 16. The above rendering is a little closer to the original than the common version. The words in *italics* have no equivalents expressed in the Greek. Comp. the translation of Bishop Ellicott, who renders "by him," instead of "through him."

‡ Such is the meaning, according to the high authority of Ewald.

P

"first-born of all creation," may allude simply to the fact that Jesus was the first *raised from the dead*, the first-born of all under the new dispensation. This idea is, indeed, expressed in the succeeding verses: "He is before all things, and in him all things subsist; and he is the head of the body, the church; who is the beginning, the first born from the dead; that in all things he might be the first."* These expressions are very different from those in which the Logos is spoken of as the eldest Son of God, which was with God in the beginning, and by which all things were created. They indicate, too, that the Apostle conceived of Christ, even in his highest character, as a creature; as in another place he even terms him "the first born among many brethren."† On the face of the subject, it is inconceivable that the Apostle could say of one to whom he attributed Supreme Deity, or the creation of the material universe, that he was "the first born from the dead, that in all things he might be the first," or (as Bishop Ellicott renders the latter words) "that in all things he might have the pre-eminence."

If, however, it be understood that Christ *is* thus spoken of as Creator, it is still evident that the Apostle did not conceive of him as possessed of an original inherent power or deity of his own. "It pleased *the Father*," he expressly adds, "that in him should all fulness dwell."‡ He is plainly, therefore, creator by the

---

* Col. i. 17, 18. † Rom. viii. 29; comp. Rev. i. 5, 18; John xx. 17.
‡ Col. i. 19. The word *Father* (or *God*) is necessarily supplied in this verse. Dean Alford observes, "The subject here is naturally understood to be God, as expressed in 1 Cor. i. 21; Gal. i. 15; clearly not Christ."—Gr. Test. *in loc.* Bishop Ellicott renders, "Because in him it pleased all the fulness *of the Godhead* to dwell" —a rendering, as the Bishop admits, involving grave, though he thinks not insuperable difficulties. One of these may be expressed interrogatively: Could he in whom "it pleased all the fulness *of the Godhead* to dwell" (the words in italics are not the Apostle's, but the Bishop's) be already possessed of Deity by his own nature? If he were so, what could that be which was pleased to dwell in him? Whatever may be meant by "all the fulness," it clearly cannot be what the Bishop supposes. On the contrary, the whole conception of the passage evidently is that it was *given* to

Divine permission and appointment, a statement in perfect harmony with all that we read elsewhere in the New Testament respecting the subordination of Christ; though far from consistent with the tenor of the popular creeds.

But, in truth, the supposition that the material creation is here intended, and that Jesus Christ is represented as the Creator, is one that is beset with the most serious difficulties. Throughout the Gospels there is nowhere any allusion to a fact which would have been so important and so marvellous—the fact that the personage who lived and taught so simply and familiarly among the people of Galilee and Jerusalem was, all the time, the Divine Creator! The Evangelists, it is to be understood, were quite aware of this wonderful circumstance; but they do not appeal to it in any way, although it was their great purpose in writing their Gospels to shew that the despised and crucified Nazarene was indeed the expected Christ, the Son of God! It will, perhaps, be said that the fact *is* referred to in the fourth Gospel. But such a statement it has been shewn, is not warranted by the language of that Gospel. It is not Jesus Christ by whom all things are there said to have been created, but the Logos; and although, in the Evangelist's conception, the Logos became flesh in Christ, acting in and through him, yet, as we have seen, this is only another way of saying that there was in and through Christ a manifestation of the power and wisdom of the Infinite Being. That mode of representation does not tell us that Jesus Christ, in his own person, was either Supreme God, or Creator of the world; but simply that he was the human instrument through

Christ, and dwelt in him by the will of another, *i.e.* of God (comp. Ephes. i. 17-23). A similar divine "fulness" (*i.e.* completeness, perfection) is attributed to Christian disciples, or said to be attainable by them, Ephes. iii. 19,—so little does the expression imply the Godhead of the possessor. The "fulness" of Christ is probably "the church, which is his body," of which he is Head and Lord: Ephes. i. 23 ; comp. Coloss. i. 18.

which the Divine purposes were effected. The line of distinction between Him who is God alone and Jesus the Messiah or well-beloved Son, is here, as uniformly in the New Testament, carefully drawn, carefully observed.

There is a further difficulty in the way of the above supposition. It is inconceivable that in the four principal and undoubted Epistles of Paul no allusion whatever should be made to the creative work of Christ. In the Epistle to the Romans, for example, or in that to the Galatians, could the Apostle have so entirely omitted to introduce, or to imply, the supposed fact? In both of these Epistles he treats of questions closely touching the dignity and authority of his Master; and he is especially anxious to uphold the importance of the Gospel, in comparison with the ancient Law of his people. Yet he nowhere mentions that which would so effectually have illustrated his argument, had it been possible to appeal to it; nowhere gives us to understand that Jesus the Christ, whose Apostle he is, whose Gospel he is recommending, was the Creator of all things.

In another Epistle, the first to the Corinthians, there is, indeed, an expression which might be thought to be inconsistent with these remarks. The Apostle writes, "To us there is one God, the Father, of whom are all things, and we in him; and one Lord Jesus Christ, through whom are all things, and we through him."* But here, again, Christ is evidently represented as the instrument, in contradistinction to what is said of God,—"of whom" ($\dot{\epsilon}\xi$ $o\dot{v}$) are all things. The latter words strictly designate the original Source, while the secondary cause or agent is denoted by the preposition "through" ($\delta\iota\acute{a}$),† followed by the genitive case, in accordance with the usual distinction

---

* 1 Cor. viii. 6.
† This force of the preposition is too well known to require illustration here. See, however, Appendix, note F.

between Christ and God. The words in this place, however, are too few, and are introduced in too incidental a manner, to be permitted to determine the meaning of the more considerable and detailed passage in the Colossians. Very probably, nevertheless, they ought to be interpreted in accordance with that passage; but they must follow, and not lead the way.

We are thus brought back to the inquiry, what does the writer mean by the remarkable words which he addresses to the Colossians? If he neither speaks in accordance with the Logos doctrine, nor attributes the material creation to Christ under some other conception of his pre-existence, what in all probability is the meaning intended?

In several instances the moral change produced by the Gospel is spoken of by Paul as a new creation. "If any man be in Christ, *he is* a new creature:" literally, "a new creation;" or, it may be, "*there is* a new creation:" "old things are passed away; behold, all things are become new." Again, "In Christ Jesus neither circumcision availeth anything, nor uncircumcision, but a new creature"—literally, as before, "a new creation." And again, "We are his workmanship, having been created in Christ Jesus unto good works."* These expressions suggest the inquiry whether the remarkable language to the Colossians does not refer to the new or spiritual creation, of which Christ was the chosen instrument.

When the Apostle speaks of the natural creation, as in the speech at Athens, he employs words in which there is no ambiguity, and refers it distinctly, not to Christ, but to God: "God that made the world and all things therein."† In such words there can be no doubt as to the meaning. Is it not, therefore, probable that in the very different phraseology of the Colossians,

---

* 2 Cor. v. 17; Gal. vi. 15; Ephes. ii. 10. Comp. also Ephes. iv. 24; Rom. viii. 19-22, where the rendering in each verse should be "creation."
† Comp. Acts xiv. 15.

he is speaking of the promulgation of Christianity and its effect under the figure of a spiritual creation? If this be the true explanation, it will sufficiently account for the remarkable terms employed. Christ was himself, the Apostle says, the "first born" of all, the first of this new creation. It was necessary that he should be the first, in order that he might be the instrument of the Almighty power in administering the heavenly kingdom into which he has now ascended: "for in him were all things created" (the words "all things" being obviously qualified in force by the connected ideas, and denoting, therefore, all things belonging to the new dispensation);—all things "that are in heaven, and that are in earth, visible and invisible." Here, undoubtedly, are terms of the most comprehensive import. But they are immediately followed by limiting words, when the Apostle adds, "whether they be thrones, or dominions, or principalities, or powers,"* all these things "were created through him and for him." Is it possible to think that this language can refer to the material creation?

The Apostle, it would appear, conceived the spiritual kingdom of Christ to contain various degrees of dignity. And it was not only an earthly kingdom, but a heavenly; not only visible, but invisible. Jesus himself, "head over all things," had been raised to heaven by the power of the Father; many of his disciples too had already followed him there; but most of them still remained on earth filling their different offices, "apostles, prophets, teachers, workers of miracles."† All these existed *through* Christ and *for* him. But, as before, it is clear that the writer of these words could not have thought of Christ as the original source of all, for he adds the words, "It pleased *the Father* that in him should all fulness·dwell."‡

---

* Comp. Ephes. vi. 12. † Cor. xii. 28, 29.
‡ On these words, see *supra*, p. 210.

The remarkable language which we have endeavoured to explain may be further illustrated by a reference to the similar passage in the Epistle to the Ephesians. The writer prays for his friends, "that the God of our Lord Jesus Christ" may cause them to know the greatness of His power, "according to the working of the might of his strength which he hath wrought in Christ, by raising him from the dead: and he made him sit" (the Apostle continues) "at his right hand in the heavenly places, far above all principality and power and might and dominion, and every name that is named, not only in this world,* but in that which is to come; and hath put all things under his feet, and he gave him to be the head over all things to the church, which is his body, the fulness of him that filleth all in all."†

Words could scarcely make it plainer than it is here, that God is the sole Cause of the exaltation of Christ. HE "made him sit at his right hand:" He "put all things under his feet:" He "gave him to be the head over all things to the church." Thus there is clearly implied, not only the absolute distinction between God and Christ, but the absolute subordination or inferiority of the latter—of the creature and instrument to the Creator and Primary Cause of all. The conception in this Epistle appears, however, to be a little different from that of the Epistle to the Colossians. In the Ephesians we are told that the Almighty Father had determined to bring all things into subjection to the Messiah.‡ Allowing for something of metaphor in the words, "all things" might be said to be created "in Christ," with a regard, that is to say, to the approaching Messianic age or dispensation. This purpose has taken effect in

---

* Literally, *age*, *i.e.* dispensation: "this age," that now existing, the Mosaic; "that which is to come," the Christian, speedily to begin, with the second coming of Christ.

† Ephes. i. 17–23.   ‡ Ephes. i. 9, 10.

and through Jesus Christ. The consequences of his life, death and resurrection, will be, and have been the establishment of his kingdom, the conversion of men of every land, and the diffusion of the Gospel among the nations. This "new creation" was thus accomplished through him, and for him. In other words, in him all things spiritual subsist, and he is head over all. But, nevertheless, it is clear, as before, that all is of God's working, God's appointment.

We have seen the difficulties which attend the supposition that the words in the Colossians refer to the material creation. They are certainly not words in which any writer who wished to be readily understood would speak of the objects of sense. On the other hand, they are not inappropriate, if we take them to express the great results that were to flow from the preaching of the Gospel in the name of the risen Christ—namely, the bringing in of the Gentiles,[*] and the subjugation of the powers of this world beneath the authority of the cross. Kindred ideas are expressed where Paul speaks of that coming time "the end," when the Christ shall have "put down all authority and power," and when, victorious over sin and death, he shall deliver up his completed work, the promised kingdom of heaven on earth, "to God even the Father."[†]

The substitution of *through* for *by*, in the rendering above given, corresponds strictly to the original. Christ is spoken of, accordingly, as the *instrument* of Divine power, not as himself its original or independent source. This cannot be too clearly kept in view, by one who would gain a just idea of these Apostolical statements. It is through his life and death, his resurrection and exaltation to be "head over all," that the results contemplated are to be brought to pass, a state of transcendent dignity, in which Jesus might even be spoken of as "the image of God,"[‡] the vice-

---

[*] See Rom. xi. 15, 25.   [†] 1 Cor. xv. 24-28.

[‡] Col. i. 15. Comp. John i. 18, "No man hath seen God at any time, the only-

gerent or representative of the Almighty Father. Yet still the distinction between the two, between God and Christ, is here, as everywhere, clear and absolute.

CHAPTER XXI.

THE APOCALYPTIC EXALTATION OF JESUS CHRIST.

It is perhaps in the Book of Revelation, more than in any other New Testament book, that a character approaching to that of supreme deity is attributed to Christ, in his risen and heavenly state. Yet this is done in such a manner as to shew us that the most positive and emphatic distinction really existed, in the writer's mind, between the person of whom he speaks and the One Almighty Being.

Thus, at the beginning of the book, Jesus is represented as calling himself "Alpha and Omega, the first and last," words which are used just before of and by the Lord God Himself.* The difference in the form of the expression, as applied to God and to Christ, is very striking. "I am the Alpha and the Omega, saith the Lord God, which is, and which was, and which is to come, the Almighty." When the Son of man uses the same words, he says, "Fear not; I am the first and the last, and the living one; and I was dead, and behold I am alive for evermore, and have the keys of death and of Hades." † In the one case, we have an expression applicable and appropriate to the Self-existent

begotten Son . . . . . . he hath declared him." In one important sense, Christ is the Divine "image" by expressing to man the moral character of the Divine Mind. Paul, it will be remembered, also terms man "the image and glory of God," 1 Cor. xi. 7.

* Rev. i. 11; comp. v. 8, in the common Version. In subsequent references to the Book of Revelation we usually follow the text of Dean Alford, which is founded upon the oldest manuscripts. See his *N.T.*, *revised version.*

† Rev. i. 17, 18.

Being; in the other, we have words which would seem almost as if intended to warn us not to think of the speaker as God; and, indeed he has just been termed in a preceding verse, "the first begotten of the dead" (v. 5).

These expressions, then, give us clearly to see that, high as was the character conceived to belong to the risen Saviour, yet that one who is said to be now "alive for evermore" could not have been regarded as, by his own nature, Eternal God. It is further evident, that the writer conceives of him as invested by *another* with whatever of power or authority the possession of the "keys of death and of Hades" may have given him. The same thing is clearly seen in another place, where he says that he will give to those who are steadfast to him, the same authority which he has himself *received* from his Father.*

He speaks, again, of God as his God; and even where it is said that he sits with the Father "upon his throne," this cannot in the writer's idea have denoted equality with God, because he represents Jesus as saying, "To him that overcometh I will grant to sit with me in my throne, as I also . . . . . . sat down with my Father in his throne."†

The highest ascription of Divine honours is to Him who is a second time described as the "Lord God Almighty, which was, and which is, and which is to come," terms of supreme veneration, which are not addressed to Christ, and in which he has no share.‡

The Son of man is next represented as a "Lamb that was slain," who alone was "worthy to take the book and to open the seals thereof." His praise is celebrated by the voices of "myriads of myriads, and thousands of thousands," proclaiming him "worthy to receive power, and riches, and wisdom, and strength, and honour, and glory, and blessing." §

* Rev. ii. 26, 27.   † Rev. iii. 21.   ‡ Rev. iv. 8-11.   § Rev. v. 6-12.

In another place, a joint and equal tribute of praise appears to be offered by " a Great multitude which no one could number," to God and to the lamb, saying "Salvation to our God, ... and unto the Lamb;" but immediately afterwards, when worship is offered by the angels, they " fell before the throne on their faces and worshiped GOD." They ascribe the highest praise to Him, "unto our God for ever and ever "—to Him alone, for in this the Lamb is *not* included.* The omission is marked and emphatic, and shews to demonstration that the Lamb does not, in the writer's conception, hold a place of real deity.

This distinction between God and Christ is maintained throughout the book. Thus in the last of the places referred to below,† the song of praise is to the "Lord God Almighty," while the Lamb is in the same verse co-ordinated with "Moses the servant of God," as he is in xiv. 10 with the angels.

The Son of man appears in another character, as the "Word of God"—not here the Logos of the fourth Gospel, but more probably one who announced, uttered, and also executed, the judgments of God.‡ He sits, in the Apocalyptic vision, upon a white horse, the armies of heaven follow him, and he treads " the winepress of the fierceness of the wrath of Almighty God; and he hath on his vesture and on his thigh a name written, King of kings and Lord of lords." The bearer of this august title is the instrument of the Divine vengeance; but the Almighty Being is clearly here, as elsewhere, a distinct object of the writer's thought. It is He who is addressed by " the voice of mighty thunderings, saying, Halleluiah ; for the Lord God omnipotent reigneth."§ There is nothing like this, in the Apocalypse or elswhere in the New Testament, addressed to Christ.

In the final chapter of the book, we are told that John, when

---

* Rev. vii 9-12. † See xi. 15, 16 ; xii. 10 ; xiv. 7-12; xv. 3.
‡ Rev. xix. 11-15. § Rev. xix. 5, 6.

he saw the wonderful vision which had passed before him, "fell down to worship before the feet of the angel which shewed him these things." The latter "saith unto him, See thou do it not ...... worship God." Was the angel who thus spoke, the same person who, at the beginning and throughout, shews the vision to the Apostle? This question has been much discussed. If due regard be paid to the immediate context, it would certainly appear that it should be answered in the affirmative.* "Behold I come quickly;" "I am a fellow-servant of thine;" "I am the Alpha and the Omega;" "I Jesus have sent mine angel;"—surely the same person is meant in all these cases, although he is also called "angel," and for a moment appears to be a different being from the "Son of man," who at the beginning appears and speaks to John. If, then, the affirmative be the correct answer to the above question, Jesus himself forbids the writer of the vision to worship him, and tells him to "worship God." At any rate, the speaker tells him to "worship GOD;" but he nowhere bids him worship the Lamb, or Jesus, or the Son of man.

This interpretation need not, however, be too confidently insisted upon. Its admission is in no way necessary for the purpose of our argument. Quite independently of this passage, the clear tenor of the Apocalypse, manifested in a large variety of expressions, abundantly proves that the author cannot have intended his readers to identify Jesus Christ with Almighty God, abundantly proves that he did not do so himself.

CHAPTER XXII.

THE WORSHIP OF CHRIST.

A VERY important question next claims our attention. Did the early Christians offer religious worship to Christ? The inquiry

* See xxii. 7-9, 12, 13, 16; and compare i. 10-19.

need not occupy much of our space, seeing that it is already answered by anticipation, if the argument thus far warrants us in making the distinction so often affirmed between the Supreme Being and Jesus Christ. Yet the presumed evidence for the worship of Christ is usually considered to be one of the strongest parts of the popular Christianity. Ill-informed persons are apt to suppose, that the disciples were accustomed to worship their Master as God, even while he lived familiarly among them in Galilee and Jerusalem—a conclusion, untenable as it is, to which the whole strain of Dr. Liddon's representation evidently leads. Thus we read, "Then came to him the mother of Zebedee's children, worshiping him.* The word used in this and other such cases does not necessarily denote religious worship, but only the respectful salutation or obeisance which one person might offer to another, probably by prostration in the oriental manner. This may be clearly seen from a parallel expression in the same Gospel, relating to the unforgiving servant and his lord: "The servant, therefore, fell down and worshiped him saying, Lord, have patience with me, and I will pay thee all."†

We have in these cases examples of the old and well-known meaning of the English word "worship"—that is all. The Greek verb strictly and exclusively denoting religious worship is a different word, and this is *never* applied to Christ.‡ It will be found that in no instance was Jesus the object of religious worship during his lifetime. Even after his resurrection, when it is said that his disciples saw him "and worshiped him,"§ the

---

* Matt. xxii. 20; compare ix. 18; John ix. 38.

† Matt. xviii. 26. An excellent illustrative example occurs in Genesis xxxvii. 6, where the sheaves are said to have "made obeisance" to Joseph's sheaf. The word thus rendered is, in the Septuagint version of Genesis, expressed by the *same* Greek word which, in the English N. T., has been so often and so indiscriminately rendered "worshiped."

‡ The word σέβομαι; Matt. xv. 9; Acts xvi. 14; xviii. 7, 13.

§ Matt. xxviii. 16.

word used is the more general word, expressive of respectful obeisance.

The case of Stephen is often cited, as affording direct and positive testimony to the worship of Jesus Christ by the early Christians, and Dr. Liddon makes the usual appeal to it. At the moment of his death, we are told, this first of the martyrs besought Jesus to receive his spirit: "They stoned Stephen invoking and saying, Lord Jesus, receive my spirit."* The words in the next verse (v. 60), "Lord, lay not this sin to their charge," may perhaps be understood as addressed to God; but there is nothing in the passage to require this; and as the New Testament writers often speak of Jesus Christ as the appointed Judge of men, it may be simply in accordance with this idea that those words are used by the dying man—and, if so, they are addressed to Christ.

In determining the meaning and value of this exclamation, it will be remembered that the Apostle, when he thus called upon the Lord Jesus, actually *beheld* him, as we are told in a preceding verse. Jesus was present to him in his dying ecstasy; and was it not therefore natural that the martyred man should invoke his risen Master, then standing before him, should call upon him to receive his spirit, and thus rescue him from the hands of his murderers? The act of Stephen is evidently not one of religious worship, properly so called. It is rather the entreaty which one friend might address to another, present to him in his moment of mortal anguish. As such, it cannot be held to authorise the modern disciple to offer his religious adoration to any other object but the One Jehovah.

The same remark is applicable to the instances brought forward by Dr. Liddon from St Paul's Epistles, in which he thinks

---

* Acts vii. 59. It is hardly necessary to observe that the word *God* in the English version is not found in the original.

it appears that the Apostle conceived of his Master as "of Divine Providence in a human form," watching over him, guiding and befriending him.* This is probably correct; but yet it should be remembered that St. Paul too had his visions of Jesus. He had, he said, seen the risen Saviour, as at his conversion; and he was personally present with him on at least one other occasion.† Moreover, he constantly speaks of Christ as of one whom he well knew to be a living person, one exalted to the right hand of God, and made "head over all things;" one too who might at any hour come again to collect and vindicate his scattered saints, and take them to reign with him in heaven.‡ No wonder, then, that the Apostle speaks as he does; that when he saw the Lord, he said to him, "Lord, what wilt thou have me do?" or that in his vision he "besought the Lord," then present before him, that the "thorn in the flesh might depart from him." All this, while it is in perfect harmony with the belief of the Apostolical age as to the continued presence of the risen Christ, yet does not shew that St. Paul, or any one else, was in the habit of worshiping him as God. Nor can it warrant the modern disciple in speaking to Jesus Christ in any similar way; much less in forgetting and violating the positive precepts of the Gospel respecting the worship of God, or in following any other example in this important matter but that of Christ himself.

The case of Stephen, however, has another lesson for us, very different from that upon which Dr. Liddon insists. We are told that his persecutors were at a loss for an effective accusation against him; for that "they suborned men" to bear witness against him. We are told that the false witnesses said, "This man ceaseth not to speak blasphemous words against this holy place [the temple], and the law; for we have heard him say that

---

* Liddon, B. L., p. 371.   † 2 Cor. xii.
‡ 1 Cor. i. 7; 1 Thess. iii. 13; iv. 16; 2 Thess. ii. 1; iii. 5.

this Jesus of Nazareth shall destroy this place, and shall change the customs which Moses delivered us."*

Now, if the disciples looked upon their departed Master as God, and were accustomed to worship him as such, will Dr. Liddon inform us why the persecutors of Stephen did not accuse him of idolatry, in that he offered religious worship to the crucified man, Jesus of Nazareth? There is no trace anywhere in the New Testament of such an accusation—although we know that it was in substance brought by the Jews against the Christians in later times, when probably the worship of Christ was growing up into an established practice.† It is impossible that it should not have been brought forward by the bigoted enemies of the early Christianity, had fitting occasion been afforded to them. But there is no trace of it in the Book of Acts, or in any other book of the New Testament. The inevitable inference is, that such a charge was not thought of, and could not be made, in the face of the fact that the disciples did *not* speak of Jesus Christ as God, nor pay him religious adoration. If they did so, they must have done it in secret, and kept it out of the sight of their implacable persecutors. But Dr. Liddon, as we have formerly seen, repeatedly affirms that Jesus " revealed his Godhead explicitly to the Apostles, and to the Jewish people;" and holds that he especially claimed to be worshiped as God, when he said that men " should honour the Son even as they honour the Father."‡ Why, then, again, if it were so—why did the enemies of Stephen, who cannot have shared Dr. Liddon's belief in the deity of Christ, never, so far as we can judge, accuse either Stephen, or any other Christian disciple, of idolatrously worshiping a crucified man, and thus setting up another as God, besides their own Jehovah of Hosts?

The true character of the worship of the primitive disciples appears in more than one place in the New Testament. When

---

* Acts vi. 11–14.   † Liddon, B. L., p. 391.   ‡ *Ibid*, pp. 177–182.

Jesus taught his disciples to pray, he said nothing about the adoration or worship of himself. He told them to say, "Our Father which art in heaven." He even said to them that, after he was gone from them, they were to ask him nothing, but to ask the Father in his name. He said to the woman of Samaria in clear and precise terms, which it might be thought that no one could misunderstand or explain away, that "the true worshipers shall worship the Father in spirit and in truth."* In the Book of the Acts we find a prayer of the disciples recorded, and to whom is it addressed? "They lifted up their voice to God with one accord and said, Lord, thou art God, which hast made heaven, and earth, and the sea, and all that in them is." It is unnecessary to quote more,† for it is evident to whom the prayer of the assembled disciples was here offered, and that it was in no sense to Jesus Christ. Similarly, on the evening before his crucifixion, our Lord himself, according to the fourth Evangelist, prayed and said, "Father, the hour is come; glorify thy Son, that thy Son also may glorify thee..... And this is life eternal, that they might know THEE, the only true God, and Jesus Christ whom thou hast sent." ‡

Wherever, in short, there is any clear statement in the New Testament as to the prayers or the worship of the first Christians, it is always to the same effect. It is in no case Christ, or the Holy Spirit, that is addressed. The great Object of religious worship is everywhere God, the Heavenly Father, even "the God and Father of Jesus Christ."

Dr. Liddon, however, brings forward one or two expressions from the Book of Revelation, in which for a moment it might appear that this statement is not wholly without exceptions; or, at least, that it is not correct, if we look beyond the earthly life of Christ to his risen and glorified state.§

---

* John xvi. 23; iv. 23. † Acts iv. 24–30. ‡ John xvii. 1–3.
§ "Of all the teachings of the Apocalypse on this subject," Dr. Liddon observes,

We have sufficiently noticed in the last Chapter those passages of the Apocalypse in which the Lamb is represented as sitting upon the throne, and, by the gift or appointment of the Almighty, even sharing in Divine honours. We have also seen that the Lamb is really everywhere represented as a subordinate Being, the instrument of God, never in any way identified with God Himself, but always distinct from Him. In one passage of that book, however, we read that "the four-and-twenty elders fell down before the Lamb." They sing his praise, as one worthy to open the book; and the writer of the vision adds, that he heard all creatures saying, "Unto him that sitteth upon the throne and to the Lamb be the blessing and the honour and the glory and the might for ever and ever."*

Unquestionably the honour here ascribed to the Lamb is of the highest conceivable kind; such as is nowhere seen paid to Jesus in any historical book of the New Testament; such as he himself, in his human life, never claimed, never received. Is it necessary to remind the reader that the whole scene occurs in a vision, or ecstasy, of the most elevated and imaginative character, —a vision of the approaching end of the then existing state of the world, and the speedy coming of the Son of man to execute a terrible vengeance on his enemies,†—a vision which has never been converted into a reality, and which, it may safely be added, never will be so? Supposing, then, the Lamb, as Dr. Liddon

---

"perhaps none is so full of significance as the representation of Christ in His wounded Humanity upon the throne of the Most High. The Lamb, as It had been slain, is in the very centre of the court of heaven; He receives the prostrate adoration of the highest intelligences around the throne; and as the Object of that solemn, uninterrupted, awful worship, He is associated with the Father, as being in truth one with the Almighty, Uncreated, Supreme God." B. L., p. 243. All that we need say, in particular reference to this highly exaggerated statement, is contained in the preceding Chapter, to which, therefore, we would again refer the reader.

* Rev. v. 8-13. † Rev. xix. 17-21; xviii.

affirms, to be really associated in worship with the Almighty Father, are we to infer that a composition of so mystical and unreal a character, in the exposition of which scarcely any two authorities have hitherto agreed, is to over-rule the plain tenor of historical writings, which give us the words and life of Christ as they were on earth, and shew us how his disciples regarded him and spoke of him, and how they paid religious worship in no case to him, but to God alone? Even, then, granting that the author of the Apocalypse, in his marvellous vision, represents the Lamb as so highly honoured, ought this fact to be received as affording a rule or law to the Christian disciple of after-times, to make him turn away from the express precepts and example of Christ himself?

But, in truth, there is no such opposition as this between the historical books and this Apocalyptic writing. We have abundantly seen that whatever worth and honour may be ascribed to the Lamb is *bestowed* upon him. They are not his of essential independent right. This appears in the passage to which Dr. Liddon appeals: "Worthy is the Lamb that was slain to *receive* power, and riches, and wisdom, and strength, and honour."* And it has been abundantly seen that the general tenor of the Book of Revelation is directly unfavourable to the supposition of the deity of the Son of Man. Nothing, therefore, can have been further from the thoughts of the writer of that book than the idea which Dr. Liddon asserts, the idea of Jesus Christ "as being in truth one with the Almighty, Uncreated, Supreme God." Such an assertion is in the highest degree unwarranted by a calm and dispassionate examination of the evidence in this book bearing upon the subject.

There remains one other expression of the New Testament, which has given a fallacious support to the belief that the early

* Rev. v 12.

disciples worshiped their departed Master. We allude to those instances in which they are said to "call upon the name of the Lord." In the Book of Acts, Saul is said to have "authority from the chief priests to bind all that call on thy name;"—that is to say, the name of Jesus. St. Paul addresses the disciples of Corinth as those who "are called to be saints, with all that in every place call upon the name of Jesus Christ our Lord."*

This phrase has been variously understood, even by orthodox interpreters. There can be no question that in the Old Testament usage, it often means to call upon Jehovah in prayer and praise. In some places of the New Testament also, where Jehovah is referred to, it may have the same sense. But it is equally certain that the word rendered "call upon" ($\epsilon\pi\iota\kappa\alpha\lambda o\tilde{\upsilon}\mu\alpha\iota$), does not properly or necessarily signify, or imply, religious worship. Whether it has this meaning or not must always depend on the *object* with which the verb is joined. Thus we find St. Paul before Felix saying, "I appeal unto Cæsar;" literally, "I call upon Cæsar," the same word.† This application of the word in question occurs several times in the New Testament. In the present connection it has been taken in a passive sense, as though denoting those who are "called by" the name of Jesus Christ. Grammatically, this is not admissible; and it is doubtless better (with Winer)‡ to regard it as a middle form. It may, therefore, denote those who *call themselves by* (put on) the name of Jesus Christ—that is to say, those who take the

---

* Acts xxii. 16; 1 Cor. i. 1; Acts ix. 14, 21.

† Καίσαρα ἐπικαλοῦμαι. Acts xxv. 11, 12, 25; comp. xv. 17, 1 Pet. i. 17.

‡ *N. T. Grammar*, by Moulton, p. 330. The words in question, "I invoke (call upon) Cæsar," imply the acknowledgment of Cæsar as Lord. This is, in reality, a force equivalent to that above attributed to the expression in connection with Christ, whom all that bore his name similarly recognized,—but the verb in question of itself conveys no idea of *religious* invocation or worship, unless, indeed, when followed by the name of the Supreme.

name of Christ, or acknowledge themselves Christian disciples. This cannot be far from the true meaning of the word.

If, indeed, it were certainly established by other evidence that our Lord was worshiped as God by the early disciples, there would be no reason to doubt that the form "call upon" might, in these cases, be used in that sense. But we have seen that there is no good reason for holding that religious worship was paid to Christ by the first Christians, but the contrary; and that their worship, like the Master's own, was always given to Jehovah alone. Hence it is reasonable, or rather it is necessary, to interpret the doubtful or neutral word in question, in accordance with that clear fact of Scripture. We have to take it, therefore, as simply denoting those who acknowledged the authority of Christ, who recognized him as Lord, and called themselves by His name.

As a conclusive testimony to the worship of Christ by the early disciples, Dr. Liddon brings forward the Letter of the younger Pliny to the Emperor Trajan, a document which has often been adduced for the same purpose. Pliny tells his imperial master that the Christians of his province of Bithynia were accustomed to meet together before day-break and sing a hymn "to Christ as God." Thus Dr. Liddon renders the words *Christo quasi deo;* but he will probably not deny that they may be correctly rendered "to Christ as if to a god." This, in fact, is the only admissible rendering, considering that the expression comes from a Roman writer, who, although familiar enough with the "gods many" of the heathen mythology, probably knew nothing of the One only and true God. Moreover, the word *quasi* (as if) really suggests the writer's denial of the implied proposition that Christ was "a god."

The words were written in the year 109, or about seventy-five years after the crucifixion; and they may certainly be accepted as shewing that the Christians of Bithynia held the name of their risen Master in the highest honour, and were in the habit of celebrating his praise in hymns. But how does it appear that they worshiped him as God?—or how does it follow, even if they did, that we, Christian disciples of to-day, should take our idea of Christian worship from the Bithynians, as reported by a Roman pro-prætor? How does it appear, because he states that they sang a hymn to Christ, "as if to a god," that *we* should worship Christ as GOD, in contravention of the plainest precepts and examples of the New Testament?

Dr. Liddon further points out that the Jews, on the occasion of Polycarp's martyrdom, "drew the attention of pagan magistrates to the worship of Jesus, in order to stir up contempt and hatred against the Christians."* He observes also that the Emperor Adrian, writing to Servian, describes the population of Alexandria as "divided between the worship of Christ and the worship of Serapis;" and he adds the remark, that it must have been very perplexing to the Roman official mind that "One who had been adjudged to death as a criminal should receive Divine honours."†

Such observations are perfectly just. But does Dr. Liddon fail to perceive the suggestion which they convey? In the Acts of the Apostles there is an entire *absence* of all indication of either Jewish or Roman perplexity at the circumstance that the Christians worshiped "One who had been adjudged to death as a criminal." Whence that absence, except only from the fact that such perplexity, from the nature of the case, could not have arisen, and never existed—seeing that the Christians did not, in truth, give occasion for it—seeing that in Apostolic times they had not yet begun to offer religious worship to Jesus Christ? Doubtless, in the later times of Pliny and of Adrian, the deity of Christ was beginning to win its way to prominence, especially among certain

* Liddon, B. L., p. 391.   † *Ibid.*, p. 392.

classes of imperfect Hellenizing Christians. It was still, however, nearly two hundred years before that peculiar development of Christianity reached its final predominance, at and through the Council of Nicæa. But such an advance as this, or anything like it, can nowhere be seen within the limits of the New Testament.

And Dr. Liddon himself may be appealed to for the amplest proof and illustration of this statement. For let any one compare the abundant and varied evidence of the worship of Christ which he cites from hymns and liturgical forms of the time of Tertullian and Origen, the third century after Christ,—let any one compare and contrast that with the total absence of everything of the kind from the Christian books. It requires nothing more to shew that the worship of Christ, like that of the Virgin Mary, was the growth of a long period of time, and of a credulous and superstitious period. It requires nothing more to shew how highly unjustifiable, on Scriptural grounds, is the modern practice of the Churches of uniting Jesus Christ in an equal offering of worship with Him "who is above all," whom our Lord himself habitually worshiped, and whom, even in the fourth Gospel, he is recorded to have addressed in prayer as "the Only True God."*

CHAPTER XXIII.

THE HOLY SPIRIT.

The conception of the Spirit of God, the Holy Spirit, was familiar among the Hebrews many centuries before the birth of

---

* The import of these most emphatic words, Dr. Liddon seeks, in his own peculiar way, to "water down"—to use an expressive phrase of his own (*supra*, p. 202). They are exclusive, he tells us (p. 237, note), "not of the Son, but of false gods, or creatures external to the Divine Essence." In other words, they *include* the person who now, in his solemn and private prayer, addresses them to the Heavenly Father; and who is, therefore, himself as much "the Only True God" as the Being of Beings to whom he prays! Can such an explanation really satisfy any serious mind?

Christ. For example, we read in very familiar words,—"Cast me not away from thy presence, and take not thy Holy Spirit from me."* The Psalm to which this verse belongs is attributed in the title to David. It is probably not so ancient; but there can be no doubt that it was written several hundred years before the commencement of the Christian era.

It follows, that the idea of the Holy Spirit,† as it appears in the Christian Scriptures, was not, and could not be, a new idea, or a new revelation of divine truth.

Some of the instances in which the Spirit is mentioned in the Old Testament are sufficiently remarkable. In one place, the skill employed in the construction of the tabernacle is said to be given by it.‡ In the Book of Job we have a similar conception, in these words:—"But there is a spirit in man, and the inspiration of the Almighty giveth them understanding." Another sacred poet writes,—"The Spirit of the Lord spake by me, and his word was in my tongue." In the Psalms, the life of the animal creation and the renewal of the earth with vegetation are attributed to the same Divine energy: "Thou sendest forth thy Spirit, they are created; and thou renewest the face of the earth."§

Such instances are very numerous; and by them we may clearly see how familiar to various writers of the older Scriptures was the great thought of the ever-active and all-pervading Spirit

---

* Ps. li. 11.

† Our English words *Ghost* and *Spirit*, the one of Anglo-Saxon, the other of Latin origin, correspond to and represent only *one* word in the original Scriptures, Hebrew and Greek respectively. This should unquestionably everywhere be rendered by "Spirit," especially in the New Testament, the word *Ghost* being, in our days, by no means free from objectionable associations. It can only tend to convey false impressions to many English readers, to use sometimes the one, sometimes the other, in an English version of the New Testament, the original word being always, without exception, the single neuter substantive πνύμα.

‡ Exod. xxxi. 1–11. § Job xxxii. 8; 2 Sam. xxiii. 2; Ps. civ. 30.

of God. All life, intelligence, mental energy and manual skill, were of its operation. The Spirit of God moved upon the face of the waters at the dawn of creation, and reduced the chaos into order. The same inspiration upholds us in being, gives us understanding and strength to do whatever man is capable of doing; and when that Divine power is withdrawn, we die and return to the dust.

It is evident that, in all such representations, what is really meant by the term in question, is no other than God Himself. It is the Almighty Being, inscrutably putting forth His power in the creation, support, control, inspiration, of the universe of animate and inanimate things—acting upon us and in us by the operation of His living will and energy. But there is nothing to shew that the ancient writers of the Old Testament, in thus speaking of the active power of God, ever attributed to it a separate personal existence. Nor has this, in fact, ever been maintained. The Holy Spirit, in the older Scriptures, is indeed the Divine Being in His action upon the material world, and in communion with the soul of man; but this fact will not justify us in saying that it is "God the Holy Spirit," as though it were a something distinct, something to be thought of and named as God, apart from Him who alone is Jehovah. The personal conception, if admitted into the Old Testament, would manifestly tend directly to weaken or destroy the proper monotheistic idea of the Mosaic religion. It will be found, that nothing approaching to so dangerous an infringement of the great characteristic principle of that religion is anywhere to be met with throughout the Hebrew Books.

The deep feeling of reverence with which the Jews regarded the Sacred Name has been formerly noticed. We have seen that they refrained from uttering it, and preferred to express it by some substituted form. Something of the same feeling makes its appearance at times, even amidst the extreme anthropomorphism of their ancient books. The sentiment referred to is, in truth, perfectly natural to the human mind. What God is, in His essential nature, man does not know, and is probably incapable of comprehending. How He acts upon the universe of material things, how He preserves, or in any way influences, the human soul, we are likewise unable to explain. This natural human incapacity has been felt in all ages. Hence the ancient idea that the Infinite cannot stand in any immediate relation with outward things, and can only act upon them by influences, emanations, angels, words spoken, going forth from Him and accomplishing whatsoever He may have ordained. This way of conceiving of the Divine activity has been already sufficiently dwelt upon in connection with the doctrine of the Logos, as it is found in the New Testament. But the same feeling in relation to Jehovah most probably gave occasion and form to expressions in the Old Testament also, as well as in the later Apocryphal books. Thus, as we have seen, in the Psalms, the "word of Jehovah" and the "breath of his mouth" are the instruments of His will; and His Spirit, or inspiration, goes forth from Him, to animate, guide, move, accomplish, according to His all-comprehending intelligence.

At the risk of a little repetition, it may be observed that this tendency to distinguish between the incomprehensible Being and His manifestations in the material universe is more marked in some books than in others. It leads occasionally to an apparent separation between Him and one or other of His attributes. The Divine Wisdom, for example, as displayed in the works of nature, is there visible to human eyes. It may, consequently, be spoken of even as a something distinct from its source. It has come forth, or been sent forth, from God; and it exists, in some sense, apart from Him. In the Book of Job (chapter xxviii.) there is an evident approach to this mode of conception. But, nevertheless, neither there nor elsewhere is Wisdom really a separate being. It is so only by a poetical metaphor. This way of speaking is *only* a mode of speech. The Divine wisdom is really and essentially in the Divine Mind; nay, it is no other than God Himself; and it would be an extreme error to make, as it were, a divine person of it, or a separate existence at all.

Such remarks as these apply not only to the personification of Wisdom in the Book of Proverbs, on which Dr. Liddon, as we have seen, lays so unreasonable a stress; and not only to the similar personifications of Wisdom found in the Sapiential Books, which he also adduces in the same urgent way; but it applies equally to instances in both the Old Testament and the New, in which the Holy Spirit might appear for the moment to be spoken of as a separate personal being. These different cases help, in fact, to illustrate and explain each other. In none of them will it be found really necessary to suppose that we are to regard the word, or the breath, or the wisdom, or the Spirit of God, as separate beings, apart from the Infinite.

The truth of these statements may be shewn by a reference to various expressions which occur in the New Testament. When Christ reasoned with the Jews respecting his own authority as a Divine teacher, and the power by which he wrought his miracles, he said to them, as reported by the first Evangelist, "If I cast out devils by the Spirit of God, then the kingdom of God is come unto you." In the parallel place in St. Luke, the same saying is reported thus: "If I with the finger of God cast out devils, no doubt the kingdom of God is come upon you."* The two forms of expression were evidently understood by the Evangelists to mean the same thing. What that meaning is cannot be doubtful, and is well illustrated by the words of the fourth

* Matt. xii. 28; Luke xi. 20.

Gospel, where Jesus says on another occasion, "The Father that dwelleth in me, he doeth the works." But this, again, cannot reasonably be taken to mean that the Infinite Father was in Christ, in the Evangelist's conception, in any other way than by the Divine help and power which He gave him; or, also, by means of the indwelling Logos; and such forms of expression simply amount, in fact, as already observed, to the statement of the Apostle Peter at the Pentecost. The Almighty Father was manifested in Christ, and, in the Apostle's conception, was seen to be so, " by miracles and wonders and signs which GOD did by him."

It is thus clear, that the "finger of God" and the "Spirit of God" are simply God Himself, the Heavenly Father, acting in and through Christ; and it is no more necessary, or allowable, to make a separate person of the Spirit, than it is to suppose such a distinction to be hidden or implied in the phrase "the finger of God."

The miraculous powers of Christ are thus denoted, at times, by the expression before us.* So it is in connection with the Apostles, who are said to "receive power" by the Holy Spirit coming upon them, and in connection with Gentile converts also, when they receive " the gift of the Holy Spirit."† In such expressions it is impossible to miss the conception really present to the mind of the sacred writers. Evidently it could not have been that of a personal agent. The gifts and powers referred to were produced by the action of the Almighty Being upon the minds of men. They were conferred by a subtle inbreathing of Divine power, such as could only be denoted in human language by the word "Spirit," no other term being equally adapted to express so refined, pervading and all-controlling a manifestation of the Divine energy.

---

* Matt. xii. 28; comp. Acts x. 38.

† Acts i. 8; x. 44–47; Heb. ii. 4:—in this last place there is no article, "gifts of Holy Spirit:" as frequently.

We read in the Book of Acts (xix. 1–6), that St. Paul found certain disciples at Ephesus to whom he said, "Have ye received the Holy Spirit since ye believed? And they said unto him," we are told, "We have not so much as heard whether there be any Holy Spirit." It is plain that they meant they had not heard of the miraculous powers conferred on the first Christians; for it is added, that "when Paul laid his hands upon them, the Holy Spirit came upon them, and they spake with tongues."

It would be easy to give a number of similar instances, by which it would be equally seen that gifts and powers of knowledge and of wisdom, sometimes of holy, guiding influence, manifested in the dispositions and the life, are denoted by this expression.* Thus the men who are chosen for the office of deacon in the primitive church are said to have been "men of honest report, full of Holy Spirit, and of wisdom." Of Stephen, also, at the time of his death, it is related that, "being full of Holy Spirit, he looked steadfastly up to heaven." We read that Simon the sorcerer offered to buy Holy Spirit from the Apostles for money. It is plain that we can only understand this of the Divine powers which the Apostles possessed, and not of a personal being. Similarly, in other places, the Spirit is said to be given, to be poured out, to be possessed, to fill, and move holy men and others;—expressions all of which correspond entirely to the statement that it is a divine power or influence that is spoken of, while they do not correspond to the theory that it is a divine person.

It is, however, alleged, that although the Spirit is nowhere expressly said to be God, or to be a Person, yet it is sometimes

---

* Matt. x. 19, 20 ; John xiv. 26 ; xv. 26 ; Acts vi. 3-5 ; vii. 55 ; viii. 18-20 ; Rom. viii. 4-12. The absence of the article in some of these instances should be particularly noted.

spoken of as possessing personal attributes and performing personal functions. It is described as understanding, willing, acting. It is represented as speaking to men, pleading with them, and interceding for them; as bearing testimony, reproving, teaching, bringing to remembrance. Are we not, then, by the use of such phrases, warranted in thinking of the Holy Spirit as a separate personal being, and, by immediate inference, as the third person of the Godhead?

To answer this question, we have first to ask another. Is it a *real* personality that is intended in such instances, or only a figurative one? Now this question cannot be reasonably answered except in one way, if we will duly attend to the manner in which figurative language is employed by the writers of Scripture, and in particular to the many cases of bold personification which occur in both the Old and the New Testament. When Joshua confirms the covenant with the Israelites, on entering the land of Canaan, he uses these words: "This stone shall be a witness unto us; for it hath heard all the words of Jehovah which he spake unto us; it shall therefore be a witness unto you, lest ye deny your God."* In this case a personal character could scarcely have been more strongly expressed. Yet no mistake is ever made as to the meaning of the passage. No one can suppose the stone to have been an intelligent being, as the words so distinctly imply—an intelligent being listening to the ratification of the covenant, to attest the fact to later ages.

Other instances might be adduced from the Old Testament, as in those parts of the Book of Proverbs in which Wisdom is so remarkably personified. But let us turn more particularly to the New Testament, as chiefly concerning our present argument. We know how the Apostle Paul personifies Sin, Death,

* Josh. xxiv. 26, 27.

the Law, in several instances. He represents them as having power, exercising dominion, reigning over men, and being enemies; yet we are never misled by such language to think that he is speaking of real persons.* The same remark may be made of his description of Charity:—Charity suffereth long, and is kind; envieth not; is not puffed up; seeketh not her own; thinketh no evil; beareth, believeth, hopeth, endureth, all things. Here this Christian virtue is represented as having the attributes of personality, exactly as happens in the case of the Spirit of God. But as we do not, in the one case, suppose that a real person is meant, so there is no necessity to do this, and no propriety in doing it, in the other. So far as the language is concerned, there is just as much reason to make Charity, or Sin, or Death, or the Law, into a person, as there is to do so in the case of the Holy Spirit.

There is one passage of the New Testament which seems to require special notice in the present connection. It is that which speaks of sin against the Holy Spirit, a sin which is declared to be unpardonable.† From the context it appears that what is meant is the denial of the Spirit of God, as manifested by Jesus to the deniers,—that is to say, as exhibited by him in his wonderful works, there done before their eyes. Blasphemy, or evil-speaking, against himself, the Son of Man, might be forgiven. But one that was so hardened as to shut his eyes and his heart to the visible manifestation of Divine power, the visible presence of the Holy Spirit in those "works,"—such a person sinned wilfully and obstinately against God Himself; and that sin should not be forgiven.

It was a severe rebuke and condemnation of the hardened unbelief which even ascribed the powers of Christ to Beelze-

---
* Rom. vi. 12, 14; v. 14-17; 1 Cor. xv. 55-57.
† Matt. xii. 31, 32; Mark iii. 28; Luke xii. 10.

bub,—powers exercised so beneficently, with so much of humility and self-forgetfulness in their possessor, and therefore so forcibly evidencing, in every respect, their own Divine origin.*

There are still one or two facts to be mentioned which are wholly unaccountable on the supposition of the truth of the popular teaching on this subject. First, there is no doxology, or ascription of praise, to the Holy Spirit, in either the Old or the New Testament. Nor is there any instance, we believe, on record, in all the Scriptures, of any prayer having ever been addressed to the Holy Spirit as a separate personality. It is inconceivable that this should be the case, had this Divine power been regarded in the early Christian times as separately God, a definite personal being, even as much so as the Almighty Father.

It is, indeed, in the second place, to be remembered, that no example can be adduced, from the first and second centuries, of the Holy Spirit being made an object of worship, or perhaps even of its being spoken of as a distinct existence—as distinguished, that is to say, from the idea of it as a power, gift, blessing, conferred by God. Even in the Apostles' Creed, which probably comes down from the end of the second century, the Holy Spirit does not appear in a *personal* character. It may be questioned whether it does so in the original Nicene Creed, although, at the time when this was composed (A.D. 325), the doctrine of a Trinity of equal persons was beginning to be held by some of the more speculative of the Church Fathers. The absence of the fuller definition of the Spirit from the Nicene Creed proper is well known. It was the Council of Constantinople (A.D. 381), which introduced the longer form now found in the English Prayer Book.† A still later addition,—that of the

* It is scarcely necessary to add, that the word *blaspheme*, and its noun, are not, in the N. T., used solely in reference to God. Hence their occasional use in reference also to Christ, as well as others: Luke xxii. 65; Acts xiii. 45; xviii. 6; 1 Pet. iv. 4.

† The original Nicene Creed, in the clause relating to the Holy Spirit, stood thus

words "and the Son,"—was the great occasion of the schism, not yet healed, nor likely to be so, between the Eastern and the Western Churches.

The following just and weighty observation, in reference to the doxology in use in the worship of the Church of England, is made by Dr. Lardner. After quoting the doxology, "Glory be to the Father, and to the Son, and to the Holy Ghost: as it was in the beginning, is now, and ever shall be, world without end. Amen," —he proceeds to observe: "Doubtless this is said by many very frequently, and with great devotion. But can it be said truly? Does not that deserve consideration? Is there any such doxology in the New Testament? Are not the books of the New Testament the most ancient and the most authentic Christian writings in all the world? It matters not much to inquire when this doxology was first used,* or how long it has been in use, if it be not in the New Testament. And whether it is there or not, may be known by those who are pleased to read it with care." †

Let us not, however, in the midst of these more controversial topics, lose sight of a very different consideration, one which has an immediate connection both with Christian faith and with Christian practice. The doctrine of the Holy Spirit is still a vital part of Christianity. And, to one who faithfully admits it, there is an effectual end to the importance of sacerdotalism, Anglican, Romish and Greek; equally an end to it in all its three

---

"And in the Holy Spirit." At the Council of Constantinople this clause was amplified as follows: "And I believe in the Holy Spirit; the Lord and Giver of Life; who proceedeth from the Father; who with the Father and the Son together is worshiped and glorified; who spake by the prophets." To this form the words "and the Son," after "proceedeth from the Father," were added at a later period, and so the Creed was completed, as it stands in the Book of Common Prayer. "So that the creed, here called the Nicene Creed, is indeed the Constantinopolitan creed, together with the addition of *filioque*, made by the Western church." Bishop Burnet, *apud* Lardner (Works by Kippis, X. p. 132).

* This was not until after the Council of Constantinople.
† Lardner, Works by Kippis, X. p. 167.

forms. For no reasonable mind can suppose that the Spirit of God is confined in its movements within the limits of those Churches, one or all of them; that it can only visit the humble, waiting soul through the person of a "priest;" or that a priest, so called, has alone the power to confer it, however exactly his outer vestments may be conformed to the style of some long past century of Christian antiquity; however elaborately he may perform enjoined ceremonies and sacraments; or however magnificent the external accompaniments of his worship.

All true religion, whether in "Church" or out of it, is founded upon, is identical with, the sense of the living presence of God with and in the human soul—that alone. Such is also the evident foundation of Christianity, as recognised in almost every act and word of Christ and his Apostles. With them, the Heavenly Father is the all-pervading Spirit of the universe, a living God, who can hear our prayers, and see our efforts to do His will; and who, by His Spirit, can help, enlighten and comfort the souls of all that faithfully look to Him, whether they shall bow down in the humblest meeting-house, or in the grandest cathedral of human Art. Not, indeed, in the presence of elaborately or superstitiously observed formalities, any more than amidst fanatical noise and excitement, can we think that the Spirit of God most effectually visits the waiting soul, or lets the "still, small voice" of His presence be most clearly and touchingly heard within the heart. It is rather in the hour of quiet and lonely meditation that this will come to pass:—when we think with penitence about our past sins, when we reflect upon the duties we have to do, and how best we may do them, when we strive and pray to give ourselves up to all God's will concerning us; then will the communion of His Holy Spirit be ours; "the grace of the Lord Jesus Christ" be with us, and the Divine Love be shed upon us. Then, too, shall we know that we are true disciples of His Son, acceptable servants and children of our Father which is in Heaven.

CHAPTER XXIV.

SACRIFICES, THEIR ORIGIN AND PURPOSE—THE HEBREW SYSTEM.

One of the earliest ideas that we meet with in the history of religion, is that of the efficacy of sacrifices to expiate sin, to propitiate the gods, and avert punishment from the guilty. The first book of the Iliad shews us the enraged Apollo, in the midst of the vengeance he is taking upon the Greeks, appeased by the offering of a hecatomb, and delighted by the singing at the sacrificial banquet by which it was accompanied. The father of history records a similar belief on the part of the ancient Egyptians, as he doubtless heard of it from their priests, in his travels among them in the fifth century before Christ. Beginning with these early notices, a long succession of passages may be cited from the classical writers, in evidence of the wide prevalence of the same idea. Among these, no statement is more definite or interesting to an English reader than that of Cæsar, in his Gallic War, where he tells us of the Galli, and of their powerful priesthood, the Druids, how given they were to religious rites, and what importance they attached to their terrible offerings of human victims.*

But, indeed, we need not go back to remote antiquity for either the belief in the efficacy of sacrifices in general, or that in the superior value of human victims in particular. A very remarkable and fearful example may be found nearer to ourselves. It is not many years since the Indian Government felt itself called upon to interfere, to suppress a system of human sacrifice prevailing among a barbarous race of people, in the province of Orissa.† It was found, in this case, that the victims were kept and reared for the purpose, and put to death, in a particular way, with circumstances of great cruelty, before an assembled crowd of people.

* Bell. Gall. vi. 16.   † Major Campbell's *Wild Tribes of Khondistan*, 1864.

The design was to propitiate some divinity, and thus to gain a victory, to obtain abundant crops, or avert calamity from the community or the individual. It is satisfactory to learn that success attended the efforts of the agents of the Indian Government to put an end to these deplorable barbarities. They serve, however, to illustrate for us the ideas of far distant times on the same subject. We cease to wonder that ancient Gauls, and Britons, and Egyptians, and others of former ages, had faith in the religious value of sacrifices, animal and human, when we find the same faith in active operation even among subjects of the British crown, and in the middle of the nineteenth century.

What has just been said shews us the wide-spread prevalence and great antiquity of the dreadful superstition referred to. It shews us more than this. We see also that the practices in question were essentially *natural* as well as heathen practices; inasmuch as they have prevailed so universally among heathen peoples, and have been, in all cases, so far as we have any evidence, the simple offspring of their own low and unspiritual ideas of the nature of the Deity, and of the worship which is acceptable to Him.

This remark is made mainly because it suggests and warrants another. Most of our older theological writers, including such men as Archbishop Magee and Dr. Pye Smith, would seem to have believed in the divine, or supernatural, institution of sacrifices. Most probably this notion is hardly yet obsolete. It is entirely destitute of reasonable evidence, and is in no way rendered feasible, but only contradicted, by the well-known facts of the case, including the miseries, and the destruction of human life to which the sacrificial system gave origin. The point is one, however, which must be admitted, at the present day, to have lost any interest or importance it may once have been thought to possess.

Among the Hebrews, sacrificial usages were in operation from the earliest period of which we have any reliable information. In the Mosaic laws, however, they are regulated and modified in such a way as to guard against some of their worst abuses. Probably no law-maker of those times would have found it expedient, or even possible, to dispense with sacrifices altogether. All that could be done was to place them under some reasonable limitations, and endeavour to connect with them better ideas than had previously prevailed. Sacrifices of animals, as well as other offerings, are accordingly prescribed by the Law; but some care was nevertheless taken to prevent the people from thinking that such things availed in themselves to expiate moral sins, actual violations of honesty, justice and truth. Although, therefore, in most cases of transgression, a sacrifice is prescribed, yet there is also some penalty or punishment connected with it. Thus, as the rule, the offender was reminded that transgression brought punishment, and was not to be atoned for by a mere ceremony of religion. Nor was the idea encouraged, that it was sufficient, in order to gain the Divine forgiveness, to turn over punishment incurred to some substituted victim. In this respect, the old law of the Jews was a better teacher than some Evangelical expounders of the modern doctrine of atonement.

An illustration of these statements may be taken from the following passage in the Book of Leviticus.*

"And the Lord spake unto Moses, saying, If a soul sin and commit a trespass against the Lord, and lie unto his neighbour in that which was delivered unto him to keep, or in fellowship, or in a thing taken away by violence; or hath deceived his neighbour; or have found that which was lost, and lieth concerning it, and sweareth falsely; in any of all these that a man doeth, sinning therein; then it shall be, because he hath sinned and is guilty, that he shall restore that which he took violently away, or the

* Lev. vi. 1–7.

thing which he hath deceitfully gotten, or that which was delivered him to keep, or the lost thing which he found, or all that about which he hath sworn falsely; he shall even restore it in the principal, and shall add the fifth part more thereto, and give it unto him to whom it appertaineth, in the day of his trespass offering. And he shall bring his trespass offering unto the Lord, a ram without blemish out of the flock, . . . for a trespass offering, unto the priest; and the priest shall make an atonement for him before the Lord; and it shall be forgiven him for any thing of all that he hath done in trespassing therein."

In this passage there are two or three things worthy of notice. First, restitution, or compensation, was to be made for injury done. Secondly, there must be an acknowledgment of the wrong, and this confession is marked and emphasized by the offering of a sacrifice. Thirdly, the victim is itself an animal of some value, insomuch that its loss was a kind of penalty upon the offender. And so it is, in most cases under the Law: actual crimes, moral offences, sins, are punished. They are not allowed to be simply expiated by sacrifice—the latter being rather a subordinate incident of the whole transaction, though doubtless very necessary in those times, as tending to strengthen the sense of guilt, and direct the mind to the idea of the invisible Ruler and Judge, whose will had been violated. The atonement made by sacrifice is constantly of the ritual or ceremonial character,—a mere appendage to something else of greater moral significance, rather than in itself possessed of an independent, all-sufficient, expiatory or propitiatory efficacy.*

It is hardly necessary to add, that the general spirit of most of the Prophets is in harmony with whatever is best and highest in the Law on this subject. The people, indeed, and probably their rulers, were long incapable of appreciating worthily these better

* Comp. Lev. v. xvi. xxiv. xxvi.

ideas. In the times of Isaiah and Micah, for example, it is clear, the tendency was to look upon the sacrifice of a victim as possessed of great efficacy to propitiate the Almighty and expiate sin. But against this, we know, the faithful prophet earnestly protests. "Will Jehovah be pleased with thousands of rams," Micah asks, "or with ten thousands of rivers of oil? Shall I give my first-born for my transgression, the fruit of my body for the sin of my soul?" Isaiah and Jeremiah are equally decided and severe on this point;* shewing us, on the one hand, how prevalent among the people of their times was the idea of the value of sacrifices to secure the Divine favour even for a guilty man, and, on the other, that such beliefs were as little encouraged by the Prophets as by the Levitical law.

A singular, but wholly factitious, importance has been attached to the sacrificial system of the Hebrews, inasmuch as it has been thought to have been intended mysteriously to foreshadow and typify the death of Christ, and the work of redemption effected by him. This theory is, in fact, only another form of the ill-founded doctrine held by so many, and discussed at sufficient length in the earlier part of this work. It is Dr. Liddon's "principle of an organic unity in Holy Scripture," applied to Hebrew sacrifices and the death of Christ; and it will not be found more valid or more tenable in the present case than in connection with the Messianic expectations of the Old Testament. A further remark is inevitable: whether the theory now in question be true or not, certainly those who profess to hold it might, at least, be expected to interpret the Christian redemption in accordance with the highest spirit of the older Scriptures to which they appeal; and this, we plainly see, does not countenance a belief in vicarious punishment, or in the forgiveness of moral transgression on account of a sacrificed victim.

* Isaiah i.; Jer. vii. Micah vi.; Amos v.

But, in truth, the theory alluded to will scarcely bear examination. The Jews themselves never so understood their ancient books. No passage can be pointed out in the Old Testament which contains an "anticipation" of anything supposed to be taught in the New Testament on this subject, or which indicates any conscious looking forward by the writer to a greater and more genuine sacrifice to come.* As we have abundantly seen, it was not expected by the Jewish people that the Messiah would die. When Jesus spoke to his disciples of his approaching sufferings and death, it would appear that they could not bear, scarcely comprehend, his words.† Thus, the crucifixion came upon the disciples very much as an unforeseen calamity—so little had it been known either to unbelieving Jews, or to Christian disciples, that the Messiah, when he came, must be offered up as a propitiatory sacrifice for the sins of the world.

In one New Testament book only does the theory now referred to find any apparent support. This is the Epistle to the Hebrews, a work, the reader is aware, of unknown authorship,‡ and which can only be received as expressing, not the belief of the general Christian community at the time when it was written, but that solely of its eloquent and fanciful author, whoever he may have been. This Epistle, addressing itself to Jews, and accommodating itself especially to their ideas, runs a kind of parallel between the ministry and death of Christ and various Levitical rites and objects. Our Lord is not only the victim

---

* We have formerly seen that Isaiah liii. really forms no exception to this remark —*supra*, Chapter V.

† Matt. xvi. 21-23; Mark viii. 31-33; ix. 10, 32; John xii. 23-26.

‡ Comp. note, *supra*, p. 5. It is unnecessary here to reproduce the ancient testimonies on the subject. Origen, it is well known, as reported by Eusebius, said of the Epistle to the Hebrews, "who wrote this Epistle, God only knows certainly. But the account come down to us is various; some saying that Clement, who was Bishop of Rome, wrote this epistle, others that it was Luke."—*Apud* Lardner, Works, II. p. 495.

offered, but also the priest who officiates. Christianity has its temple, its altar, its Holy of holies, its sacrifice, even as Judaism itself had: but in what sense? Evidently in no real or literal sense; but in an imaginative, allegorical sense only, similar to that which we so easily attribute to the "Pilgrim's Progress." Thus, again, the typical or predictive significance attached to the ancient rites by the Epistle to the Hebrews is purely imaginary, and cannot justify us in thinking that those rites were, in their institution, consciously designed by any one to prefigure or anticipate the life and death of Jesus Christ.

The remembrance of the probably Alexandrine origin of the Epistle equally warns us against the error of accepting its representations as literal statements of fact and history. In various points, indeed, its whole conception is essentially different from the leading ideas of the writings of St. Paul:—a conclusive reason, both against its Pauline authorship, and also for declining to allow the views which it sets forth to exercise any determinative influence in the interpretation either of those writings, or of any other part of the New Testament.

Passing on from the older times of the Law and the Prophets to those of the primitive Christianity, we find the ancient system of worship in operation in the time of Christ, and long afterwards. The smoke of the morning and evening sacrifice still ascended daily from the temple court; and, probably, there prevailed widely throughout the nation a belief in the sacredness of such rites, and in their value as the means of propitiating the Almighty and obtaining the forgiveness of transgression, national and individual. Hence the writer to the Hebrews can declare, "Almost all things are by the law purged with blood; and without shedding of blood is no remission."* To the Jewish mind of that time, doubtless this was true. The people had been

* Heb. ix. 22.

accustomed for many centuries to such ideas, in common with most of the nations of ancient times. But, however natural it was to the childhood of the human race so to think and so to worship, the old ideas and practices are incompatible with increased knowledge, and a better understanding of moral and spiritual truth in particular. When our Lord so plainly and emphatically spoke of God as the "Heavenly Father," and taught that we must worship Him, not with ceremonies and sacrifices, but "in spirit and in truth;" when he repeated to the people around him those ancient words, "I will have mercy and not sacrifice;" when he said, "If thou bring thy gift to the altar, and there rememberest that thy brother hath ought against thee, leave there thy gift before the altar, and go thy way; first be reconciled to thy brother, and then come and offer thy gift;" when he declared, as he plainly did, that the tears of the penitent sinner are better in God's sight than all the boastful pride of Pharisaic righteousness;—in such teachings as these he struck at the root of those long-descended ideas and practices of his countrymen in connection with sacrifices. These may, indeed, still linger for awhile in the world; for the world is slow to learn the lessons of a simple, non-mystical, and truly spiritual religion. But it will learn them in time. In proportion as men become truly able to look up to God as the Heavenly Father, and to trust in Him as a God of love and mercy unspeakable, they will put away from their thoughts the old heathen belief in the necessity of sacrifices to propitiate Him, or to expiate sin. Especially must this be so, if, as may easily be shewn, Christianity itself does not really teach or enjoin any doctrine of the forgiveness of sin, other than that of its being a free gift of the Infinite mercy. Forgiveness is not, indeed, offered in the Gospel without conditions on the side of man;* but we may well believe that it is so on the side of

* Matt. vi. 14, 15; xviii. 35.

God. He, we are taught, forgives freely, of His own unbought grace and goodness. If, in short, we may place any reliance on the plainest declarations of Christ himself—such as we have, for example, in the parable of the Prodigal Son—the ancient and widely-diffused belief in the efficacy of sacrifices, in every form, must sooner or later die out from the thoughts of devout men, giving place to what is higher and better, more worthy of the Divine love, and of the worship and service which He who is a Spirit Himself asks from us.

We know, however, that there are numerous expressions in the New Testament which connect together the forgiveness of sins and the shedding of blood,—in particular, the shedding of the blood of Christ. Our purpose must now be to ascertain the meaning of this language; and, if possible, to find an interpretation of it, not drawn from any modern theories of the Atonement, whether of this church or of that, but founded simply on a fair consideration of the circumstances and feelings of the times from which the expressions referred to come down to us. Dr. Liddon speaks of "writers who carry into their interpretation of the Gospels ideas which have been gained from a study of the Platonic Dialogues, or of the recent history of France.* The remark is just, and the warning which it conveys perhaps more widely applicable than its author suspects! It is at least a remark the spirit of which is especially worthy of remembrance in connection with the present subject. For the danger is obvious of introducing into its discussion ideas gained, not from the New Testament, but rather from Augustin, Anselm, Luther, to say nothing of various Creeds and Articles which are still nearer to us, and not unlikely to have their weight even with a Bampton Lecturer. This error, then, let us here duly bear in mind, and carefully endeavour to avoid.

* Liddon, B. L., p. 100.

CHAPTER XXV.

THE DEATH OF CHRIST—POPULAR THEORIES FOUNDED UPON IT.

THE language in which the death of Christ is spoken of in the New Testament is richly varied in its forms. Him, says St. Paul, "God hath set forth *to be* a propitiation through faith, by his blood." "Ye were not redeemed," writes another Apostle, "with corruptible things, as silver and gold, from your vain conversation received by tradition from your fathers, but with the precious blood of Christ, as of a lamb without blemish and without spot." And so the first Epistle of John: "The blood of Jesus Christ his Son cleanseth us from all sin."[*] Similar expressions might be multiplied; but these are sufficient to enable us to state, in one of its principal forms, the doctrine of redemption which has been founded on such language.

The human race, we are told, was guilty of manifold sin before God, both as being descended from Adam and partaking of his guilt, and also on account of actual transgression: "As it is written, There is none righteous, no, not one." All men were thus guilty and deserving of punishment. The wrath of God was aroused against them, and would, in due time, have fallen upon them, in the form of eternal damnation. It would now also be impending over all of us, without any chance of escape, had not Christ, by suffering and dying, borne it for us. He, however, suffered and died upon the cross, for sin. Thus by his death he appeased, propitiated, or made "satisfaction" to, the wrath of the Almighty Father, by himself enduring the punishment which must else have been inflicted on men. From that punishment he has, therefore, redeemed us; by his stripes we are healed; or, in

[*] Rom. iii. 25; 1 Pet. i. 18, 19; 1 John i. 7.

other words, we have redemption through his blood. Thus God, it is further said, forgives us our sins. He has manifested His love to the world in giving and accepting Christ as our substitute. At the same time He has manifested His justice, because He does not pardon sin without punishing for it. The sovereignty of the Divine Law is vindicated; man does not sin with impunity; for though *he* may escape the penalties he has incurred, yet these fall upon an all-sufficient substitute, and the requirements of justice are satisfied.

In giving an account of the doctrines of others, there is some danger of overstating or understating what they teach—a fault which ought always to be guarded against. The doctrine of Atonement, and its subsidiary doctrines, have been variously laid down by different writers, of older and more recent date. In the above statement we have sought to express fairly the substance of prevailing ideas of the forgiveness of sin, and the connection of that forgiveness with the death of Christ. Probably few persons familiar with modern Evangelical preaching, whether among the clergy or the Methodists and other Nonconformist sects, would say that there is any overstatement in the brief summary just given. But that this may further appear, we will quote a few sentences from certain works and documents well known and widely accepted at the present time. The first of these, though not possessed of any official authority, may properly be regarded as the representative of an important phase of the common doctrine, seeing that it comes before us with all the authority of one of the heads of the National Church. Speaking of the death of Christ, Archbishop Thomson writes as follows:—

"How came this exhibition of Divine *love* to be needed? Because wrath had already gone out against man. The clouds of God's anger gathered thick over the whole human race; they discharged themselves on Jesus only. God has made Him to be sin for us who knew no sin; He is made 'a curse' (a thing accursed) for us, that the curse that hangs over us may be removed. He bore our sins in his own body on the tree. There are those who would see on the page of the Bible only the sunshine of the Divine love; but the muttering thunders of Divine wrath against sin are heard there also; and He who alone was no child of wrath meets the shock of the thunderstorm, becomes a curse for us, and a vessel of wrath; and the rays of wrath break out of that thunder-gloom and shine on the bowed head of Him who hangs on the Cross, dead for our sins." *

In another page the Archbishop says, speaking of Christ, "He came to reconcile men and God by dying on the Cross for them and bearing their punishment in their stead. He is 'a propitiation through faith in his blood.'† He is the ransom, or price paid, for the redemption of man from all iniquity. The wrath of God was against man; but it did not fall on man. God made His Son 'to be sin for us,' though He knew no sin; and Jesus suffered, though men had sinned. By this act God and man were reconciled."

Once more, the Archbishop describes a main point of "this mysterious transaction" in the following words:—" God the Father laid upon His Son the weight of the sins of the whole world, so that He bare in His own body the wrath which men must else have borne, because there was no other way of escape for them; and thus the Atonement was a manifestation of Divine justice."‡

* *Aids to Faith*, 4th ed., p. 332.

† Rom. iii. 25—but, we are persuaded, a mis-rendering of the words, which may be correctly translated thus, "Whom God hath set forth to be a propitiation through faith, by his blood." So Prof. Jowett, *Epistles of St. Paul*, I. p. 121. Meyer observes that the words "his blood" belong in sense to the verb "set forth," and not to the word "faith." So, in effect, Bunsen, De Wette, and various other authorities. The phrase, "faith in the blood of Christ," is very familiar, and very essential to the popular theology, but it is nowhere found in the New Testament, unless it be in this very doubtful instance.

‡ *Aids to Faith*, pp. 336, 337.

It it evident that the writer of these passages holds the doctrine of Atonement in no undecided form. He does not, however, expressly tell us the nature of the *punishment* which impended over man; but there can be little doubt as to what is meant. It is easy to see that the Archbishop, if he had spoken more fully on that point, would have said, with many before him, that the "terrible wrath" of God could only have been "appeased," or found "satisfaction,"* by and in sinful man's endurance of endless suffering in hell.

What, however, this eminent expositor of the Church's doctrine fails to explain for us on the point in question, may be found very fully set forth in other quarters. It may be well, too, not to pass over and neglect more "popular" statements. We therefore take the following from one of the Methodist Catechisms. Referring to the Fall, question and answer run thus:

"Wherein consists the misery of that state into which man fell?—The misery of the state into which man fell consists in this, that all mankind, being born in sin, and following the devices and desires of their own corrupt hearts, are under the wrath and

---

* *Aids to Faith*, p. 351. "The wrath of God" is a favourite expression with the Archbishop of York, judging from the frequency of its occurrence in his Essay, where it may be found, we believe, much oftener than in the whole of the New Testament. In the latter, it is used to denote especially the condemnation and destruction awaiting the wicked on the great judgment-day of the Messiah, at his second coming. But there is no instance in which it denotes abiding wrath hanging over human kind, and threatening to find its consummation in their eternal misery. Ephes. ii. 3 affords no exception to this remark. The persons here addressed had been *Gentiles* before their conversion, and therefore both virtually and actually "sinners," and deserving of the punishment of sin. "By nature" (or in their former heathen state) "they were children of wrath," according to a well-known Hebraism. But neither here nor anywhere else does the Apostle *say* that "the clouds of God's anger gathered thick over the whole human race." On the contrary, he immediately goes on to speak of the "great love" of God, who, even when men were thus "dead in sins," had no wrath towards them, but only mercy and grace, having by Christ made known His will to receive even guilty men "through faith." (Ephes. ii. 1-10.) Comp. *supra*, p. 20.

curse of God, and so are made liable to the miseries of this life, to death itself, and to the pains of hell hereafter."

After pointing out that Christ, by his death upon the cross, "offered a full satisfaction and atonement to Divine Justice for the sins of the whole world," the Catechism proceeds:

"How did the death of Christ satisfy Divine Justice?—The death of Christ satisfied Divine Justice, in that our sins deserved death; but Christ being both God and man, and perfectly righteous, there was an infinite value and merit in his death,—which being undergone for our sakes and in our stead, Almighty God exercises his mercy in the forgiveness of sins, consistently with his justice and holiness."*

There is evidently a very substantial agreement between the Archbishop and the Methodist Catechism, while yet the latter is the more explicit of the two in regard to the punishment from which man has been delivered.

The "Declaration of Faith" issued by the Congregational Union is in harmony with both, and it may be cited here as shewing us what is no doubt the usual doctrine of a large and important section of English Nonconformists. The Congregational churches, we are told, believe "that Jesus Christ, the Son of God, revealed, either personally in His own ministry, or by the Holy Spirit in the ministry of His Apostles, the whole mind of God for our salvation; and that by His obedience to the Divine law while He lived, and by His sufferings unto death, He meritoriously 'obtained eternal redemption for us;' having thereby vindicated and illustrated Divine justice, 'magnified the law,' and 'brought in everlasting righteousness.'"†

There is, it will be observed, a little vagueness in this document. It does not speak of the "wrath of God," nor tell us at

---

* *Wesleyan Catechism*, No. 2 (published by the Conference), pp. 10, 13.
† *Congregational Manual*, p. 104.

all definitely *what* mankind have been redeemed from, nor even state that Christ suffered and died in our stead, as our substitute. It is, in short, altogether less decided than either the Archbishop or the Wesleyan Catechism,—as if its writers had been especially careful to keep close to the phraseology of Scripture, and commit themselves to no idea which had not at least an apparent sanction in its statements. But, nevertheless, it may safely be assumed that the doctrine intended by this " Declaration," and now widely or generally received in the denomination, is little different from that contained in the previous quotations on this subject. If, indeed, the vaguer statement just given be interpreted by the doctrinal Schedule annexed to the model Trust-deed of the Independents, there can be no question as to what is meant. That schedule speaks plainly of "the fall and depravity of man;" of Christ's "sacrificial death for the sins of mankind;" and of " everlasting punishment."

Finally in this enumeration, may be mentioned the two Articles of the Church of England in which the effect of the death of Christ is more particularly spoken of. To these it may be supposed that some importance is still attached by many—how much, or how little, it would be presumptuous here to attempt to define. Article II. declares, in reference to Christ, that he "truly suffered, was crucified, dead and buried, to reconcile his Father to us, and to be a sacrifice, not only for original guilt, but also for actual sins of men." Article XXXI. runs thus: "The offering of Christ once made is that perfect redemption, propitiation, and satisfaction for all the sins of the whole world, both original and actual; and there is none other satisfaction for sin, but that alone."

It is not necessary for our present purpose, to notice in any way the sense in which the various expressions of these Articles are either admitted or denied by different persons. It is enough to lay them before the reader in their plain and obvious signification. So taken, it would seem that there can be little question as to the fact of a doctrine of substitution and propitiation being held in a very definite form—or if not held, at least professed—by a considerable and important section of English people at the present time, as it undoubtedly was by the generation from which the Thirty-nine Articles have come down to us.

In whatever form the popular doctrine may be stated or professed, we suppose it would, by very many of those who hold it, be thought but a light consideration to urge in reference to it, that it is out of harmony with the dictates of reason, and with that natural sense of right which the Creator Himself has given to be the guide of man in the ordinary affairs of human life.*
Such persons may say, and have said, that human reason is only depraved, and unfit to be the judge of any question of right or wrong in the dealings of God. But surely, on the other hand, if what is believed to be Divine revelation is to have weight and influence among men, it is of very great importance that its principal teachings shall not appear to be in opposition to man's cultivated sense of right, or to the usual promptings of his rational nature. In the interest, therefore, of Christianity itself, it may be well to ask respecting the doctrine now under notice, whether it is really a part of Christianity; and if it should appear to be so, then a further question will remain, and will press for an answer: Is it possible, is it right, that the cultivated reason and conscience of man should submit to an unjust or irrational doctrine? Our spiritual faculties are as much the Creator's gift as any written revelation can be, and we are

* A popular author, a Congregationalist minister, thus wonderfully writes—"With regard, first of all, to natural reason, it may be enough to remind ourselves that the whole history of Jesus Christ removes itself as far as possible from the court in which natural reason presides." Dr. Joseph Parker's *Ecce Deus*, Chapter XVI., "On the Cross of Christ," p. 268.

evidently called upon to render obedience and honour to *them*, as much as we can be to receive any truth or doctrine whatsoever, handed down to us from old times in a written form of words. Hence the question just suggested returns upon us with redoubled force, and in various forms: Is the doctrine of substitution and redemption expressed in the above cited passages really, in its different particulars, in accordance with the sentiments of reason and justice on which men usually act in their ordinary conduct? Can it be right to inflict upon man an everlasting and infinitely terrible punishment for the sins of a short lifetime? Can it be right to inflict the equivalent of such a punishment upon an innocent Christ for the guilt of others, even with his own consent? But indeed, in this case, it can scarcely be said to have been inflicted with his own consent; for we are told how he prayed and said, "If it be possible, let this cup pass from me," although it is true he immediately added the words, "not as I will, but as thou wilt"—a consent certainly, but one of submission and resignation, rather than of willing or eager acceptance, as required by the creeds. If, again, it may be asked, a human father were to send his innocent son to be crucified, in order that a band of evil-doers might escape, would this be felt to be a righteous deed on the part of the father? And is God less just than man? "Shall not the Judge of all the earth do right?" If the father, as an earthly sovereign, wished to pardon the criminals, to be merciful to them and let them escape punishment, would it not be more gracious and merciful, as at the same time more just, to pardon them at once; without exacting punishment from an innocent substitute? How, again, does it vindicate or "magnify" the Divine law to let the guilty escape, and put their punishment on another who has done no sin? Does not this really make God indifferent to justice? For, provided the punishment falls somewhere, it would appear that he does not care who it is that suffers. And can that be right in God, the Heavenly Father, which would be so fearfully wrong in man, in any human father, in any earthly sovereign? Or can that really "reconcile the Father to us," which, as between two human beings, could only tend to greater bitterness, distrust and alienation? Moreover, if such be really the Divine proceeding and idea of right, how can man feel assured that some terrible punishment for his sins shall not hereafter still fall upon him? May not a Being who can punish the innocent instead of the guilty, be thought likely, on second thoughts, to punish the guilty nevertheless, according to their just deserts?

That the last inquiry is perfectly apposite, appears from a remarkable passage in the Archbishop's Essay,* in which he explains how Christ bore the curse for us. "The curse under which man labours" shews itself, we are told, "in his social relations, in his relation to nature, and in his relation to God;" and then the writer goes on to speak of some of the inconveniences and miseries of human life, the evil habits, the weakness, and the sins of men, in which the curse is exemplified. He proceeds to explain how Christ partook of these. He was poor; his life was spent among "lepers and lunatics," with men afflicted and possessed. After a career, in which "all the sufferings of our social state . . . . . . were brought around Him," he was betrayed by a disciple, and crucified, while "His disciples fled in terror from His side." "He shared our curse in tasting the bitterness of death." There is more to the same effect, upon which we refrain from entering; but we venture to add the expression of our surprise that the Archbishop should have failed to note that if Christ thus indeed *bore* "the curse" and "the wrath of God" for us, he has yet by no means released the human race from the enumerated evils. Do they not all press

* *Aids to Faith*, . 357, *seq.*

upon our lot, much as before? Social suffering, selfishness, indolence, passion, the bitterness of death, the fear of death, manifold wickedness and sin,—these, alas! are all here in our human life, just as of old. How then has Christ *borne* them in "our stead," or redeemed us from them, or, by taking them from us, changed the earthly state into a heavenly paradise? No such effects have followed, and so far as this world is concerned, it is evident that they are non-existent, the merest dreams of theological system-makers.

Shall we, then, say that the Almighty Ruler *has* changed His mind?—and even though it be that Christ bore our punishment, "the just for the unjust," that the Incomprehensible One, nevertheless, still inflicts upon men the dread consequences of their sins?

The only refuge from this alternative is evidently in the proposition, that the whole efficacy of the Atonement belongs to the *next world*, for truly it is little to be traced in this. It is from eternal misery that man is saved by the sacrifice of Christ,—if from anything at all. The Archbishop, however, does not tell us, as theologians of a former generation would have done, that suffering equivalent to the eternal misery of the whole human race was inflicted upon Jesus Christ; that he was made a curse for us, and bore our sins, in that unspeakably fearful sense. This he does not say, and his reticence is not to be wondered at. But nevertheless, even this, and nothing else, is what a consistent development of his theory required him to say. For, if Christ has not borne the *future* punishment of sin due to a guilty world, and so redeemed man from bearing it, what else is it that he has done or suffered "in our stead"? In what other way has he, as our substitute, released or shielded us from "the wrath of God"? *

---

* The old reformers were less scrupulous than the Archbishop. Flavel says, "To

But such inquiries as these have been often made. Natural or unavoidable as to some minds they may be, to many others they will appear as the mere dictates of carnal and "unsanctified" reason. They will be deemed, therefore, wholly superfluous and uncalled for, as well as inconsistent with the reverence due, whether to Holy Scripture or the teaching of "the Church." The one question with the numerous religionists of this class will be simply this—What is the doctrine of the New Testament respecting the death of Christ, and its connection with the forgiveness of sin? Let, therefore, even this be now the great question to be here considered.

And let us begin with a remark which might be expected to surprise those who are accustomed only to the ordinary Evangelical teaching. When the New Testament is carefully read, with a view to learning what it says on this subject, we nowhere find it *stating* that men are under the wrath and curse of God, in consequence of the transgression of the first pair. We *nowhere* find it stating that Jesus Christ "suffered, was crucified, dead and buried, to *reconcile his Father to us*, and to be a sacrifice not only for original guilt, but also for actual sins of men." Such we have indeed seen, is the proposition of the Second Article of the English Church; and such, we know, was the belief of that darker age of English history, the sixteenth century, in which that Article was drawn up; but it cannot be found, nor anything really like it, in the New Testament.* Nor is it there declared

---

wrath, to the wrath of an infinite God without mixture, to the very torments of hell, was Christ delivered, and that by the hand of his own Father." (Quoted in *Six Lectures on the Atonement*, by R. L. Carpenter, B.A., 1860.) So, without any hesitation and with fearless consistency, Luther, Calvin, Beza and others, in various and dreadful terms. The late Bishop Jeune tells us that the worst suffering which Christ had to bear occurred when "he had fallen into his Father's hands"! Sermon on the Death of Christ, 1864.

* Comp. 2 Cor. v. 18-20. It is clear that the "reconciliation" (atonement) of St. Paul is that of *man to God*, and not the reverse.

that Jesus Christ, being God as well as man, was therefore able to bear the infinite amount of suffering required to "satisfy" the claims of Divine justice, to "appease" the wrath of the Almighty Father against the human race, on account of inherited or actual sins; or that he suffered, "the just for the unjust," the innocent for the guilty, in order to redeem the world from hell-fire. Nothing of this kind, no ideas of this kind, can be found in the Christian teachings, as they lie before us in the New Testament. Such ideas are but the human theory, devised by speculative theologians to explain and harmonize certain expressions which, though many persons still think they are only to be interpreted in that way, are, nevertheless, capable of an interpretation far more simple and rational, as well as infinitely more in harmony with the Christian idea of God, the Heavenly Father.

What has just been said, as to the absence from the New Testament of some of the most essential ideas involved in the popular doctrine of Atonement, has been very effectively set forth in recent years by a certain portion of the national clergy, some of whom have spoken out on the subject with a freedom and clearness of language which it has been pleasant to see. These writers tell us very explicitly, that there can be nothing meritorious in mere suffering; that punishment, in the form of physical or mental agony, cannot be thought peculiarly acceptable to God. The sufferings and death of Christ are not, therefore, to be regarded as that which pleased or satisfied the all-merciful Father; nor did the Saviour, in short, suffer and die (as the Article says) "to reconcile his Father to us." It was not *this* which constituted the propitiatory efficacy of the atonement by Christ, but rather his voluntary obedience and humiliation, his perfect submission even unto death, his renunciation of his own and acceptance of his Father's will. This moral element it was, which made his death an acceptable sacrifice, and upon this the

Almighty Father looked down with grace and satisfaction. "In the whole of the two Testaments (we are told) there is not a single passage which states unambiguously the doctrine, that Christ received at God's hands the punishment decreed to our sins, and thus enabled God to forgive us."*

These representations are no doubt, in substance, perfectly correct. Yet they are by no means so new as to many persons they might appear. Similar enunciations of the Christian teaching, and similar protests against the popular doctrine, have long been familiar in certain quarters; among those, however, who have not had the advantage of speaking from the national pulpits,—who, indeed, have usually been looked upon as the merest heretics, if deemed to be within the pale of Christianity at all. In illustration of these statements, the publications mentioned in the note below are referred to,† and from the last of them the following passage is offered to the reader's consideration:

"It is nowhere declared that the death of Christ . . . . . . enabled God to forgive; that God could not forgive sins without a satisfaction by the vicarious punishment of an innocent person. It is nowhere declared that the sufferings of Christ were a punishment at all. . . . . . . It is nowhere declared that the death of Christ appeased the wrath of God, rendered Him propitious, made Him merciful, or disposed Him to forgive."

Thus it is plain that the theory now referred to, in its more

---

* *The Work of Christ*, by the Rev. J. Llewellyn Davies, M.A., Pref., p. xxv. See also Garden on the Atonement, in *Tracts for Priests and People*, No. III. (1861), and comp. a *Sermon* preached in York Minster (1868) by the Rev. Canon Robinson. From this (p. 8) we take the following: "No, the essence of the sacrifice of our Lord lies in the life-long surrender of His will to God, in the way in which the whole current of His being set towards His Father, in that absolute and unwearied obedience of which His death was but the consummation and the crown."

† *The Sacrifice of Christ*, by the Rev. Edward Higginson (1833); *The Scheme of Vicarious Redemption inconsistent with itself*, by the Rev. James Martineau (1839); *The Scripture Doctrine of Redemption*, a Tract, from the pen of the late Dr. Lant Carpenter (1837).

material negative positions, is new only as regards the quarter from whence it proceeds. That part of it, moreover, which may appear to have somewhat of novelty, will be found to afford no adequate key to the numerous passages of the New Testament in which the death of Christ is spoken of. It does not give any real solution of the difficulties of the case; although, as may be readily admitted, it has much the advantage of the more popular scheme represented by the Archbishop, in being at least rational, and not out of harmony with the higher Christian conceptions of the character of God. The two modes of explanation appear, however, to be about equally far from being based, as they ought to be, upon the historical circumstances of the primitive Christian times. Their respective expounders are also equally open to the objection of bringing a theory to Scripture, and putting it into Scripture expressions, rather than gathering the meaning of these by any legitimate process of interpretation.

The essence of the atonement, we are told by the class of writers now more particularly in view, lay in the satisfaction, complacency, delight, with which the Divine Being saw the beloved Son give up his own will to the will of his Heavenly Father. By this it was that He was propitiated; and Christ offered himself as a sacrifice and propitiation in this sense alone. If this be true, is it not an obvious remark that the Divine Being was very easily satisfied, and allowed his guilty creatures to escape on very easy terms? And further, how does this explain for us the various expressions of the New Testament?—as when, for instance, we read of the Ephesians, "Now in Christ Jesus ye who some time were afar off, are made nigh by the blood of Christ: for he is our peace, who hath made both one, and hath broken down the middle wall of partition . . . . . . and that he might reconcile both unto God in one body by the cross, having slain the enmity thereby;"—or when Peter writes, "Who his own self bare our sins in his own body on the tree . . . . . . by whose stripes ye were healed;"—or when John writes, that God "sent his Son to be the propitiation for our sins."* It is impossible to see how any adequate or reasonable interpretation of such language as this is given by the doctrine that the atoning work of Christ consisted simply in the perfect surrender of his own will to that of God; even though it be added to such statements that Christ was "the head and root of all mankind," and that therefore "mankind now stand accepted before God, and every sharer in the kind (*sic*) may plead and occupy the righteous position which has been won for it by the accepted sacrifice of its great representative."†

This theory, then, may be said to fail by defect, as that of the Archbishop, in common with the popular beliefs, by excess. And, indeed, it is only fair to note that the writers referred to themselves express their strong sense of the difficulty of explanation, and of the obscurity or mystery of the whole subject. "In a matter like this," observes Mr. Garden, "we have still much to learn." The same author quotes with approval the words of Bishop Butler, "How and in what particular way it (Christ's sacrifice) had this efficacy, there are not wanting persons who have endeavoured to explain; *but I do not find that the Scripture has explained it;*" and for himself he remarks, on another page, "Our Lord's redemptive act is indeed deeply mysterious." In similar terms the Archbishop speaks of "this mysterious transaction;" and the same epithet, "these mysteries," is used by Mr. Llewellyn Davies.‡ Thus it really appears as if the repeated discussions of these eminent and learned writers do not avail to clear away the obscurity in which the whole subject is evidently to their minds involved.

* Ephes. ii. 13-16; 1 Peter ii. 24; 1 John iv. 9.
† Garden on the Atonement, *Tracts for Priests and People*, III. p. 18.
‡ *Ibid.* XIII. p. 72; Davies, *ibid.* p. 51; *Aids to Faith*, p. 337.

We take the liberty of suggesting that this unsatisfactory result really arises from a very simple cause—the neglect of those historical considerations to which we have just alluded. It cannot be expected that any one should succeed in obtaining from the Epistles the meaning of their varied expressions respecting Christ's death, while he passes over and takes no notice of the circumstances, the feelings, the prejudices, of the early Christian times, in which those expressions have their original force and application. Writers on this question, as we presume to think, involve themselves and their subject in helpless perplexity, simply from not observing the conditions on which alone it can be profitably discussed. Starting from some received doctrine of this nineteenth century, applying some already constructed theory to the ancient language of the Christian books, and seeking to obtain from these a meaning in harmony with their several preconceptions, no wonder that they differ from each other, and fail to find any common ground on which to stand together; one, at times accusing another even of teaching "heathenism in its most terrible form."[*] No such common ground is obtainable, except by a careful consideration of the particular state of belief and feeling among Jews and Judaizing Christians, in connection with which the expressions in question are first used. If such consideration be duly given, preconceived ideas being put away, whether it be the crude speculations of various early Fathers, the legal phraseology of an Anselm, or the "masterly dissertation"[†] of an eloquent theorizer like Coleridge, to say nothing of the different established formularies of modern churches—this question of the atonement, or reconciliation, by the death of Christ will probably prove no more a "mystery" or "a mysterious transaction," than any other historical question arising within the limits of the New Testament.

[*] Words of the Rev. Newman Hall, quoted in *Garden*, Tract XIII. p. 5.
[†] *Ibid.* III. p. 11.

CHAPTER XXVI.

THE DEATH OF CHRIST—ITS PURPOSE AND EFFECT AS SET FORTH IN THE NEW TESTAMENT.

It would seem to be going back to the merest elements of Biblical learning to speak of the necessity of interpreting the Apostolical writings by the light of contemporary circumstances, so far as these are historically known to us. This point may, therefore, be dismissed with the citation of a few words from two eminent writers of very different ways of thinking in theology, whose authority, nevertheless, on such a subject no one will think of calling in question. "Illustrate" (says Bishop Ellicott) "wherever possible, by reference to history, topography and antiquities;" and the same author sums up the four rules of interpretation which he gives under this " one general canon;"— " Interpret grammatically, historically, contextually and minutely." Still more, perhaps, to our purpose are the following words of Professor Jowett: "Of what has been said this is the sum;— That Scripture, like other books, has one meaning, which is to be gathered from itself, without reference to the adaptations of Fathers or Divines; and without regard to *à priori* notions about its nature and origin. It is to be interpreted like other books, with attention to the character of its authors, and the prevailing state of civilization and knowledge, with allowance for peculiarities of style and language, and modes of thought and figures of speech."*

Following, then, the guidance of these undeniable rules, we have now to proceed to the inquiry, why it is that the death of Christ is so much dwelt upon in the New Testament, and what is the connection between that event and the forgiveness of sin; or,

---

* Ellicott in *Aids to Faith*, pp. 430-439 (4th ed.); Jowett in *Essays and Reviews*, p. 404 (6th ed.).

to put these two questions together, in what way the world is or was redeemed by the "blood of Christ."

In the first place, then, it was not expected by the Jews, or the first Christian disciples, that the Messiah would die at all. We may recall the statement in the fourth Gospel: "The people answered him, We have heard out of the law that the Christ abideth for ever: and how sayest thou the Son of man must be lifted up?" If this may be relied upon as shewing the belief of the contemporaries of Jesus, it is evident what was the popular idea. And so, when Christ spoke to his disciples of his going up to Jerusalem, and said that he should there be crucified and put to death, we are told, "they understood none of these things."* Various other evidences occur to the same effect, shewing us that the early disciples did not expect that their Master would die as he did; nor understand why he died, until their eyes were opened by the course of events.

In the second place, however, they learnt, in due time, why and how it was, by the teaching of events and circumstances. They were brought to see that Jesus died in his mortal body in order that he might be raised again, and, "ascending up on high," might become the spiritual "Head over all things to the church;" that he might become the spiritual Christ, "a Prince and a Saviour, to give repentance to Israel and forgiveness of sins;"† and this not only to Israel, but to all the world besides. He was by birth a Jew, "under the law," and necessarily subject to the same restraints in regard to intercourse with the sinful heathen which were conceived to affect all others of Jewish race. None, therefore, of the outcast nations could be disciples of Christ as the Jewish Messiah, and the limitation appears to have been recognised by our Lord himself during his personal ministry.

* John xii. 34; Matt. xvi. 21, 22; Luke xviii. 31-34.
† Ephes. iv. 8; i. 20-22; Acts v. 31.

"I am not sent," he said, "but to the lost sheep of the house of Israel."* The same thing is recognised in connection with the centurion Cornelius, who, though "a just man and one that feared God," was yet ritually "unclean," and not, it was thought, admissible as a Christian disciple, without previously adopting Judaism. Even a Peter could say to him and others, "Ye know that it is an unlawful thing for a man that is a Jew to keep company, or come unto one of another nation;" but God had shewed him (he added) that he must rise above this prejudice.

found it difficult, nevertheless, to do so, as we may see in what took place between him and Paul at a later period. But in this "he was to be blamed," and the Apostle of the Gentiles "withstood him to his face."† Thus, it is evident, all who were not Jews, were looked upon by the latter, and by Judaizing Christians, as "aliens from the commonwealth of Israel," and as "strangers" who had no part in those "covenants of promise" which God had given to His chosen people. They could not, therefore, in that their state "by nature," be disciples of a Hebrew Messiah.‡

It is easy in these days to see that all this was, to a large extent, mere prejudice. But, like many another prejudice, it was very powerful. And it was founded upon ancient laws, and privileges enjoyed for centuries past by the chosen race. So they believed. We can see, too, that if such ideas had prevailed, they would simply have restricted Christianity to persons of Jewish birth. In other words, they would have led in a short time to the perversion, and ultimately to the extinction, of the new religion.

In time, however, the disciples began to understand, that when

---

* Matt. xv. 24. † Acts x.; Gal. ii.
‡ Ephes. ii.; comp. Acts xv., where the strength and importance of the feeling in reference to the Gentiles are clearly exhibited.

his own people rejected the Messiah, and put him to death, a great change had necessarily ensued in his relations towards both Jews and Gentiles. Being dead to the world, and ascended to his heavenly throne, he was no longer a mortal man, a Jew under the law of his people. St. Paul alludes to this result in several expressions: "Know ye not, brethren (for I speak to them that know the law), how that the law hath dominion over a man so long as he liveth?" So writes the Apostle, and he goes on to shew, in his own manner, how one that is dead is released from the law, just as a wife, who had been bound to her husband, is freed from similar restraints by his death. In a previous passage he speaks of those who are "baptized into Jesus Christ" as being "baptized into his death;" as partaking, therefore, of his death, and being "dead with Christ."* Christ's death had thus, to the Apostle's mind, a twofold operation. It released him from the law, and it released *others* too, who by baptism into his name partook of his death, from the same control, and from any concern for it, so that they might live now, not to the law, but "in newness of spirit," and "unto God."

Hence, then, by his death, Jesus the Christ was taken away and made free from the restraints imposed by his birth as a Hebrew. Whatever rendered him, as the Jewish Messiah, the exclusive property of a single people, and virtually disqualified the rest of the world from discipleship to him, all this, by his death, ceased to affect him and them. He rose to heaven, a glorified, spiritual being, and there he is now, says the Apostle, "far above all principality, and power, and might, and dominion." Such was the mystery of "a crucified Christ;" "the mystery which had been hid from ages and from generations." The risen and exalted Saviour now reigns over all men alike, accessible, not by Jewish rites of circumcision or other ritualistic works, "vain and beggarly

---

* Rom. vi. 1–14; vii. 1–6. Comp. Coloss. ii. 20.

elements" as these are, but by simple faith.* Jew and Gentile are henceforward alike to him. "There is no difference" in God's sight or in Christ's. If they will only receive the Messiah by a true faith in him,—joining with it the practical obedience which it necessarily implied,—such faith will admit them to be his disciples. God will freely forgive past sins of disqualification to all, the Apostle writes, for that faith of theirs in the risen Christ.†

Such, then, was the change of relations between the Christ and the world which came to pass in and through his death. It has sometimes been said, that without the atonement for sin made by Christ (in the popular and so-called "evangelical" sense), there was no need to lay so much stress on *his* death. The death of Peter or of Paul would have been equally important to the Christian world, might have been equally spoken of, and have done just as well.‡ The remark is obviously void of force. Neither Peter nor Paul was the Christ. The cross of these apostles, eminent as they were, would have had no more significance or effect than the cross of any ordinary man. The "cross of Christ" was a totally different thing, even because this was the medium through which the Messiah was made a spiritual being, and a legitimate access to him was given to the otherwise outcast and ritually unclean heathen peoples.

Let it now be observed how intense was the feeling of the Jews in reference to their own righteousness and the sinfulness of the Gentiles: "Sinners of the Gentiles;" "dead in trespasses and sins;" "by nature children of wrath;" such are the phrases in which this feeling is expressed. But the Apostle, who thus speaks of Gentiles, could not, on the other hand, admit the

---

* Ephes. i. 9-23; Col. i. 17-27; 1 Cor. i. 23-30; Gal. iii. 24-29; iv. 9, 10.

† Rom. iii. ; viii. 34; x. 9; and comp. *supra*, Chapter XVIII.

‡ See the *Sermon* by the late Bishop Jeune, "Was Paul crucified for you?" 1863. Comp. Liddon, B. L., p. 476.

righteousness of his own people. The latter had, indeed, the adoption, the covenants, the law, the service of God, the promises, the fathers, and of them the Christ came. But, nevertheless, they too were "under sin," as much as the Gentiles. "By the deeds of the law there shall no flesh be justified" in God's sight, "for by the law is the knowledge of sin." But a merciful God had opened out a new way of justification, and all who would accept Jesus as His beloved Son, as the anointed Christ, might be admitted to discipleship, becoming "children of God by faith in Christ Jesus."

This, however, He, the All-merciful, did and allowed "freely, by His grace." It was in no way purchased of Him or of His justice. It was not because His "wrath" was appeased, or satisfied by the sufferings of an innocent substitute, but because of His own essential fatherly goodness and "great love." "It is the *gift* of God," not a thing bought from Him with any price,* except in so far as this might be figuratively said,† in reference to that death of the Messiah through which he and his disciples, for all time to come, had been released from the claims of the Law. Nothing in all the New Testament is clearer than the doctrine of the free and unbought character of the Christian redemption, as on the side of God. It can only be the strongest exigencies of theological system which have prevented the Christian world from seeing so plain a truth—the central truth, in fact, of the "glad tidings." ‡

The disqualification, therefore, caused to both Jew and Gentile by their own sins, whether ritual or moral, a merciful God deter-

* Rom. iii. 9, 20, 24, 25 ; Ephes. ii. 4, 8.   † 1 Cor. vi. 20 ; vii. 23.

‡ In confirmation of these statements may be noted the fact, that the common orthodox expression, "for Christ's sake,"—an expression continually used, both in prayers and in graces before and after meat—is never found in the N. T. God is nowhere there represented as doing anything "for Christ's sake." The one instance (Ephes. iv. 32) in which the expression is found, is a well-known mistranslation ; the words really being, "even as God *in Christ* hath forgiven you."

T

mined of His own free grace to overlook; giving to sinful men, on condition of their faith in the risen Christ, a justification which at once qualified them for discipleship. The barrier of the Law, which would have kept Jew and Gentile apart, was broken down by Christ's death, "the enmity" abolished. And this was so, and could be so, as we have seen, only by the death of the Messiah. Thus, then, he died *for* them; for Gentiles as well as Jews; he died for *all*. The death of the Christ operated as much for the Jew as for the despised and outcast heathen. The former had no claim, of right, to an exclusive possession of the Messiah, for he was equally concluded under sin. But the Messiah's death was for *his* benefit also, inasmuch as it necessarily abolished, for one that was dead, the dominion of the law, and made it possible even for those who had broken the law, or who had been without the law, to become Christian disciples.

It may now be seen, without further exposition, in what sense Christ died for others, "the just for the unjust;" how he died, in fact, not only ὑπὲρ ἡμῶν, but even ἀντὶ πολλῶν.* He died for their benefit, and he may be said to have died even in their *stead*, though not in the usually received sense. For his death, admitting men to a new "justification" by faith in him risen, may easily be conceived of as saving them from the penalty due to their unrighteousness. In strict justice, they ought to have suffered; but God was merciful, and allowed His Son to suffer instead— not in order to bear their punishment, but simply to open a new way of admission for them.† The Scripture, however, as noted below, usually speaks of Christ as dying ὑπερ, not ἀντὶ; and it is equally clear that it was not in their stead—as their substitute—

---

* There is only a single instance in which ἀντὶ is used in connection with the death of Christ, Matt. xx. 28 (parallel with Mark x. 45). In this instance the sense of *substitution* is not at all needed. The word may be used exactly as in Matt. xvii. 27: "Give unto them *for* (ἀντὶ) me and thee."

† Rom. iii. 21-25.

that he died for men; not to redeem them from eternal misery; not (as Archbishop Thomson would affirm) because the clouds of God's wrath had gathered thick over the human race, and required a victim, and could find that victim only in the innocent Jesus. It was simply that all men, of every nation, might be admissible, by a new way of justification, to the fold of the spiritual Christ, even though *they* were " sinners," and even though *he* were the Jewish Messiah, born " under the law."

Readers who are accustomed to the ordinary doctrine of atonement, with all its affluence of mystery, suffering, and prospects of damnation for the whole human race, will naturally be shocked at the simplicity of the above exposition, and find it fatally deficient, by comparison with the stronger food on which they have hitherto been living. Objectors and objections of this kind are easily met with. But this is evidently not the great consideration. The question, after all, is this, What is the truth? Is the exposition proposed sufficient to account for the Scriptural phraseology? Is it the more in accordance with historical circumstances? Is it the more in harmony with the Christian idea of a just and merciful God? These are very weighty considerations, and the reader ought to ponder them well before he rejects the simpler doctrine. And, let him remember, it affords little reason against the latter, that it may not at first be quite agreeable to his taste; for is he sure that this may not have been vitiated by the stimulating and artificial diet to which he has grown accustomed?

The effect of the death of Christ, above spoken of, though, as might be expected, nowhere described in formal or express terms, is yet alluded to in a great variety of language, partly literal, partly figurative. Everything which the ancient sacrifices were supposed to do, in connection with the pardon of sin, is naturally said to result equally from the death of the Messiah, and a great deal more. Those sacrifices were effectual only for Jews; but

Christ's death is so for all the world. He is "the Lamb of God which taketh away the sin of the world." "He who knew no sin was made sin for us,"—condemned, or treated as one guilty, for us. He "was made a curse for us," for the law declared that every one hanged on a tree, as he was, is accursed. He "his own self bare our sins in his own body on the tree, that we, being dead to sins, should live unto righteousness; by whose stripes ye were healed." This is said, it will now be manifest, not of a substitutionary punishment of sin inflicted on the innocent Christ, and not of any expiation of sin wrought in God's sight by his death, but of the admission, or admissibility, of all men by faith to be his disciples, notwithstanding the sins, ritual and moral, which, had he remained alive and under the law, would necessarily have prevented the access of Gentiles to him. His death opened the way of release from that kind of disqualification. Hence, by an easy metaphor, he "bare" the remitted sins "on the tree." It was, in short, the sins of others which made it necessary for him to die, if those who were guilty of them were to be his disciples. Those who were thus released might now, without care for the condemnation of the law, "live unto righteousness;" they were "healed" by his "stripes," whatever might be alleged to the contrary by the Law and its bigoted adherents. So again, "He is our peace," and "Ye who sometime were afar off are made nigh by the blood of Christ." He is "a propitiation," "set forth in his blood," and "through our Lord Jesus Christ" . . . . . . "we have now received the atonement,"—reconciliation to God.*

In some of these passages, Gentiles only are referred to, and language is used which is applicable only to them—persons, as they were, who had been living out of the dominion of the law, not only ritually condemned, but in the midst of positive "tres-

---

* John i. 29 ; 2 Cor. v. 21 ; Gal. iii. 13 ; 1 Pet. ii. 24 ; Ephes. ii. 13, 14 ; Rom. i. 25 ; v. 11.

passes and sins." But "all" men by faith in the risen Christ might have admission to the privileges of the Gospel, and receive the forgiveness of "sins that are past."

Thus, too, dying as he did for sinful men, he was in a certain sense a *sacrifice* for them, and for their sins. It is evident, however, that he was so in no literal way, for Christ was not offered up as a victim on the altar by the hand of a priest, but crucified by Roman soldiers. Hence the word *sacrifice*, which in connection with Christ's death is of rare occurrence in the New Testament,* can only be figuratively used. The question is, what literal fact does such a metaphor veil or convey? There is absolutely nothing in the Christian teaching to justify the supposition that the Heavenly Father needed *propitiating* by a sacrificed victim, and that victim the Christ in whom He was well pleased. There is nothing to tell us that the sacrifice of Christ was offered "to reconcile his Father to us," or that he might suffer a *punishment*, whether for "original guilt," or for "actual sins of men." An idea of this kind, in reference to heathen gods, may easily be found in the Iliad, or in Herodotus, or in a Greek play; but, orthodox as it may be with many, it will not really be found in the New Testament, either as an expressly described and enjoined truth, or as one of inference, reasonably deducible from a fair consideration of the various circumstances of the case. What may be learnt is simply this, that Christ's death was a sacrifice for sin, because it was required for the admission of sinful men to the privilege of being his disciples in spite of the Law which excluded them, so long as he was in life. It is unnecessary to add that Christ's sacrifice did not consist merely in the surrender of his own will to the will of God, although unquestionably this was included, and was freely given.

It may be well to apply the interpreting idea now before us to

* Ephes. v. 2; comp. 1 Cor. v. 7; Heb. ix. 26; vii. 27; x. 12.

one or two of the more remarkable expressions of the New Testament relating to this subject. Paul writes respecting Christ, that it is he "whom God hath set forth *to be* a propitiation through faith, by his blood"—that is, "by his death."* In this place, the word "propitiation" is a little uncertain. It is, for one thing, too abstract after the preceding verb "set forth," which requires a concrete object. The original word ἱλαστήριον is used in the Septuagint to denote the *mercy-seat*,—the lid or cover of the ark, on which the high-priest sprinkled the blood of an appointed victim, in expiation of sin, on the great day of atonement.† The same word is used once in the New Testament (Heb. ix. 5) in the same signification. Hence it is by no means impossible that the Apostle may here designate Christ as the "mercy-seat," set forth in his death, and sprinkled with his own blood, for the remission of sin. But if so, the representation is clearly figurative only, and must involve the same literal meaning as before pointed out. It is more probable, however, from the general analogy of related expressions, that the rendering of ἱλαστήριον should here be "propitiatory offering," or "propitiatory sacrifice;" but still, as before, we have to ask for the literal fact intended by this figurative phrase. That fact is, simply, what has been so often stated, namely, that the Messiah by his death, by shedding his blood, ceased to be under the Law, became a spiritual being, and was thus enabled to receive all men as disciples, by faith, their sins notwithstanding. In other words, and figuratively speaking, their faith in him may be said to have constituted him a sacrifice of propitiation for them; or again, he, by dying, nullified the effect of the Law in excluding them from discipleship on account of their sins. Their sins are thus virtually forgiven through his death,—a result similar to that which the ancient sacrifices were conceived to work under the Law of Moses. Hence the possi-

---

* Rom. iii. 25; comp. *supra*, p. 254, note. † Lev. xvi. 13, *seq.*

bility and the propriety of applying to the death of the Christ the sacrificial language so familiar to the Jews under the older dispensation.

A similar explanation holds in regard to another of the most remarkable expressions of St. Paul. "Christ our Passover," he writes, "is sacrificed for us." The rendering should rather be "killed for us,"*—the Passover not being a sacrifice. It was a lamb which was killed and *eaten*, but there is nothing to shew that any expiatory efficacy was connected with it. We thus see that in one place Christ is a "sacrifice;" in another, he is a "Passover;" while in others, again, he is both sacrifice and "high-priest" at once.† But is it not equally plain that all this is pure *metaphor*? He might, however, be very fitly likened in his death to the Passover lamb, inasmuch as that event was a pledge and emblem of deliverance from the bondage of sin and the law, as well as from the state of exclusion from the Messiah's kingdom necessarily attaching to Gentiles,—a deliverance similar to that effected in the olden times from Egyptian oppression, and so carefully commemorated by the literal Passover ceremony.

There is no passage in short, relating to this subject, which may not be adequately explained by a reference to the peculiar ideas and circumstances so often noticed.‡ It was perfectly natural and inevitable that the New Testament writers, familiar as they were with the sacrificial usages of their nation, should speak of their Master's death, the Messiah's death, and the effects which resulted from it, in phrases and figures drawn from those usages. The error of our time is in taking so many of the expressions referred to in a literal sense; in allowing so little for Jewish forms of thought and feeling; and, above all, in over-looking,

---

* 1 Cor. v. 7 ; comp. Mark xiv. 12 ; Luke xxii. 7.   † Heb. ix. 11, and *passim*.
‡ This was long ago pointed out with careful detail by Mr. Martineau, in the masterly lecture before referred to, "The Scheme of Vicarious Redemption inconsistent with itself."

as is so commonly done, the historical considerations which alone can give a true life and meaning to those expressions.

The popular theory, in reality, is largely the product of dark and ignorant ages; coming down in some of its elements from Fathers who held that the redemption secured by Christ was a release from the Devil, and the ransom paid, a recompense to *him*. No wonder, then, that this theory, even as represented by an Archbishop, is utterly misleading, that it involves so much that is unspiritual and difficult to reconcile with the idea of a merciful God, so much that distorts the true meaning of Scripture, and substitutes mere human speculation for Divine truth.

It remains for us, nevertheless, to qualify the foregoing exposition by an admission which may, to some readers, appear scarcely consistent with it. A few passages occur, the sense of which, it may be, is not sufficiently explained or accounted for by the doctrine of Atonement, or reconciliation through the death of Christ, as here set forth. Even readers who do not assent to the popular doctrine may thus think; holding that, after all that can be said, there *is* more or less at any rate of the expiatory idea in some of the expressions, even though many or most of them are adequately interpreted by a due regard to the historical circumstances here appealed to.

In this qualified view of the case there is very probably some degree of truth. The expiatory idea could hardly fail to occur sooner or later to Jewish writers, in connection with an event which operated so plainly, though indirectly, for the remission of sins;—an event by or through which that remission was proclaimed to the world. This idea, in short, may be intended in the Epistle to the Hebrews, and also in a few places in the Book of Revelation, but hardly, except as pure figure, in any other book. If, however, any other New Testament writer held it, so as to regard the death of Jesus Christ as really of the nature of an expiatory sacrifice, in virtue of which, or for the sake of which, God forgave the sins of men,—much as the old Greeks believed that Apollo or Jupiter could be propitiated by a hecatomb, and induced to forgive one that had offended him,—if such an idea were really held by any other New Testament writer, is it not in the Gospel and Epistles of John that it is to be met with? At least such passages as John i. 29, and 1 John ii. 2, and a few more in these writings, may be fairly understood as conveying a real expiatory sense; and it may even have been a part of the Evangelist's conception of Jesus as the Word "made flesh," to attribute a peculiar expiatory efficacy to the death of so important and unique a personage. But, if so, this latter idea must be regarded as necessarily partaking of the essential non-reality of the whole conception.

There are, however, serious difficulties in the way of this admission. For example, the fourth Gospel, in the account of the trial and crucifixion, contains no allusion to the death of Christ as being, in any sense, a "sacrifice" possessed of some occult propitiatory or expiatory efficacy. How is such an omission, in such a subject, and on such an occasion, to be accounted for? The same is true of the other Gospels;—except only, as some may think, in the case of the words of Christ at the Supper.* These, it may be said, indicate his knowledge of the mysterious value of his death. But it is evident from the foregoing exposition, that all that can be safely inferred from the words in question is, that Jesus himself anticipated the effect of his death, not in propitiating God or expiating human sin, but in releasing himself from the Law, and so throwing open the Gospel to all the world. It may well be believed that he did so.

---

* Compare Matt. xx. 28, "Even as the Son of man came .... to give his life a ransom for many." The sense of the latter words is explained by the exposition we have given—Christ by his death secured the admissibility of the Gentile world to discipleship. His life given was thus (as it were) the ransom price paid for their redemption from their outcast state.

However this may be, it may still be reasonably held that, even if the writings of St. John contain the expiatory idea, they can do so only in a kind of ideal, metaphorical sense. Even in their strongest expressions, something of figure must be admitted. Jesus was not literally a "lamb;" not a victim offered upon an altar; nor was his "blood" shed or applied after the manner of the ancient sacrifices, but only drawn, in an accidental way, by the spear of the soldier, as related by the Evangelist. Everywhere there is figure;—in John as in other writers. So that here, again, the true question is, how much, or how little? If, then, the reference to historical circumstances, much as we have made it, supplies an adequate key to the various expressions, and suggests to us the literal truth of fact lying at their basis, it is surely reasonable to accept the interpretation thus afforded—to discard, as it were, the mere figure, or form of words, and penetrate down to the real sense which lies beneath. It is right and necessary, above all things, to guard against taking figurative language in a literal way, and so, in many a case, making the sacred writers speak sheer nonsense.

It is hardly necessary, in conclusion, to call attention to what must be so obvious, namely, that the various expressions of the Christian Scriptures respecting the death of Christ arose out of very special feelings and circumstances of the primitive Christian times. This appears to be one of the most undeniable facts connected with the subject. Those expressions formed, therefore, it is true, an *argumentum ad Judæum* very suitable to St. Paul's time. But their permanent value is unimportant;—except only, of course, that they imply, or set forth in a peculiar way, the essential impartiality and comprehensiveness of the Gospel. There is nothing in the actual or natural relations of God to man, or of man to God, which can make it incumbent upon the modern disciple to return to the forms of thought embodied in such language. Its entire force and propriety belonged to, and are exhausted in connection with, circumstances, feelings, institutions, persons, that have long since passed away from the stage of mortal existence, leaving nothing behind them in which such phraseology can, in our times, have any fitting use or application. Nobody now, however "ritualistic" he may be, will doubt that a man may be a Christian without being "circumcised," or conforming in any other way to the law of Moses.* If there were a great sect among us maintaining this, then we might plead that Christ "died for us;" that he redeemed us from the curse of the law, "being made a curse for us;" that we have redemption "through his blood;" that a new "justification" has been provided for us, admitting to discipleship "without the deeds of the law." But such phrases cannot now be used with any rational force or sense. They belong to the past alone; and the sooner the past is left in quiet possession of them by popular teachers and preachers of every name and degree, the better surely it will be for the credit of Christian learning and the peace of the Church.†

CHAPTER XXVII.

RELATION OF THE BIBLE TO THE REASON AND CONSCIENCE— INSPIRATION—TRUE AUTHORITY OF SCRIPTURE.

That mankind are naturally prone to religion, that their own nature, sooner or later in the course of its development, leads

* It may be a question how far this remark applies to the Congregationalists. At least they appear to find it expedient to announce that "they are justified through faith in Christ," . . . and *not* by "the works of the Law."—It might seem, therefore, that some one among them had been seeking to impose the ancient yoke, as happened to the Galatians of old! (*Dec. of Faith*, xiii.)

† It is proper to mention here that the substance of this and the preceding Chapter appeared as an article in the Theological Review for October, 1869. It is now republished with considerable alterations and additions.

them to think of God, to seek Him, "if haply they might feel after him and find him," is a proposition at least as old in substance as the speech of St. Paul upon Mars' Hill. It is one also which, probably, few thoughtful persons of the present day would care to dispute. Theories of human depravity and incapacity may, indeed, be held by many, and may, in certain quarters stand in the way of its full and cordial admission. But yet the evidence of manifold observation in almost every part of the world, as well as of numberless ages of past history, points uniformly to the one conclusion, and will doubtless prove sufficient in the end to overcome even long-established and widely prevailing doctrines of an opposite import.*

This natural religiousness of man exists in him by virtue of the moral and spiritual capacities which he possesses, stimulated and developed as these are by their contact with the outward universe. From the dawn of his reflective powers he is conscious of frailty and dependence. His own life, he feels, is not altogether within his own control, but has mysteriously come to him, and goes from him again, without any command of his. He sees around him in the world, or believes that he does, numerous marks of a great and marvellous power; while many things in his outward condition, and in the natural phenomena amidst which he lives, are subject to "laws," which indicate the appointment, or the action, of a controlling Will, similar to that which he is conscious of exercising himself. Thus the idea of God, of one God or of many, begins, in its germ, to be formed in his mind; and when, later, he becomes more capable of reasoning and reflecting, he is sure that this creative and controlling Being must

---

* It is scarcely necessary to observe that the above remarks have in view the usual teachings of the popular orthodoxy, rather than the opinions expressed in such works as Sir John Lubbock's *Origin of Civilization*,—while yet they are not advanced without a recollection of the conclusions of that able and learned investigator, and of their bearing upon the great question of the origin and validity of religious belief.

be far superior to himself. That on which he feels himself dependent, to which in the last resort he owes his own spiritual nature, endowed with faculties of intellect, affection, conscience, and other capacities of the most excellent kind,—that great Parent Mind to which he is thus indebted must, at all events, however mysterious and incomprehensible, be something unspeakably higher and better than he is himself.

Thus it appears that the belief in God, which is the central thought of religion, comes to man, in at least its rudimentary forms, by the natural operation of his own moral and spiritual faculties—stimulated, doubtless, and trained by the manifold influences of outward nature. The process of the argument, so far as it is a process of argument at all, may be a sound and valid one or not. With this point we are not now immediately concerned. But, at all events, it is a natural process. It shews us that religion is not a something implanted in us from without, any more than it is dependent for its existence on the Bible, or any other book reputed sacred—as some persons might suppose. In other words, it shews us that the Creator of men has not left Himself without a witness in the hearts of His human creatures, or in that great universe of existences wherein He has assigned them their dwelling-place.

As a matter of fact, however, the religious belief which prevails in the Christian world is not simply a product of the mental faculties of the individual persons who hold it; that is, it has not been formed by the independent working or exercise of their mental powers; but, in a large degree, it has been communicated to them from without, and also transmitted to them historically. One generation has handed down to another, from the most distant times, its belief in God, with its conceptions of His nature and will; and so our religion, we may say, has come into our possession from our immediate forefathers and instructors, as they in their turn had received theirs from those who had gone before them. By this it is not meant that individuals have not employed their minds on religious subjects, or that individual thinkers have not often contributed to the purification or further development of long-descended ideas; but that the substance, so to speak, of religious belief,—that is to say, the idea of God as Creator and Ruler, equally with our recognition of the moral law as His will for us, and of our obligation, as His creatures and servants, to obey it,—has been very largely transmitted from parents to children, and from one generation of men to another.

And when we go back as far as we can in this ascending series, we find that, to all practical intents and purposes, in relation to the present belief of the Christian world, this process of transmission commenced in the Bible; and that, for many ages in the past, religious belief was forming, and has been handed down, in a considerable section of the human race, from and through and under the influence of that Book. The Bible has thus, in effect, been, if not the producer, at least the influential interpreter, of the spiritual instincts of men, giving form and expression to the religious belief now existing throughout what we usually term the Christian world.

How this has come to pass, we may read in the Bible itself. That book, of various and unknown origin as so much of it is, is yet manifestly the Record preserving for us the early history of religious knowledge; shewing us how this was gradually strengthened and purified among a particular people, and how from them it has come forth and been proclaimed among the nations, and so been preserved and made a light and a help for our later times.

Thus it cannot be denied by any Christian man, that the true religious life of the world commences in, or perhaps with, the

Hebrew nation. This is not a theory of any kind, but a manifest fact of history. Of this the Bible is itself both the record and the witness. And, indeed, every existing congregation of Christian worshipers is a visible testimony to the same effect; for they meet to worship the same God whom Abraham and the patriarchs worshiped, the God whom Moses, Samuel and Isaiah and all the prophets worshiped, even, "the God and Father of Jesus Christ."*

It is unquestionably a long and a striking "succession"—and not only "apostolical," but prophetical and patriarchal as well. The religious influence of all these ancient, earnest, devout men is preserved for us in the Bible, and is exercised, we may also say, through that book. In stating this fact, we have, however, to recall another fact, which is of equal importance as shewing us the true character of the Bible. It is, that the Book manifestly offers itself to *us*, the people of these later times, virtually as a book of History. It never professes or claims to be anything different; never, in truth, makes any profession or claim at all on the point; but stands before us there, simply as it is, essentially a book belonging to the past history of a particular people.

To a considerable extent, the Bible is actually a history in its outward form,—a history in which we may see what different persons have done and said in the past, by whose example we may often be taught and shewn what is right, or warned against what is wrong. This is evidently true of a large proportion of the Biblical books, from Genesis, on through the Mosaic writings, through Joshua, Samuel, the Kings and some minor books. All these are books of history, coming down from different ages; and though, in nearly every case, by unknown writers, as formerly

---

* The proper limitations of some of these statements, and the sense, in particular, in which we intend to use the words "the same God," has appeared in preceding Chapters of this work: *supra*, Chapters VIII. IX.

pointed out, there is no reason to think that what is written is not, in its main outlines, substantially trustworthy.

In certain parts, indeed, these books are books of law, that is to say, they contain the laws of the Hebrews; but it is a Law which we can only regard as a portion of the Biblical history. It is nowhere enjoined upon us who read; and, indeed, it would no longer be possible for us, even if we wished, to obey it, or carry it out in many of its details. Great moral principles, contained or expressed in the law of the Hebrews, so far as they are in harmony with the reason and the cultivated sense of right, are necessarily permanent and will remain and impress themselves upon our lives, even by their own vitality and power. This sway, however, they will have quite independently of the fact that they may once have been embodied, or recognised in some way, in the laws of the Jews.

In other books of the Bible,—in the Poetical Books and the writings of the Prophets,—we have compositions which show us what their authors thought and said on, and in accordance with, the ideas and the circumstances of their own times. They are thus, again, intimately related to the history of the Hebrews, and cannot be understood without frequent reference to it,—excepting, indeed, by a peculiar class of our modern preachers, of whom such men as Lord Radstock and Dr. Cumming may be referred to as typical examples. Thus in reading even the Psalms, or the Book of Job, or the Proverbs, we must often bear in mind the contemporary ideas and circumstances amidst which, or in reference to which, those books, or their component parts, were respectively written. The same remark is eminently true in reference to the Prophets, who, while they faithfully warn, exhort, condemn, the kings and people of their own day, speak to us of later ages only through them.

Then, when we come to the New Testament, we have what is

essentially of the nature of history again, at least in its relation to our modern times. It is very largely a thing of the past, at which we can only look as distant spectators, seeking, so far as may be, to draw instruction, inspiration, guidance, from its lessons. We have, first, the four Gospels, setting forth the life of Christ. We have next the Acts of the Apostles, which purports to be simply a history of what the Apostles did in their early labours to preach the Gospel. We have then a series of letters, written by Apostles and apostolical men, in reference to topics of interest at the time to those whom they address; the whole closing with the mystical Book of Revelation, the aim and application of which unquestionably belonged to the age of Cæsar Nero, in which it was most probably written.*

Throughout this long succession of books and writers, it is evident that the Bible presents itself to us, not as a code of laws, nor as a system of theology, which we of these later times, and men of all times, ought to receive and assent to but rather as a great historical record of what has been thought and done by men of times long past—a record of what they have thought and believed, in connection often very particularly with the subject of religion, or under the influence of religious feelings and motives. And in this its character of a historical record it shews us, by such examples, as we have formerly seen, how the Hebrew people were led on from rudimentary and imperfect beginnings to a more adequate apprehension of great religious truths; and how, therefore, they have been instrumental in helping to establish religion among Christian men as it now exists.

It is, then, manifestly a great mistake, to do what, nevertheless, there has been and is so great a tendency among Protestants, in

---

* As indicated by the number of the Beast, Rev. xiii. 18, which was no doubt meant to denote the emperor above named. See *Theological Review*, July, 1871, p. 311.

spirit or in letter, to do,—namely, to infer that what was established and approved among and by Biblical leaders and teachers, must be either right, or deserving of approval by us,—more especially in case it should not have been expressly disowned or condemned by Christian authority. Some things, as we are told, were permitted because of the hardness of their hearts. The Mosaic law, for instance, allowed of polygamy; and it made divorce an easy matter, depending on the will of the husband alone. This may remind us that those who were under it lived nearer to the beginning of civilization than we do; and that if we were to imitate them in such matters, we should be going backward in the direction of the ignorance and barbarism from which mankind have been slowly rising through many past centuries. So in regard to the observance of the Sabbath and the institution of the Goel. Under the law of Moses, one who did not keep the Sabbath with the enjoined strictness was to be put to death; and the next kinsman of a murdered man was permitted to avenge his relative by slaying the murderer, wherever he might meet with him outside of certain cities of refuge. Ought Christian nations to return to that state of things, seeing that the Jewish law on these points is nowhere expressly repealed by the Gospel? Such cases shew us clearly that the Bible, even where it is expressly a Code of laws, is not so, cannot be so, for us, however sacred and binding it may have been to the Hebrews of ancient times. To the modern reader, as before, it is simply a great historical picture, providentially given to us—in which we may see what former generations of men have thought and said and done, and how they have been led, in a special case, from their primeval ignorance, to the better ideas of moral and religious truth embodied in Christianity.

We might, therefore, be led into grievous error by looking upon the Bible, as the old Puritans did, and as some of the Anglican

Bishops seem still to do,* as a sort of Law-book, binding upon us, without regard to altered feelings and circumstances, or improved knowledge. Even, then, if it were admitted, for example, that the Book of Leviticus forbids marriage with a deceased wife's sister, that question should, nevertheless, be argued upon its own merits, and in reference to the character and necessities of modern civilized life. Yet, in connection with this subject, we have known the book just named spoken of in the columns of an influential English newspaper as a "revelation" of the Divine will, and as such binding upon the conscience!

A similar appeal to the New Testament was made, not many years ago, in behalf of American slavery. Because the "institution" is recognised in the Bible, not being expressly condemned even in the New Testament, certain ministers of religion in the Southern States represented it as not only allowed, but also sanctioned, by the authority of the Scriptures. But, even admitting that an Apostle approved of slavery as it existed in his own day,† it does not follow that we are to approve of slavery as it exists, or has existed, in modern times. There may be other and higher principles of right and wrong known to us, according to which slavery must be condemned and put away; and our circumstances, too, may be different from those of the Apostle, rendering it altogether sinful for us to sanction various things which might by possibility have appeared allowable to him. We can, therefore, only read such passages as the one referred to, not as containing laws or principles to regulate our conduct, but simply as equivalent to historical examples recorded for us, and as in this respect "profitable" for our instruction or our warning. They

---

* See the debate in the House of Lords (1870) on the Bill respecting marriage with a deceased wife's sister.
† See 1 Tim. vi. 1-5.

may be there, in short, to arouse our disapprobation, and to forbid, rather than to attract, us to approve and imitate.*

Such remarks as these are applicable to the New Testament as well as to the Old. Various matters there, too, involving perhaps no moral principle, or none that would be available or practicable in our modern life, can only be looked back upon with an historical interest, as something belonging to a past state of society. Such, for example, are the question of eating the flesh of animals offered in sacrifice to idols, that of circumcision, and of the observance of other Jewish institutions, including the Sabbath and the rite of baptism. Even in the words of Christ himself there are some things of this kind; as there are in the writings of Paul and other Apostles.† Thus it is not possible, however willing a man might be, blindly to receive and carry out many even of New Testament ideas and principles. Thought, care, discrimination, are necessary in reference to these also. If such qualities be not exercised, we shall be in constant danger of bringing ridicule or disrepute upon a cause we would honour and support.

But how, then, are we to know? How are we to decide as to the truth, wisdom, justice, applicableness to ourselves, of what we read in the Sacred Books, if we are not blindly to accept all and seek to obey all? This question has been virtually answered. Clearly, we can only do this by the light and under the guidance of the Conscience within us, and by the free and faithful exercise of our own reasoning powers. That this is so, we may see by the case even of those who are the most determined opponents of the right of private judgment in religion. They surrender their own judgment, we will suppose, to the decisions of an infallible church. In doing so, they *exercise* the very right which they

---

* In illustration, see 1 Sam. xv. 32, 33 ; 2 Sam. i. 13-16 ; iv. 9-12 ; xxi. 1-14 ; Judges xv. xvi. xvii.

† Matt. v. 39-42 Luke vi. 20-24; James v. 1 ; 1 Cor. vii. 32-40 ; xiv. 34, 35 ; 1 Tim. vi. 8-10.

would condemn in others. They prefer, deliberately or otherwise, *not* to think, reason, judge, for themselves. But that preference itself implies the very judgment which they deprecate. At least, if it be not utterly worthless, it does so.

If, then, a precept, a principle, or a statement of the Bible, be not such as will stand the test of this rational criticism, it will be our duty simply to neglect it, and pass it by, or even, it may be, to condemn it and act in opposition to it. The Scriptures, if they may be the guide and light of the spiritual nature, are clearly not to be as an opiate to it, to put it asleep, or make it insensible to even the nicest shades of distinction between right and wrong, true and false. What they contain of good and evil example, of true or false thoughts of God, His providence and His relations to mankind, or of man's duties and responsibilities,—these things, although written, in some sense, for our instruction, are yet not to be accepted and followed, or put aside and neglected, thoughtlessly and mechanically, but with the aid and sanction of our own reason and moral faculties. If it were not so, we might be drawn away, as doubtless many are by their excessive deference to priestly authority, even to cherish error and unrighteousness; we might turn warnings into examples; we might be led, in short, to approve and follow principles, both religious and moral, which are really false, sinful, injurious and contrary to the Highest Will.

Some of these statements might easily be illustrated, had we the space, from the history of religion in our own and in other countries. But it is more, perhaps, to our present purpose to observe, that the Conscience and the Reason are God's gift to man certainly not less than the Bible, and that their free and healthy action are quite as essential as the teachings of any book can be, not only to the practical guidance of life, but also to the right apprehension of religious truth. The Almighty Parent who has given us these faculties, must have intended that we should use them; that we should seek to cultivate them and make them more strong and pure; that we should live and act as moral and intellectual beings who are capable of discrimination and progress in the knowledge of things spiritual. The Bible, we may well believe, is able to aid us in this great work of life; and we shall best perform our duty towards the Giver of that and every other good gift, by using His bounty, not to prevent, or render needless, the deliberate and responsible action of our own higher powers, but to assist us to cultivate and develop them, and obey their suggestions.

And abundant warrant for thus thinking may be found by the Christian disciple in the memorable words of the Christian Master, when he said, "Why even of yourselves judge ye not what is right?"

In recent times, much has been said on the subject of Inspiration—the inspiration of the Scriptures. It is remarkable that the Bible does not itself give us any definition, or description, either of that word or of the *quality* which it is used to denote. It nowhere, in truth, claims inspiration, or says anything definite about it.* The Biblical inspiration, whatever it is or was, would seem, like the genius of Shakspeare, to be unconsciously possessed. The phrase, "Thus saith the Lord," and its equivalents, are most probably to be understood simply as indicating the prophet's belief that what he was about to say was conformable to the Divine Will. At the utmost, such expressions, whatever their full import, are valid only for the immediate context in which they stand, and do not affirm or imply anything for the

---

* Comp. 2 Tim. iii. 16. This verse is thus rendered by Dean Alford: "Every Scripture inspired by God is also profitable for doctrine, for conviction, for correction, for discipline which is in righteousness." The allusion is no doubt to the O. T. Scriptures, but what precisely is intended by the adjective θεόπνευστος, rendered "inspired by God," we are nowhere informed.

entire Biblical collection. We cannot, for example, infer the "inspiration" of Genesis xxxvi., or of Psalm cix., of Solomon's Song, or of the Book of Jonah, from the circumstance that Jeremiah or Isaiah sometimes spoke to their contemporaries as direct messengers of Jehovah, and used forms of speech corresponding to that character. Many a modern preacher in his excitement and earnestness does the same, but no one misunderstands him.

So, again, in such portions of the New Testament as the Epistle of Jude, or the anonymous Epistle to the Hebrews, or the unfulfilled anticipations of the Book of Revelation, we could not infer the "inspiration" of these, because the Apostle Paul may have lived and acted and spoken under the special impulse of the Spirit from on high.

It is scarcely allowable, in short, to think of inspiration as being or acting in the dead words of any book; while yet it is natural and easy to us to think of the Divine Spirit as influencing and moving the living soul of a man; as being, for example, in Abraham, in Moses, in Isaiah, in Paul, enabling them to act effectually and wonderfully among the men of their time, according to the ideas and circumstances of the age to which they belonged. But this living inspiration was primarily for them and their day. When their thoughts, in all their complexity and specialty, come to lie before a future age, and are read among people differently trained and circumstanced, they are found in large measure to be practically inapplicable—or applicable in principle only. Human language is at best an imperfect vehicle for the transmission to distant times of Divine thoughts and impulses—the subtle, indescribable inbreathings of that Spirit which, like the wind, cometh and goeth "where it listeth." At any rate, that the writers of Scripture, whatever their "inspiration" may have been, were not preserved from the consequences of using human language as the means of expressing their ideas, is clear from the fact, that there are so many, not only difficulties and obscurities of one kind and another, but discrepancies or contradictions,* in the sacred page—a fact which ought to warn us against the common superstition about inspiration in the vague or irrational sense in which this is maintained by some writers of our time.

Yet, while saying this, let us not lose sight of that which may still claim to be the durable inspiration even of the written Word. The living men of old, whose thoughts are preserved for us in the Scriptures, and in whom the Spirit of God was eminently present, have doubtless left sufficient traces and proofs of this fact to the attentive reader. But such indications are not to be seen in every separate sentiment of individual speakers or writers,—much less in every sentence or word which a Scriptural author may have written. The Biblical inspiration is not, therefore, verbal. It is something far greater and higher. It consists, surely, in the great moral and religious thought or thoughts which the different parts of the whole Scripture combine to give us, as the common and harmonious result of their various utterances. In this sense, therefore, again, both the unity and·the continuity formerly spoken of must be admitted to be prominent features of the Bible.

If we would illustrate this position from the Old Testament, we have at once suggested to us the leading idea of that part of the Bible—the idea of the One God, Jehovah, the Creator and Lord of heaven and earth. We find the chief men of the Hebrews, their legislators and prophets, constantly, and the more decidedly as time passes onward, holding up to their people this first and greatest fundamental of true religion ; and from them, through

---

* For example, 2 Sam. xxiv. 9, compared with 1 Chron. xxi. 5 ; Mark xv. 25, compared with John xix. 14 ; also the accounts of the birth of Jesus Christ in the first and third Evangelists, as well as those of the resurrection in all four.

the medium of Christianity, the same has been handed down to our day. And under this Biblical idea of God should be included, not only His oneness, but also the clear intimations given respecting Him as a living and conscious Mind. The God of the Bible is not a mechanical force, or a diffused principle or tendency of life and motion in the universe. He is One of nature in some sense kindred to our own; He is the Supreme Disposer; His providence sustains us; He sees us; and He approves or condemns in righteousness. Such is the idea of the Divine personality and character conveyed to us, as the clear result of the Old Testament teaching—a result evidently accepted by the Founder of Christianity, and by his influence perpetuated in the world. Shall we be wrong, therefore, if we say that the *inspiration* of the Old Testament is mainly or precisely in this very point?—that it is not in separate words or phrases, not in ideas expressed in natural science, in geology or astronomy, or other such subjects of ordinary knowledge, all of which were necessarily imperfect, and such as belonged to an early age of the world?—but simply in those incomparably greater ideas of God, His character, His will and providence, which the Hebrew Scriptures have been so obviously the means of recording and preserving for us?

Christian people will undoubtedly be relieved of much difficulty by admitting this more simple and natural idea of the inspiration of the Scriptures. We can see, for one thing, how it is that individual writers are left so free to express their individual thoughts and feelings; to give utterance even to angry passions and evil wishes, or to ignorant, ill-founded hopes and anticipations; while yet the grand idea of Jehovah, the Creator, Sovereign, Righteous Observer and Judge of men, comes forth uninjured from the midst of all such utterances, and, with the progress of the ages, gradually obtains a higher and clearer recognition, in the thoughts of successive generations, from Abraham to Christ.

Similar observations may be made respecting the New Testament. Here, too, certain great elements of religious truth present themselves and form the abiding result, after many local and temporary peculiarities are laid aside. Chief among them is the ancient doctrine of the One God,* in its Christian form of the Heavenly Father, with its related spiritual truths and principles. Shall we be wrong, again, if we say that the inspiration of the New Testament consists essentially or solely in the great lessons respecting God, Providence, moral duty, retribution, purity of life, which its various parts combine as they do to impress upon the mind of a reader?

The chief addition made by the New Testament to what has descended to us in substance from the Old, consists in the doctrine of a Future Life. And yet this doctrine was clearly no "revelation" first given through the Christian teachers. It was already known and acknowledged among the people before Christ came.† The utmost, therefore, that can be alleged is, that the Christian Master and his disciples accepted the ancient belief, and gave it the seal of their approval;—accepted it, also, so far as the *form* of it was concerned, much as it was already held by those among whom they lived. It was left to time and the growth of knowledge to supply any correction needed, to bring the doctrine in question into a truer harmony with the highest suggestions of the reason and the moral sense.

It is remarkable, however, how closely accompanied, and moreover, how much embarrassed, is the great Christian hope by an idea of marked prominence in the New Testament;—the idea, that is to say, of the speedy second coming of Christ. This expectation has been manifestly proved by the lapse of time to have been erroneous. Whatever, therefore, its origin, whether in

---

* Matt. vi. 9 ; Mark xii. 28-30 ; Luke x. 27 ; John xvii. 3 ; 1 Cor. viii. 6 ; Ephes. iv. 6 ; 1 Tim. ii. 5.
† Mark xii. 18-27 ; Matt. xxii. 23-33.

the misapprehension by the disciples of some declaration of their Master, or really in express words of his, and however important its influence upon the early Christianity, it ought now to be passed by as a merely temporary incident of primitive Christian faith. Like many another error, it has answered its transitory purpose in the providential plan, and may well, at length, be left to rest in peace. It *is* in truth thus put aside by considerate readers of the Bible. For they can no longer say, with James, "The coming of the Lord draweth nigh;" or with Paul, that when the Lord cometh, we shall be "caught up together with him in the air;"*—they can no longer say this in the sense in which those Apostles said it and believed it.

And there is this further difference between the expectation referred to and the doctrine of a future life. The former is in no way demanded or sanctioned by the reason or the sense of right, while the latter is so. On this ground, therefore, it may be allowable, or rather necessary, to reject the one, while accepting the other. As may again be observed, it is not the office of the Scriptures to supersede the action of our spiritual nature, by imposing upon us beliefs or laws of conduct which are not perceived and felt to be right. Their function is rather to afford us a helpful guiding influence, and even, in some cases, to supply, as it were, the materials out of which we may select and assimilate to ourselves what is best adapted to our spiritual nutriment and our onward progress in the divine life.

Although, therefore, the belief in the second coming of Christ was so prominent and influential a part of the early Christianity, and is strongly affirmed by several New Testament writers,†— although it stands also in very intimate connection with the Christian hope of the life to come, insomuch that the one seems to

---

* James v. 8 ; 1 Thess. iv. 17.
† 1 Cor. xv. 23-28, 51-53 ; 1 Thess. i. 10 ; iii. 13 ; iv. 13-18 ; 1 Pet. iv. 7 ; 2 Pet. iii. 4, 10-13 ; Rev. i. 7.

involve and to stand or fall with the other,—although, too, the former has been plainly proved to be unfounded, by remaining unfulfilled through the lapse of more than eighteen centuries, and cannot, therefore, any longer be held to be a credible or essential part of Christian faith,—still and nevertheless it may be competent to us to hold fast the hope as a sure one, while we dismiss the expectation as only a temporary misunderstanding. And we may do this the more easily and confidently, even because the one is in harmony with the dictates of reason and conscience, while the other is not, or, at any rate, is very much less so. We may do it, in other words, even because the one receives the sanction of the supreme approving and verifying faculties of our nature, while the other does not; and because, too, it is largely and necessarily left to us, in reading the Scriptures, to discriminate between one thing and another, between the temporary and the permanent, the good and the evil, the true and the false. It is left to us to do this; we are called upon, and it is our obvious and individual duty, thus to discriminate. We cannot act by proxy in this matter, and turn our duty over to another; for unless we will think and act for ourselves, we must be made, and shall deserve to be made, the sport of every wild "wind of doctrine," from the highest of high ritualism and superstitious priestcraft, down to the lowest depths of the most ignorant scripturalism.

We are not called upon, then, to accept an irrational or immoral doctrine merely because it is contained in the Bible—supposing, for the moment, any such doctrine to be really contained in that book—that, for example, as so many allege, of eternal punishment. The true alternative course, in such a case, would appear to be, to receive the statements of the Scriptures on that subject simply as a part of the *history* of the growth of religious knowledge, preserved for us in their pages. Thus we may look upon the doctrine just referred to, not as a permanent truth of religion, but only as belonging to the days of the world's earlier experience, like those alluded to by the Apostle Paul;* as a something therefore of past times and forms of thought, which, by its own nature, could have only a temporary existence, and was destined to pass away as soon as the strengthened and purified intelligence of man should be able to rise up to the conception of higher and better ideas of divine truth.

And doubtless this will be the case with every doctrine, whether Biblical or not, which is in serious discordance with the true dictates of reason and the moral sense. Such things, even if contained in the Bible, will have to pass away and give place to what is better, as soon as ever the Almighty Father shall, by the course of His providence, have led on His children of mankind to more spiritual views of His works and ways and will. For, be it not forgotten, the Almighty Spirit is alive, and not dead. God is still and ever the Living God; and our human part must be to embrace the highest forms of Truth of every kind, the highest ideas of Right and Duty which may become known to us, through whatever channel we may obtain them, whether through the pages of Scripture, by the teaching or the experience of others around us, or by the secret intimations of our own souls.

If this were not so, how should we know that we were not setting ourselves against the very Spirit of God itself within the heart, and what would the Bible be but a mere drag upon the steps of human progress?—as, alas! it has too often been made by the ignorance and unwisdom of past times.

In speaking thus freely, though we hope not irreverently, respecting a Book which is without doubt, in its influence, the most remarkable known to us in this part of the world, we should make a great omission if, on the other hand, we failed to acknowledge the elements of divine life and guidance which the same

* Acts xvii. 30.

book contains. This must be said in large measure of both the older and the later portions of it. We have in the former, among other things, the history of the early introduction and growth of the idea of One God, and many traces of the prolonged conflict of prophets and others against the various wickedness of rulers and people; shewing us how the Hebrews were brought, almost in spite of themselves, from and through imperfections, prejudices and obstacles, to what was better and truer; until, finally, a suitable preparation was made among them for the coming and the life of Jesus Christ, with all the rich practical lessons of moral and religious teaching which are identified with his name or due immediately to his influence. These are mostly of a character not, certainly, to offend or do violence to the natural reason or sense of right, but rather to awaken, purify and strengthen the conscience, and so win the approval of the intelligent and thoughtful mind. There are many things of this kind in the Christian teachings, of the very highest character, such as are completely above the ordinary thoughts and practices of men, but which we feel, nevertheless, within our hearts to be right, and deserving of our obedience.

When Christ, for example, gives us the parable of the Good Samaritan, and tells us to go and do likewise, do not our best reason and sense of right assent, respond and sympathize? When he tells us to love our neighbour even as ourselves, to do good to those who hate us, and to forgive those who have injured us; when he tells us that the peacemakers shall be called children of God; that the pure in heart shall see Him; and that they are blessed who do hunger and thirst after righteousness, for that they shall be filled;—when Christ not only speaks and teaches in this spirit, but also manifests a perfect faithfulness in his own devotion to the work of duty which he was called to do; —when we see him going straight forward, even to the painful death of crucifixion, without faltering, and even on the cross carrying out his own precepts by praying to God to forgive the men who were putting him to a cruel death;—in all this, and such as this, do we not feel that we have a divine spirit in the Bible, which it will be good for us to admit into our hearts, and exemplify in our lives, if we can?—a spirit which the secret intimations of the soul assure us is altogether right and beautiful, and worthy to be received; which, in short, in its perfectness, is far above man's ordinary doings, and which we can only hope and pray to be enabled faithfully to receive and make our own?

And things of this kind in the Bible, which awaken our sympathy and lay hold of our moral nature, evidently constitute the true value of that book, and its true claim upon us; not, however, because they are there laid down before us in the form of laws and creeds, but because they are great spiritual principles, which we *feel* to be such; because they are in harmony with the best dictates of our nature; not opposed to these, or in any way inconsistent with them. The true authority of the Bible consists, in a word, just in this and in nothing else, that our secret hearts, in our best and most serious moments, acknowledge and testify to its truth and power in so considerable a portion of its teachings.

CHAPTER XXVIII.

SUMMARY OF RESULTS WITH ADDITIONAL REMARKS—THE CHRISTIANITY OF CHRIST—HIS TRUE DIGNITY—HIS DEATH—THE LORD'S SUPPER, WHAT IT IS—THE FUNCTION OF THE BIBLE: PRIESTLY AUTHORITY—THE CHURCH AND THE CHURCHES—PROPER BASIS OF CHRISTIAN COMMUNION—QUESTION OF A NATIONAL CHURCH—WHAT UNITARIANS WORSHIP—WHAT IS A UNITARIAN?—A PARTING HOPE.

The principal conclusions which appear to be established by the foregoing argument may now be very briefly recapitulated.

In the first place, the Almighty Being whom the Bible would lead us to acknowledge and worship is, in the strictest sense of the words, ONE GOD. He is a Living Spirit, of "loving kindness and tender mercy," our Father in heaven; while yet He is at the same time a God of righteousness, "who will render to every man according to his deeds."

Into this ancient idea of one Divine personality, there is nowhere introduced, throughout the Scriptures, any change or qualification whatever. The Jehovah of Abraham and of Moses is the Jehovah of Isaiah and Jeremiah, of the latest as of the earliest Prophets. The same Almighty Being is the Heavenly Father of the Gospels, and He it is who is also spoken of by the Apostles Paul and Peter as the God and Father of Jesus Christ. Throughout the Bible it is everywhere the same; the most strict and literal conception of the oneness of the Divine Mind, of the sole deity of Jehovah of Hosts, being constantly expressed or implied, in much variety of phrase.

It is true, nevertheless, that various little peculiarities of a plural character occur in the Hebrew writers in immediate connection with the Sacred Name. Thus their word for *God* is grammatically plural in form. But however this may have originated, it came to be a mere idiomatic expression of the language. As such only it stands before us, and it is employed in the Bible, like other plural forms, to denote a single object. So much is this the case, in reference both to this word and to some kindred expressions on which Dr. Liddon so anxiously insists, that all such things are absolutely insignificant, in comparison with the overwhelming force of the argument for the strictest doctrine of the Divine Unity. The citation of such small evidence by him and by other defenders of the popular orthodoxy proves nothing, in fact, but the extreme poverty of their general argument from the Old Testament. It is simply indicative of the absence of all direct testimony to the theory which they seek to uphold.

In the second place, Jesus of Nazareth is nowhere in Scripture represented as God, but simply as the Christ—that is to say, the anointed, the chosen instrument, the well-beloved Son, of the Almighty Father. In this character he was received by his own immediate disciples; more or less of the temporal or political conception of his office most probably attaching to their earliest confession of him. By his death, however, and in the course of years, that grosser element was removed; yet for a long period something of it remained, in the lingering expectation of his second advent. But this, too, in time, and by the course of events, was proved to be only a misapprehension. With few exceptions, Christian men have now outgrown it and put it away. For eighteen centuries and more it has been left unfulfilled, and hence, we may reasonably infer the will of the overruling Providence that Jesus was to be Christ in no temporal or worldly sense. He is thus simply the Spiritual Christ, and all who will may be disciples of his—not, indeed, by virtue of any outward rite, such as circumcision, or baptism, or the confession of a creed, but by Faith alone, carrying with it, as a matter of course, the Obedience which is better than sacrifice, and the Christian love which is greater than faith.

But what then is Christian Faith to the modern disciple? It can be no merely intellectual state, voluntary or involuntary. It is a thing, in truth, of manifold character. It is the affectionate reverent trust of the disciple towards the Teacher; it is the earnest desire to sit at his feet, and learn of him the virtues and the graces of the Christian character; it is the humble yet hopeful aspiration to obey his precepts, to follow his example, and to imbibe the spirit of his life. From this definition of Christian faith, it easily follows that Christianity is not a mere dogma, whether about Christ or about God, about heaven or hell, or Adam, or sin, or the devil; that it does not consist, in any essential degree, in a particular form of church government, or in submission to a priesthood, or in the observance of holy days, forms of worship, ceremonial rites and sacraments. Christianity cannot consist in things of this kind, or be dependent either upon their presence or their absence; although it may be freely confessed that such things as dogmas, ceremonies and priests, may be a help and a stay to many, even though also a hindrance to many others. If, then, a man should feel them to be such, let him cling to them; but, as the Apostle reminds us, "let every man be fully persuaded in his own mind." *

Thus, to vary the form of definition, it follows, again, that Christianity, objectively considered, is Christ himself—the mind, life, character and spirit of Christ. The best expression of it is in *him*, in his words and deeds; by the side of which every human creed and test of discipleship is but an impertinent intrusion. He then is the truest Christian, not who is readiest or loudest in saying, "Lord, Lord," but who most closely and practically follows the Master in doing the Heavenly Father's will;—who strives and prays to do this Divine will in Christ, so far as it is given to frail and tempted man to imitate so lofty an example, to manifest so righteous and so holy a spirit.

But between Jesus as the Christ, thus set before us, and Him who is the "Only True God," there is the same infinite distance as between the Divine Creator and every other created intelligence. Christ is indeed, in apostolical phrase, the "first born of many brethren," the well-beloved Son of the Almighty Being, but he is not himself God—nor is he ever really represented as such in the New Testament. "There is one God the Father," and "one Lord Jesus Christ;"† but these are not in any sense one being or one nature; they are two beings and two natures; two distinct, self-conscious minds—a fact which cannot be got rid of,

---

* Rom. xiv. 1-6. † 1 Cor. viii. 6.

or ignored, even by the most zealous upholders of the deity of Christ and the oneness of divine nature in him and in God.* It thus further appears as a marked and evil feature of the popular theology, that it tends so directly to weaken, or also to perplex and obscure, proper monotheistic feeling,—turning away the mind from one true and only Object of devout trust and worship, to the acknowledgment as divine of other beings which are not really God in any allowable sense of the word, and which can never by the nature of the case be shewn to be so.

This remark applies, not only to the doctrine of Christ's deity, but to that also of the personality of the Holy Spirit. For the Holy Spirit, although, indeed, as we have seen, it is truly God Himself, more especially as manifested in His intercourse or communion with the soul of man, yet it is not, in any real sense, a separate divine "person," that is to say, a separate God; nor, consequently, ought it ever to be so spoken of by one who has a regard to the teaching of Christ. It ought not, therefore, to be separately addressed in prayer or praise, for such acts are, in effect, a detraction from the honour which is due to Him who alone is God. And this statement is enforced by the unquestionable fact that there is not a single instance in the Bible in which the Holy Spirit is so addressed, or invoked, or presented to us as an object of worship.

It is further to be observed—for we are here endeavouring to speak the whole truth in very plain words—that Jesus Christ, as *man*, as the first and noblest of the sons of God, the spiritual Head under HIM of the "Communion of Saints," is a far greater, more attractive and more commanding object, than when looked up to as a derived or secondary God, as he is represented in the Nicene Creed; or as one, again, whose Godhead is for ever a

---

* In particular illustration of this statement, see the remarks on Canon Lightfoot's exposition of Philip. ii. 6-11, Appendix, note E.

doubtful and disputed thing. This it now is, and this it always has been, from the day when it was first heard of, downwards to our time. For has the Godhead of Christ ever been universally acknowledged in the Christian world, except, perhaps, in the darkest periods of the Middle Ages, when, along with the Virgin Mary and innumerable saints,* Christ also was made the object of Divine honours which he had never received in his lifetime, and against which he would certainly have protested, as due not to him, but to the Father alone? Jesus Christ, then, most certainly, as MAN, the patient, steadfast, righteous servant of the Almighty Will, raised up by the power of God to a glorious spiritual throne, is a being calculated to awaken and to help the love and trust and courage of every faithful soul. But Jesus Christ as GOD, doubted or denied in that character by many, and by many more received only with a secret fear, half acknowledged to themselves, lest in so honouring him they are guilty of idolatrous treason towards the Lord of the universe,—what shall be said of such a doubtful Deity as this? How can a God with a disputed title permanently command the faith and homage of the world, or rule effectually in the hearts of men?

On the subject of the death of Christ, it may be enough to remind the reader that this is nowhere represented as possessed of a propitiatory or expiatory efficacy, in the old heathen sense of such expressions. It was simply the Providential means by which the admission of the Gentile world was secured to the faith of

* "When the grand hereditary truth of Judaism, which is transmitted to Christianity, was lost sight of in the third and fourth centuries of our era, polytheism and idolatry in new forms sprang up forthwith, and multiplied with rapid increase through the whole mediæval period. First, the Son, then the Holy Spirit, then the Virgin Mother, and at length countless hosts of saints and martyrs, rose into the rank of Deity, and were invoked with fervent prayers—the last personage so exalted being usually the most popular object of worship; till, finally, at the altars which filled the churches before the Reformation, the name of the Father Himself was never heard."
—*From an unpublished Lecture by the late Rev. J. J. Tayler, B.A.*

the Gospel. The phraseology in which it is spoken of is, indeed, at times very largely figurative—arising naturally out of the Levitical ideas and institutions of the Jews. But, while this is true, one literal fact is usually expressed by it. That fact is what has just been stated—not the incredible doctrine that the All-merciful God, in His " wrath," required to be propitiated by the death of an innocent victim; nor the equally incredible doctrine that Christ's death has redeemed men from everlasting sufferings in hell, because he has borne their punishment, and thus given " satisfaction" to Infinite Justice. No such barbarous ideas as these are anywhere either plainly stated in the New Testament, or veiled and conveyed, as in a parable, under its more figurative expressions.

It follows by necessary consequence, that the Romanist and high Anglican doctrine of the Sacrament of the Lord's Supper is a huge mistake; and that all the miserable animosities and controversies to which it has given origin have been only so much energy misapplied and wasted, or worse. There is no Scriptural evidence whatever, no evidence at all which rises above the character of early Christian superstition, by which the Lord's Supper can be shewn to be of the nature of a sacrifice for sin, requiring to be perpetually renewed by a " sacrificing priest." There is no evidence, in truth, worthy of the name, by which it can be shewn to be anything else, in its institution and nature, but a simple service of devout commemoration. " Do this in remembrance of me," are the words of Christ himself, when he founded the rite. Whatever, in modern doctrines concerning it, passes beyond this, in form or in spirit, can only be set down as misunderstanding, or as the inherited remains of ancient error. But from these, it may be added, the Christian world is gradually and surely, though it may be slowly and painfully, releasing itself.

The Lord's Supper, then, being thus a service of grateful

commemoration and reverence towards the Christian Head, is naturally, at the same time, a testimony of sympathy and fellowship among those who partake. And, it must be added, alas for that Church which fences round this simple rite of faith with terms of communion unknown to Christ himself, and thus in effect forbids the approach to him of any who would seek to come in and sit down in the reverential spirit of Christian discipleship!

The collection of writings which form the Bible is, in its greater part, the remains of the ancient Hebrew literature; the rest, or Christian portion, being of much later date, and, in some cases, hardly less fragmentary in its character. In both divisions we have many documents of uncertain or unknown authorship, which are yet of the highest interest, both for the record which they preserve of the history of an ancient and peculiar people, and for the picture which they give us of the manner in which the Hebrews were led on from very gross and imperfect ideas in religion and other subjects to the higher moral and spiritual standard of Christ and Christianity. In the Christian literature, moreover, we have in substance the record of a great revolution destined in the course of time deeply to affect the ideas and the material condition of the civilized world. We have also the only historical or biographical outline left to us of the life and teaching of that remarkable personage from whom so wonderful an influence was to proceed. At the lowest estimate of its character, the Bible is not less than this. To many persons, and not without reason, it is much more; but it is not a Creed or a Creed-book, which men are called upon to receive under penalty of damnation. It nowhere claims to be so. Nor is it a body of immutable laws for our time, or for any other. Many of its ideas on creation, on the Divine Being and His intercourse with men, and on various other subjects, are simply such as were suited to the infancy of the human race—some of them are such as can only be passed over in silence by readers of any refinement or delicacy of mind. The Book, in short, in many parts, is one of which, more perhaps than of any other within ordinary knowledge, we may reasonably be expected to remember the old Baconian maxim about antiquity being only the youth of the world. The Bible may, nevertheless, if wisely used, be a help and an influence to guide and enlighten the conscience; as it is a channel through which the Unseen Spirit has often spoken to men, and may still speak to us, if we will listen. But it is not, and ought not to be made, a substitute for the free and earnest action of our own higher nature; nor an opiate to stupefy, or put it to sleep. The Bible never claims to exercise any such function as this; but rather, in its usual tenor, appeals to us and bids us stand up as intelligent, moral and religious beings, to judge for ourselves what is right, and act faithfully in accordance with the highest dictates of our inner sense of duty.

It is scarcely necessary to add, that nothing in the letter or the spirit of the Bible commands, or even permits us to devolve this duty upon others—upon "priests" of this church or that. Such a course may have been necessary, or becoming, in some of those darker ages which lie between the present time and that in which Christ lived. But when a priest or a Pope puts forth the claim to spiritual allegiance, or seeks to dictate either what men ought to believe, or how they ought to act, what is there to shew that he has a rightful authority to do this? Surely it is not so ordered either in the words of Christ, or even in those of any Apostle. Is then the priest's word to be taken for it? Even when he urges it under the impersonal name of the "Church," there is still a weighty question to be resolved. For the Church, as usually put forward, is only the people, priests or laymen, of a darker age than ours; and on what reasonable ground can a man be required to give up his own judgment for theirs?—to accept their conclusions on the great subjects of religious inquiry, and forego the exercise of his own faculties? What is to shew that the priestly claimant of our time is morally and spiritually worthy to be a guide of men in matters of faith and duty?—that he is even a man of pure and upright life? From every point of view the pretension is untenable; or, to speak plainly, it is absurd in the highest degree—a thing from which the cultivated reason and conscience will more and more revolt and turn away with scorn. Witness to this effect the present religious condition of Italy, Spain and France.* Who does not see that in these countries priestly pretensions have been pushed to their natural vicious extreme?—that they have produced the fruits to be expected from such a tree?—that they are now, therefore, simply to be rejected by reasonable people?—that they are able to maintain their ground only by virtue of ancient prescriptive right, and, even by the aid of this, mainly among the more ignorant and superstitious classes of the population? It cannot for a moment be supposed that the thoughtful and well-informed of the English people will ever, in any great numbers, be reduced to this kind of subservience to a priestly class. Every year that passes, with every new step in the path of popular education, renders such a supposition more impossible.

The great question of the Church and the Churches cannot here be discussed at any adequate length. It may, however, be noted that no basis of Church union that is likely to be permanent can anywhere be found, except only in the ever-enduring words of Christ. The ancient creeds are clearly inadmissible, and this for more reasons than one. For example, it is impossible to

* On this painful subject the Bishop of Argyll has recently said,—"Catholicism, substituted for Christ, has turned the thought of Southern Europe to simple infidelity, if not to atheism; let us take heed that Protestantism does not bring about the same thing, in another way, in the North."—*Letter* in the Spectator of April 8, 1870.

learn who wrote them. The Apostles' Creed is a document of unknown authorship, and can only be traced, in any form, to the latter part of the second century. It really, therefore, stands before us under false pretences. It is *not* the Apostles' Creed, and never was so in any proper sense of the words. Moreover, many of its clauses are now popularly misunderstood, and, from the nature of the case, can no longer be accepted in their proper signification. A similar statement is eminently true of the so-called Creed of Athanasius;* and in regard to the Nicene Creed, although some knowledge is easily accessible, not indeed as to the hand that wrote it, but at least as to the credulous and narrow-minded ecclesiastics whose opinions it embodied, yet will any one allege that this knowledge tends to recommend the document to the faith or reverence of any thoughtful and free-minded man? The proposition, then, remains true, that the ancient creeds cannot form a permanent basis of Church communion among instructed men; and the same thing may be equally said of the Thirty-nine Articles of the English establishment.

A formidable question remains to be asked in regard to Creeds and Articles alike. Does any considerable number of Christian people now *believe* them, honestly and fairly believe them in their natural sense, as they lie before us? Of those who use them, doubtless some do so, but it is equally undeniable that multitudes do not. How, then, can they serve as a basis of Church union for the whole English nation, or even for the religious portion of it?

But even if the number of believers in the Creeds and Articles were far larger than it is, no one has *authority*, or, by the nature of the case, can ever have *had* authority, to impose these

* See Riddle, *Christian Antiquities*, 2nd ed., p. 463, *seq.*; Nicolas, *Le Symbole des Apôtres*, 1867; Dean Stanley's *The Athanasian Creed*, 1871.

standards upon others — except, indeed, a usurped authority. And, above all, they are not *needed*. We may well believe that had precise dogmatic statements been required as the foundation of his Church, the Christian Master would himself have given them to his followers, and not have left to them the invidious and fruitless task of setting up rival creeds and dogmas. But he, the Christian Master, has taken no such course. The confession of himself as Christ is all that he appears to have contemplated. "On this rock," he said, "will I build my church."* The acknowledgment, therefore, of him as Christ in things spiritual, is the only true foundation of his Church on earth. Yet the Anglican communion persistently supersedes and obliterates the true principle of Christian fellowship by the complicated formularies just spoken of, imposing assent to these, if not upon its ordinary members, at least upon its ministers, and thus perpetuating the inculcation of what multitudes in the nation can no longer accept as truth, but simply regard as antiquated and pernicious error.

It is not, however, to be concealed that the great Nonconformist sects are quite as chargeable with doing this as the National Church; that their proceedings in this respect are animated by precisely the same spirit. The Congregationalists, for example, by means of doctrinal schedules attached to chapel trusts, and by other well-understood means,† of which it is not necessary here to speak in detail, provide very effectually that no one shall be minister of a church who does not teach and preach according to the little scheme of Calvinistic doctrines specified in the schedule.‡

---

* Matt. xvi. 16–18 ; and comp. *supra*, Chapter XVIII., "Jesus the Spiritual Christ."

† Such as restricted admission to the Lord's Supper, and little sets of Articles imposed upon teachers and students, in some of the colleges.

‡ Such, after much inquiry, we understand to be the usual practice of the Congregationalists. Of exceptions we have never heard, and should be very glad to be informed of their existence — if there are any.

The Wesleyan Methodists, and probably the minor sects of the same generic name, pursue a similar course. Not contented with the teaching of Christ as it lies before us in the Gospel, or not willing to trust their ministers with a real freedom of speech, they have set up or accepted their venerable founder as a kind of Pope, and make the candidates for their ministry declare at ordination that they will not depart from the doctrines of his Sermons and Notes on the New Testament.* The Baptists, it is well known, are not far behind in the same narrow path; maintaining, as they do, that no one shall partake of the Lord's Supper, or, in other words, enter into church communion with them, who has not been wholly immersed in water,—thus applying to the people of our cold northern climate an injunction which can only have contemplated the inhabitants of the semi-tropical lands in which Christianity was first preached.

The natural consequences of this unseemly sectarian spirit are seen partly in the bitterness, dissension and intolerance which now unhappily prevail within the established Church itself, and partly in the irreligion, ignorance and manifold vice, which, alas! exist so largely throughout the lower strata of the English nation. For such evils, it cannot be doubted, English sectarianism is greatly to blame. The remedy, however, is not to be found, as some might tell us, in a self-degrading submission to priestly authority—supposing, for a moment, such a thing to be possible. It is rather in the combination and the organization of all religious men, of every sect, for united Christian work in one grand national whole on the simple basis of Christ's teaching. It is in the concentration of energies, now too much divided and wasted, for the instruction and evangelizing of our people. But this union can never take place, can never even commence, until at least the National Church shall open its doors wide enough to

* See Grindrod's *Laws and Regulations of Wesleyan Methodism.*

admit, without test or creed of human devising, all who "profess and call themselves Christians," and who desire to come in and unite as brethren in Christ on the broad and simple principle of the acceptance of his words—his words alone—as the test of their discipleship.

The day has perhaps gone by, when such a renovation of the religious and ecclesiastical life of the English people was still within reach—within the power of some great statesman to propose, and of the Church and nation to accept. At least, this desponding view of the case is held and urged by some leaders of public opinion from whom a different course might have been expected. They are willing, it would appear, to give up the battle for a united and comprehensive Church as already lost, even before it has been fought. But, on the contrary, let us beg the reader to consider whether this question has yet been fitly discussed—whether a true commencement has been even made of its discussion. The short-sighted policy of the Liberation Society has, indeed, been long and amply agitated; but the great idea of a common Church for the whole English people, founded upon some simple and intelligible Christian principle admitted by all,— a Church in which the first duty of its ministers would be to speak out what they believe to be the truth, without fear of consequences,—this idea surely has not yet been fairly placed before the nation,—and possibly, we must add, it is destined never to be so, or it is destined to be so in vain.

One thing, at all events, seems plain. To disestablish the existing Church, after the manner of the Church of Ireland, will only be to add an additional sect of overwhelming influence to the numerous "denominations" already existing. It will be to set up this sect in all its ancient prestige, and in all the power conferred by the possession of a large portion of national Church property, which must of necessity and in justice be given to it.

If, as some expect, the body thus relieved of its national character, and no longer held together by Parliamentary and other restraints, shall split up into three or four different sections, this will only be to make matters worse; adding so many new sects, instead of one, to those which now exist, with all the waste of power consequent upon the competition for influence among the people, which will naturally attend such a state of things. And so the nation will be given over, for an indefinite period, to a sectarianism more intense than ever. Can such a policy be a wise one? Is it one that is worthy of a great Christian people? Would not the better course be to open wide the doors of the existing Church, to abolish, or greatly simplify, the ancient creeds and articles,—or at least to offer them for acceptance only so far as the individual conscience finds them to be in accordance with the teachings of Christ,—thus, in effect, requiring no test of membership, except only the profession of allegiance to him as Head?

But, it must be added, with such a revolution as this should be united Justice in the distribution of national Church endowments and revenues. There is no reason why all should be in the hands of a single sect, while others are left to shift for themselves. These, however, are questions of detail which cannot be adequately discussed in these pages, and a few words on one other point may close this part of the subject.

Is it objected that the principle of Church union above proposed is too vague, not definite enough for united worship or united action? The answer is evident. The Gospel and the Church have been left to us by their Founder precisely in this position, in this all-comprehensive spirit. Why should any one seek to limit and lower what He has left so free, so lofty, and so broad? Who, moreover, of our day, or of any age since Christ lived, has, or has had, the right to define more exactly than he has done, what are the essentials of Christian faith, or the conditions of admission to the Christian Church? It may, indeed, be true that in a National Church built upon the foundation of Christ alone, there would be great diversities of opinion on many speculative points. But do not such diversities of opinion exist now, under the old, long-tried, narrow and broken-down system? We should then be in no worse position in that respect. Nay, we should be in a better; for, although people would naturally group themselves round various centres of instruction and influence, as they found spiritual food suitable to their different wants, yet all might still feel, and this far more truly than at present, that they are equal members of the one Body of Christ, and all members one of another. Differences, within the Christian fold or outside of it, cannot be got rid of; but, in one comprehensive Church, injurious influences arising from them would probably be reduced to a minimum; while a true freedom of thought and speech, fully and legally allowed to all, could only tend, among honest men, to the destruction of error, the speedier discovery and the surer establishment of Truth.

If any of our highest Anglican or "Catholic" friends could not be members of such a re-constituted National Church, the more would be the pity,—at least for themselves. But, in any case, the door would be open for those who preferred to go out. They could become Dissenters! And probably the change would be good for their spiritual health; while many would be ready to acknowledge, that such a turning of the world ecclesiastical upside down would, in their case, be no unfitting "Nemesis" of spiritual arrogance,—all things considered. Moreover, a harbour of refuge, and more than one, would still remain to them. The Roman Church and its Greek sister (or rival) would doubtless receive them with open arms; and thus would the particular "re-union of Christendom" for which many of them are understood to long, be at length happily accomplished, so far, at least, as they were concerned—a result, it may be supposed, far better, in their eyes, than so unorthodox a thing as a re-union, on a common Christian basis, between themselves and the sects and churches of Protestant England.

It is scarcely necessary to add, that in the ecclesiastical renovation here contemplated, there need be no place left for any injurious "State control." Certainly the State ought not to set itself up as a theological dictator, either to the present or to a future generation. But neither ought this to be done by any little knot of chapel-founders, by the committee or deacons of a congregation, or by the select body which may call itself "the church," whether among Baptists or Independents. The utmost possible liberty of thought and speech ought to be allowed to all who accepted the fundamental principle of union,—any control that might be exercised being solely in regard to material arrangements. It is perfectly reasonable, and would be necessary for peace, that things of the latter kind should be subject to definite national laws; but let no court, or committee, or conference, or parliament, arrogate to itself the function or the place of Christ, by attempting to impose what he has left open and free to the conscience and reason of each individual disciple. Liberty to inquire, and to express the results of honest inquiry, cannot, therefore, fail to be one of the most prominent characteristics of a church which desires to serve and worship God "in spirit and in truth;" and this principle we would heartily commend to the attention of the members of the Liberation Society.

The outlines of Christian doctrine sketched in the preceding pages are, in substance, the same which have been usually designated by the term *Unitarian.* It would appear that they are in themselves very simple,—not complicated, or full of mystery and apparent contradiction, as may, with some degree of reason, be alleged of the prevailing orthodoxy. It has usually been allowed, indeed, that the Unitarian form of Christian belief, however wanting it may be in *truth,* is at least rational and intelligible. In this, doubtless, Dr. Liddon and many more will only find an additional ground for rejecting it, perhaps without examination. Such persons, like Naaman the Syrian, would prefer "some great thing." To wash even seven times in the waters of Jordan will be a light thing with those who can find peace only in baptismal regeneration, apostolical succession, or (if attainable) some sort of infallibility, documentary or personal—only *not* that of the Pope!

It is not, therefore, to be greatly wondered at, that so many, even of thoughtful and intelligent persons, are unable fairly to appreciate Unitarian theology, or even to make out very clearly what a Unitarian can be. Of those who appear to be afflicted with this kind of incapacity—to use the mildest word which the circumstances permit—may be mentioned the learned and venerable Dr. Hook, the present Dean of Chichester. In his widely circulated Church Dictionary, he describes Unitarians as "certain persons who do not worship the True God."* We scarcely know what remedy can be suggested for this curious case of theological blindness. But we venture to ask any candid reader whether it does not appear from the preceding pages that Unitarians are at least desirous to worship the True God? Do they not say in their prayers, as Christ taught his disciples to say, "Our Father which art in heaven"? Is it not also their earnest wish to keep "the first of all the commandments," that "the Lord our God is one Lord;"—as well as to render the love and obedience which are not to be dissociated from it; to remember that "God is a Spirit,"

* *Church Dictionary* (10th ed.), article "Unitarian."

and that "they that worship him must worship him in spirit and in truth"? How, then, if this be so, can it be truthfully said that they are persons "who do not worship the True God"? Has Dr. Hook some God of his own still truer than the "God and Father of Jesus Christ"? If he has, it behoves him to reveal this "unknown God" more fully to the world. He may be assured that the Unitarians of England will not be slow to turn away from what they now so "ignorantly worship," to that Greater and Truer Being which the author of the Church Dictionary may be able to declare to them!

Another case of the same remarkable kind is seen in what a recent very able writer has said in the pages of the Contemporary Review.* The Rev. John Hunt there declares how difficult he thinks it to define a Unitarian. "To define a Unitarian," he says, "would be about as difficult as to explain the primal essence of the universe." What degree of difficulty may attend the latter explanation, Mr. Hunt does not explain; but this volume can scarcely, perhaps, be more suitably concluded than by endeavouring to help him, so far as is possible, out of his perplexity. A definition may be given of the term at which he stumbles which will probably be level even to the humblest capacity. A Unitarian, then, it may be said, is one who follows Christ in holding the doctrine of the Divine Unity without explaining it away. This definition will probably be admitted to cover the whole question of Unitarian or not Unitarian.

It is true, indeed, as some of the Bishops and other speakers in recent debates in Convocation observed, that there are considerable differences among Unitarians on various theological subjects; just, in fact, as Trinitarians differ from one another on some points

* *Contemporary Review*, April, 1871, article on "The Bishops and the Revision of the Bible," p. 91.

Y

—do they not?—while remaining Trinitarians nevertheless. One, for instance, will hold the Trinity of the Athanasian Creed; another, that of Sabellius; another, as Mr. Hunt himself once pointed out, that of Proclus—although the last-named teacher was not even a Christian. So doubtless it is, to some extent, with Unitarians. On many points they hold different opinions; and they ought certainly to do so peacefully and charitably. Indeed, no Unitarian would prosecute another for heresy in any Court of Arches, although such a thing *has* happened among Trinitarians. Yet while Unitarians may thus differ from each other, still on the great point of the Divine Unity they do not differ. They none of them believe in more Gods than one; or admit that Jesus Christ was God, always holding that he was a distinct being, distinct in mind and consciousness, from the Almighty Father whom he worshiped, and whom, as has been shown, he taught his disciples to worship.

It may be hoped, therefore, that it has been made plain to both the eminent writers just named, not only what a Unitarian *worships*, but also what a Unitarian *is*. If not, the failure can only be attributed to one cause. Eyes, it is said, which are much in the dark, or accustomed to a subdued, imperfect light, have difficulty in bearing the full daylight, and will fail to perceive objects as clearly as they ought to do, even in the bright sunshine of noonday, simply because they are so much accustomed to a different medium. Does something like this occur in connection with Religion? Do those who are long accustomed to the sacred obscurity of Nicene and Athanasian theology gradually lose the faculty of seeing clearly and appreciating rightly more simple doctrines? Can *this* be the reason why the Dean of Chichester thinks that Unitarians do not worship the True God, and why the Rev. John Hunt has found it so much beyond his power " to define a Unitarian"? If such be their state, it can only be hoped that the scales may be taken from their eyes; that before many years have elapsed, their blindness or dimness of sight will have passed away; and that, like Saul of Tarsus, they will be strengthened to stand up in the synagogues (that is, in the churches), and with converted Paul proclaim and prove " that this is very Christ."*

* See Acts ix. 10-22 (in a revised version).

GENERAL APPENDIX.

Note A, p. 36.

Isaiah vii. 14.—The Scriptural usage appears scarcely sufficient to determine the meaning of the word rendered, Septuagint, παρθένος, English *virgin*, and quoted in Matt. i. 23. The word is found only in Gen. xxiv. 43; Ex. ii. 8; Prov. xxx. 19; Ps. lxviii. 26; Cant. i. 3; 1 Chron. xv. 20; Ps. xlvi. 1; Cant. vi. 8. In all these instances it may be used simply in the sense of *young woman*, whether married or not. The Hebrews had a different word to denote the stricter meaning, as, for example, in Gen. xxiv. 16; yet even this was sometimes used in the wider sense (Joel i. 8). Hence it may be supposed that the other too, even if usually and properly corresponding to παρθένος, may also have been occasionally employed with the same latitude. It follows, that the rendering *young wife* may be the right one. It is a very obvious remark that the prophet by using the definite article, and thus referring to a definite person, must really have meant to designate his own wife (Gesenius, Kommentar *in loc.*), much as he does in the next chapter, in connection with the birth of Maher-shalal-hash-baz. In the latest English work on Isaiah (*The Book of Isaiah chronologically arranged*, &c., by T. K. Cheyne, M.A., Fellow of Balliol College, Oxford, 1870), the verse under notice is rendered thus: "Behold, the damsel shall conceive and bear a son, and call his name God-with-us." Mr. Cheyne observes, in his note on the word rendered *damsel*, "So far as the etymology of this word is concerned, ... there is nothing to prevent us from interpreting it of the wife of the prophet;" and on the rendering "shall conceive," he adds, "or 'is with child,' thus bringing the fulfilment a little nearer the time of the prediction." This is in exact agreement with what has (quite independently) been said above, and in the text (*supra*, pp. 36, 37).

Note B, p. 47.

Isaiah lii. 13–liii. 12.—It is observed in the text (*supra*, p. 38, *seq.*), that the prophet, when he speaks of the sufferings of the Servant of Jehovah, uses *past tenses*, and *futures* only when he refers to the exaltation which is to come. This distinction may be best seen by an inspection of the passage. The following version is taken from the work of Mr. Cheyne, already referred to. It has been published since the section of the present volume on the passage in Isaiah was written; and is here given simply because it is from the pen of an independent translator, and is the latest English version of the passage known to us. It will be at once plain to the reader from Mr. Cheyne's rendering, how entirely historical, and not predictive, the passage is, and how impossible it is to refer the words to Jesus Christ,—except, indeed, in the usual New Testament manner of accommodation.

Isaiah lii. 13–liii. 12.

13 "Behold my servant shall be prosperous; he shall be exalted and extolled, and be very high. 14 According as many were astonished at thee (his visage was so marred unlike to a man, and his form unlike to the sons of men), 15 so shall he cause many nations to admire; kings shall shut their mouths at him; for that which had not been told them shall they see, and that which they had not heard shall they consider.

liii. 1 Who hath believed our revelation? and to whom was the arm of Jehovah disclosed? 2 He grew up before him as a tender plant, and as a root out of a dry ground; he had no form nor majesty, that we should regard him, and no beauty, that we should desire him. 3 He was despised, and forsaken of men, a man of pains and acquainted with sickness; and we hid as it were our faces from him; he was despised, and we esteemed him not.

4 Surely he did bear our sicknesses and carry our pains, whilst we esteemed him stricken, smitten of God, and afflicted. 5 But he was pierced for our transgressions, bruised for our iniquities; the

chastisement of our peace was upon him, and through his stripes we are healed. 6 All we like sheep did go astray; we turned every one to his own way; and Jehovah laid upon him the iniquity of us all.

7 He was tormented, but he suffered freely, and opened not his mouth, as the sheep that is led to the slaughter, and as the ewe that before her shearers is dumb; and he opened not his mouth. 8 From oppression and from punishment was he taken,—and as for his generation, who considered that he was cut off out of the land of the living, for the transgression of my people he was stricken? 9 And his grave was appointed with the wicked, and his tomb with the oppressor, although he had done no violence, neither was any deceit in his mouth.

10 Yet it pleased Jehovah to bruise him, and to smite him with sickness: for if he should make his soul a trespass-offering he should see a seed, he should prolong his days, and the pleasure of Jehovah should prosper in his hand; 11 he should see the gains of his soul, and should be satisfied; by his knowledge should my righteous servant make many righteous, and he should take up the burden of their iniquities. 12 Therefore will I divide him a portion among many, and with a great company shall he divide, because he poured out his soul unto death, and was numbered with the transgressors, though he had borne the sin of many, and made intercession for the transgressors." (Cheyne's *Isaiah*, pp. 189, 190.)

In a few instances the above version may be open to some slight verbal correction, but the historical character given to the passage is beyond question. On the last verse Mr. Cheyne observes, "The chapter concludes, as it commenced, with a Divine oracle. The personification is now completely dissolved, and the spiritual recompense of God's 'Servant' is divided among a great company." In reference to the words, *the sin of many*, he adds, "The 'many' and the 'transgressors' are evidently the Jewish exiles, on the analogy of similar expressions in an earlier paragraph." (*Ibid.*, p. 193.)

Note C, p. 202.

1 Tim. iii. 16.—Bishop Ellicott, in his valuable Commentary on the Pastoral Epistles, renders this verse as follows:—"And confessedly great is the mystery of godliness; 'Who was manifested in the flesh, justified in the spirit, seen of angels, preached unto the Gentiles, believed on in the world, received up into glory.'" The whole of the verse, from "Who" to the end, may, he conjectures, be a quotation from some ancient *hymn* or *confession of faith*. This supposition is interesting, and would account for the somewhat abrupt and difficult character of the passage as it stands. But it is without evidence, except only the fact that the six clauses may be arranged stichometrically. This may be pure accident, as in the case of Coloss. iii. 19, in the English Version, where we have a good hexameter verse.

The reference of the relative ὅς *who* (masculine) to the immediately preceding word μυστήριον *mystery* (neuter) is difficult, and hardly admissible, though adopted by Dean Alford in his revised version of the New Testament. So Sharpe, *New Testament translated from Griesbach's Text*. If, however, this be the correct rendering, *Christ* is still without doubt the subject alluded to. He is the "mystery who was manifested in flesh," whatever may be the meaning of these words. The reader who consults the Commentary above referred to will see that the distinguished author is by no means perspicuous or satisfactory in his explanation of either σαρκί (flesh) or πνεύματι (spirit); and indeed the difficulty of explanation is acknowledged by him, as it must be by every one—except perhaps Dr. Liddon.

The question whether or not the passage necessarily implies the pre-existence of Christ, we have sufficiently answered in the text (*supra*, p. 203). But even if *this* question were answered affirmatively, it would not follow that Jesus Christ was conceived of by the writer of the Epistle as Supreme God. Such a conclusion would be contrary to the uniform tenor of the New Testament, as we have abundantly seen in connection with Rom. ix. 5. Comp. *supra*, p. 199.

Note D, p. 204.

In the Epistles there are two passages to which Dr. Liddon attaches great importance, as direct testimonies for the deity of Jesus Christ. They have not been noticed in the body of this work, chiefly from the desire not to burden the text with too many critical details; but a few brief remarks may properly be introduced here. The passages referred to are Titus ii. 13 and 1 John v. 20.

(1) Titus ii. 13.—In the common version this runs as follows: "Looking for that blessed hope, and the glorious appearing of the great God and our Saviour Jesus Christ." Dean Alford (*New Testament, revised version*) varies thus: "And the manifestation of the glory of the great God and of our Saviour Jesus Christ." Mr. Sharpe (*New Testament, from Griesbach's Text*, 6th ed.) agrees with this, only substituting "appearing" for "manifestation." The three translations (like many others, for example, those of Bunsen and De Wette) distinguish between "the great God" and Jesus Christ; intending, in their respective renderings, to denote two separate subjects or persons, and not one merely.

Dr. Liddon, however, as might be expected, renders thus: "Looking for the blessed hope and appearing of the glory of our great God and Saviour Jesus Christ," exactly following the translation of Bishop Ellicott (*Pastoral Epistles*, p. 259).

The question then is, which of these two forms of translation is correct, the received form, or that of Dr. Liddon and the Bishop? In reply to this inquiry, we would first ask the reader to refer to the remarks on Rom. ix. 5 (*supra*, p. 199), and in particular to the notes (pp. 199, 200) which repeat the decided statement of Meyer to the effect that St. Paul has nowhere designated Jesus Christ by the word θεός, and that such an application of this word to him is not met with until after we leave the apostolical age. Thus, the analogy of Paul's usual expressions is clearly *against* the supposition that he here means to speak of Jesus Christ as "the great God."

Further, it is on all hands acknowledged that there is nothing in the grammatical form of the passage to determine its translation the one way or the other. It may be correctly represented by either rendering; the one or the other being simply determined by the degree of force which any one may choose, in this place, to attribute to the article standing in the Greek before the word rendered "great." * In the presence of this doubt, the ordinary reader may be well satisfied to follow the guidance of such scholars as Meyer and Winer, who are agreed in telling us that *two* subjects of thought are here designated, and that Jesus Christ accordingly is *not* described as "the great God." The guidance of these scholars, we repeat, is what the reader should follow; and this may properly be urged upon him because their conclusion, as they tell us, has been dictated simply by a due regard to the usual tenor of St. Paul's language, in reference to God and to Christ.

The following are the words of Winer, taken from his *Grammar of the New Testament* (edited by Prof. Moulton, 1870):—"Considerations derived from Paul's system of doctrine lead me to believe that σωτῆρος [Saviour] is not a second predicate, co-ordinate with θεοῦ [God],—Christ being first called ὁ μέγας θεός [the great God], and then σωτήρ [Saviour]. The article is omitted before σωτῆρος because this word is defined by the genitive ἡμῶν [rendered *our*], and because the apposition *precedes* the proper name: *of the great God and of our Saviour Jesus Christ.*" Winer adds to this in a note:— "In the above remarks I had no intention to deny that, in point of *grammar*, σωτῆρος ἡμῶν may be regarded as a second predicate, jointly depending on the article τοῦ; but the dogmatic conviction derived

---

* The usuage of the N. T. in regard to the Greek article is quite insufficient to settle the question as against the rendering of the received version. In reply to the appeal to that usage, it is quite enough to recall the well-known words of Bishop Pearson : "We must not think to decide this controversy by the articles, of which the sacred penmen were not curious, and the transcribers have been very careless."— Pearson on the Creed (1842), p. 229, note.

from Paul's writings, that this Apostle cannot have called Christ *the great God*, induced me to shew that there is no grammatical obstacle to our taking the clause καὶ σωτ. . . . . . Χριστοῦ by itself, as referring to a second subject." To this note the English translator and editor of Winer appends these words:—" This passage is very carefully examined by Bishop Ellicott and Dean Alford *in loc.;* and though these writers come to different conclusions (the latter agreeing with Winer, the former rendering the words, 'of our great God and Saviour Jesus Christ'), they are entirely agreed as to the admissibility of both renderings in point of *grammar*." Winer, Gram. N. T., ed. by Moulton, p. 162.

Probably nothing more is needed to enable the English reader to decide for himself that the rendering of our English New Testament is perfectly correct; although, at the same time, it is not to be denied that the rendering of Dr. Liddon and Bishop Ellicott might be admitted, provided the analogy of St. Paul's writings required it, or would even justify it. But, as we have sufficiently seen (*supra*, Chapter XIX.), the direct *contrary* is the case.

Indeed, both these learned writers virtually admit this, speaking as they do with manifest hesitation as to their own rendering. Thus Dr. Liddon observes, "Here the grammar *apparently*, and the context certainly, oblige us to recognise the identity of 'our Saviour Jesus Christ' and 'our Great God.' As a matter of fact, Christians are not waiting for any manifestation of the Father." (B. L., p. 315.) As to the latter remark, we would remind Dr. Liddon that in Paul's time Christians *were* waiting for a "manifestation of the Father." Our Lord himself in the Gospel expressly says respecting himself, that "he shall come in his own glory and *in his Father's*" (Luke ix. 26). These words amply explain the terms used by Paul ("the manifestation of the glory of the great God"); and they shew us how vain it is, on the grounds put forth by Dr. Liddon, to hold that Jesus Christ was regarded in apostolical times as "the great God."

Bishop Ellicott, on his side, is equally hesitating with Dr. Liddon, and, we must add, more than equally candid, in regard to the rendering which he has adopted. "It must be candidly avowed," he writes, "that it is *very* doubtful whether on the grammatical principle last alluded to [the union of two substantives under the vinculum of a common article] the interpretation of this passage can be fully settled." The Bishop goes on to give in detail the reasons which have determined him to render as he has done, and he concludes his comment in these words: "It ought not to be suppressed that some of the best versions, Vulgate, Syriac, Coptic, Armenian (not, however, Æthiopic), and some Fathers of unquestioned orthodoxy, adopted the other interpretation. . . . . the true rendering of the clause really turns more upon exegesis than upon grammar, and this the student should not fail clearly to bear in mind." (*Pastoral Epistles*, p. 201.) This last remark, that the true rendering "turns more upon exegesis than upon grammar," is one to which every fair-minded reader will at once assent; but he will remember that exegesis, in this connection, ought unquestionably to be illustrated and confirmed by the usual strain of St. Paul's writings, and should not be in opposition to it. In other words, the distinction which the Apostle everywhere observes between God and Christ should here be duly kept in sight. The point in question is by no means to be settled by the analogies or the exigencies of the established theology, however ancient and venerable this may appear to any one to be.

(2) 1 John v. 20.—Here we read:—"And we know that the Son of God is come, and hath given us an understanding, that we may know him that is true; and we are in him that is true, in his Son Jesus Christ. This is the true God, and eternal life."[*] It would here certainly appear as if Jesus Christ were termed the true God. But, on the other hand, it seems plain that the writer is referring to two objects. One is "him that is true;" there can be

---

[*] It is worth noting that the Alexandrine MS. omits the words "Jesus Christ." The order of the preceding Greek words is "in the Son of him." Hence, omitting "Jesus Christ," the word "this" would refer to the antecedent "him," *i.e.* to God. But no great weight need be attributed to this circumstance.

no question that by this is meant the Almighty Father. The Apostle adds, that "we are in *him*," when we are "in his Son;" that is, we are in God through and in Jesus Christ. But then come the words, "This is the true God," as if the writer meant to reduce the two objects just spoken of to *one*. But such a meaning would be self-contradictory, and can hardly be what is intended. Dr. Liddon, however, has no hesitation about it. The Apostle, he tells us, "leads us up to the culminating statement that Jesus himself is the true God and eternal life" (p. 239). He adds in a note, "After having distinguished the ἀληθινός [true] from his υἱός [Son], St. John, by a characteristic turn, simply identifies the Son with the ἀληθινὸς θεός." With all due deference to Dr. Liddon, we do not think that the Apostle wrote such nonsense as is thus attributed to him. The whole difficulty is at once removed by referring the word "this," not to Jesus Christ, but to the Being denoted by the words, "him that is true." This yields an easy and self-consistent sense. By being in Jesus Christ, we are in Him that is true; this is the True God and eternal life.

But is there, then, in the Epistles attributed to this Apostle, any other case of the kind, in which the word "this" is similarly used —referred, that is, not to the nearer, but to a more remote, antecedent? Such an instance there *is*, and one of a very remarkable kind. In 2 John v. 7, we have these words: "Many deceivers are entered into the world, who confess not that Jesus Christ is come in the flesh: This is a deceiver and an antichrist." Here, in strictness, "This" refers to Jesus Christ, who accordingly is termed a deceiver and antichrist. But this cannot be the meaning. We see, therefore, that the author of these two Epistles writes with a certain carelessness or inaccuracy; but it does not follow that he writes nonsense. A little discrimination, on the part of his readers, will prevent them from making him say what he cannot have intended to say. It is perfectly reasonable, then, in the former of the two expressions, to conclude that the word "This" must be referred to the more distant antecedent. If, in short, the writer does not intend us to understand that, in the one case, he terms Jesus Christ a deceiver and antichrist, neither can he intend us to understand, in the other, that he terms him "the true God."

Dr. Liddon has a further remark, which ought not here to be passed over. He tells us that ὁ ἀληθινὸς θεός; [the true God] " is the Divine Essence, in opposition to all creatures;" and he adds, " Our being in the true God depends upon our being in Christ, and St. John clenches this assertion by saying that Christ is the true God Himself." He does not inform us where he has learnt that ὁ ἀληθινὸς θεός; means "the Divine Essence;"—an omission of some significance, considering that the assertion is strangely inconsistent with certain words of Jesus Christ himself. He, we may remember, speaks to the Heavenly Father in prayer, addressing him by the appellation "Father;" and he calls HIM not only "the true God," but the "Only true God." Is it allowable to "water down" such words into the meaning of "the Divine Essence;"—or virtually to contradict them, by declaring that he who addressed them to another, even to God, in one of the most solemn moments of his life, " is the true God Himself"? (Comp. *supra*, p. 231, note.)

Note E, p. 205.

Philip. ii. 5-11.—This passage is paraphrased as follows by one of the latest and most learned of our English commentators: " Reflect in your own minds the mind of Jesus Christ. Be humble, as He also was humble. Though existing before the worlds in the Eternal Godhead, yet He did not cling with avidity to the prerogatives of His divine majesty, did not ambitiously display His equality with God; but divested Himself of the glories of heaven, and took upon Him the nature of a servant, assuming the likeness of men. Nor was this all. Having thus appeared among men in the fashion of a man, He humbled Himself yet more, and carried out his obedience even to dying. Nor did He die by a common death: He was crucified as the lowest malefactor is crucified. But as was His humility, so also was His exaltation. God raised Him to a pre-eminent height, and gave Him a title and a dignity far above all dignities and titles else. For to the name and majesty of Jesus all created things in heaven and earth and hell shall pay homage on bended knee; and every tongue with praise and thanksgiving shall declare that Jesus Christ is Lord, and in and for Him shall glorify God the Father." (*St. Paul's Epistle to the Philippians,* a Revised Text, &c. By J. B. Lightfoot, D.D., Hulsean Professor of Divinity, &c., Cambridge, 1868, p. 108, *seq.*)

This exposition is open to what must, to every Christian mind, be the gravest of all objections. It really assumes and asserts the existence of *two* Gods! Jesus Christ, we are told, existed "in the Eternal Godhead;" that is to say, he was *God,* for the words can mean nothing else. But he did not cling "to the prerogatives of His divine majesty." He divested himself of them, humbled himself, by becoming a man and allowing himself to be crucified, and dying the death of a malefactor. All this occurred to the God Jesus Christ, but not to the Almighty Father: the humility was in the mind of the one, but not in the mind of the other; and for that divine humility of his, the God Jesus Christ has been exalted to a pre-eminent name and glory by the other Divine Being, who did not humble himself or suffer or die.* Is it possible that two separate existences can be more distinctly affirmed than in such a representation as this? Nor does it at all relieve the matter to add a verbal

---

* Similarly, in reference to Mark xiii. 32, Bishop O'Brien writes as follows:—"All things that the Omniscient Father knows,—that is all things,—doubtless were known to the Son, when he was *in the form of God.* But it appears that when He became man, and dwelt among us, of this infinite knowledge He only possessed as much as was imparted to Him."—*Charge* (1863), p. 110. It is as plain here as words can make it, that the writer is thinking of *two* Gods, one of whom is possessed of knowledge, which the other, during a particular interval of his existence, is without, and only receives as the former imparts it to him. Is it *possible* more strongly to convey the idea of two distinct minds? Yet these writers profess to be monotheists, and to believe in the existence of only one God! Such expositions are about as truly monotheistic as the old Greek story of Apollo and Admetus. The god served the mortal as a shepherd for nine years, and he too kept his deity "in abeyance" during the interval. So Bp. O'Brien declares of Christ, "His infinite attributes and powers seem . . . . . . to have been in abeyance, so to speak."—*Charge,* p. 105.—So to speak, indeed!

reservation against being supposed to intend to speak of two Gods, or three. Of course, Trinitarian theology does not intend or desire to do this; but it does it nevertheless, if the language it employs has its usual meaning. We cannot understand how this most fatal difficulty can be left out of sight as it is by able and learned men, in the usual orthodox expositions of this, and indeed of other passages. The same objection applies with equal force to the explanations of Bishop Ellicott and Dean Alford.

Professor Lightfoot has a long and elaborate note (p. 125, *seq.*), the drift of which is to establish the conclusion that the word μορφή (form) really means *essential nature*. But, whatever be the peculiar shades of meaning sometimes attached to this word by the philosophical and others writers appealed to, it is perfectly clear that in the passage before us it refers to outward condition and circumstances only. What else is meant by "took the form (μορφήν) of a slave"? Clearly this cannot refer to essential nature; although, strangely enough, in the above quoted paraphrase our Lord is said to have taken upon him "the *nature* of a servant." The Apostle does not say this; nor can the word "form" in this latter expression be reasonably held to have a different force from that conveyed by "form of God." The word has evidently the same meaning in the two clauses. If, then, "form of God" denotes the essential nature of God, "form of a slave" must denote the essential nature of a slave—and this, we venture to submit, is a simple *reductio ad absurdum* of the whole exposition.

The word ὑπάρχων (rendered "being"), Professor Lightfoot observes, "denotes prior existence, but not necessarily eternal existence." Dr. Liddon seems to go a step further, and says, "The word ὑπάρχων points to our Lord's 'original subsistence' in the splendour of the Godhead." (B. L., p. 317.) But does it not here denote simply a prior *condition*, upon which something else was conceived to supervene?—a prior condition, whether actual, or only imagined and potential? Jesus as the true Messiah was, in the conception of his disciples, of right possessed of all the dignity and power properly appertaining to his exalted office. This is what is meant by the ἐν μορφῇ θεοῦ ὑπάρχων. And most probably, as formerly pointed out, we ought to distinguish here between θεοῦ and τοῦ θεοῦ. The former may be used in that subordinate sense which was perfectly familiar in the days of St. Paul, and which is alluded to, we have seen (*supra*, p. 165), by Philo, Origen and Eusebius; as perhaps also it may be employed in the first verse of the fourth Gospel. Jesus, then, as Messiah, was of right entitled to the position of a God upon earth; but he did not regard this Messianic power and dignity as a prize to be seized; he emptied himself of it,* humbled himself and died; and for this his self-renunciation He who alone is God has rewarded and exalted His servant.

The expression τὸ εἶναι ἴσα θεῷ is no doubt equivalent to μορφῇ θεοῦ. It literally means, "the being equal [or in equal circumstances] to God," or "to a God." But surely this, again, can only refer to outward condition; for no one maintains that there was any change in the Divine nature, or that Jesus (if he were truly God) could have ceased to be so. Professor Lightfoot admits "He divested himself, not of His divine nature, *for this was impossible*, but of the glories, the prerogatives of Deity." We acknowledge ourselves quite unable to attach any definite meaning to the latter part of this statement. How could the infinite God lay aside "the glories and prerogatives of Deity"? Dr. Liddon scarcely ventures to be so precise as Professor Lightfoot on this part of the subject. He says, "The point of our Lord's example lies in His emptying

---

* The words "likeness of men" (v. 7), and "found in fashion as a man" (v. 8), may reasonably be understood to convey an implied allusion to some higher condition. The suggested contrast, however, is simply that of the Messianic dignity which rightfully belonged to Jesus, and which he did not deem "a thing to grasp at," but renounced. There is nothing here, or elsewhere, to shew that the writer of the words was thinking of an abandoned "Eternal Godhead." The word ἄνθρωπος (rendered *man*, *men*), probably has its lower meaning here, and is used somewhat like the corresponding Hebrew word (see Isaiah ii. 9) to denote an ordinary mortal man, a human being. Jesus, therefore, the Apostle writes, lived in the lowly condition of an ordinary man, humbled himself and died, although all the time he was the Christ! The appeal to his example was evidently natural and forcible in the highest degree. Can the same be said, on the orthodox theory of Paul's meaning?

Himself of the glory or 'form' of His Eternal Godhead," and He thinks that his example would have been worthless had he been only a created being. (B. L., p. 317.) But, in reply to this, may it not be asked as before, How could God empty Himself of the glory of "His Eternal Godhead"? Is not Dr. Liddon rhetorically using words here, as sometimes elsewhere, without any real sense? Or, if not, what sort of a changeable God must He be who can empty Himself of His Eternal Godhead? And in regard to the force of the example given, are we to think that a created being cannot be humble, or set an example of humility?—a king or a queen, for instance, an earl or a bishop? Surely the possibility of this does not depend so entirely upon the nature of the person as created or uncreated, but only upon his circumstances and disposition. On the other hand, is it rational to suppose that the Infinite can be humble?

In any case, what the Apostle gives us to understand that Jesus renounced, or did not grasp at, was τὸ εἶναι ἴσα θεῷ; and as, by the orthodox admission, he could not have divested himself of deity, so conversely τὸ εἶναι ἴσα θεῷ (which, again, is the same as μορφῆ θεοῦ *) cannot with any consistency be understood to mean a state of pre-existent deity, or, in the words of both Dr. Liddon and Professor Lightfoot, one of "Eternal Godhead."

And here, again, the old objection recurs with undiminished force. In such expositions we are really called upon to believe in two distinct Gods, one of whom divests himself of the glories and prerogatives of Deity, while the other does not; one of whom suffers humiliation and is put to death, while the other looks on with approval, conferring upon his co-deity the glorious reward which he has won for himself by his submission. May it not be asked, whether in such ideas as these we have not the old Homeric plurality of Gods over again, under a different name—the thing having, as Prof. Lightfoot might say, changed its σχῆμα, though not

---

* Dr. Liddon expressly says, "The expression ἐν μορφῇ θεοῦ ὑπάρχων is virtually equivalent to τὸ εἶναι ἴσα θεῷ." B. L., p. 317, note.

its μορφή? To speak more seriously, is it not too plain that Christian monotheism is not the ruling spirit of the theology which can tolerate or require such representations? In the name of our common Christianity, let us, at least, protest against ascribing to the Apostle Paul anthropomorphism so gross as this, and so lamentably destructive of spiritual religion.

Prof. Lightfoot observes, that "between the two expressions, ἴσος εἶναι and ἴσα εἶναι, no other distinction can be drawn except that the former refers to the person and the latter to the attributes." Does not the latter refer rather to the *manner?*—or, in other words, as before, to the external circumstances? The vagueness of the neuter plural, or adverbial form, corresponds exactly to this explanation; while ἴσος θεῷ, as Prof. Lightfoot justly says, "would seem to divide the Godhead." We greatly wonder that it does not occur to so candid and thoughtful a writer that his whole exposition is open to the same objection; for that it really "divides the Godhead" into at least two equal divine beings, each of whom is God precisely and essentially as much as the other.

The late Dean Alford, it may be noticed, in his revision of the New Testament, thus renders Philip. ii. 6: "Who, being in the form of God, deemed not his equality with God a thing to grasp at." On this translation it may be enough to observe, that there is no "his" in the original; nor is there anything in the form of the expression to justify its introduction. The rendering can only be regarded as a singular illustration of the power of an established system to bias even the most upright and truthful mind. On the true force of the article with the infinitive, comp. Winer, N. T. Grammar, by Moulton, p. 406.

Note F, pp. 212, 216.

The Instrumental Force of the Preposition Διά.

The following passage, taken from the work referred to, affords an excellent and exhaustive illustration of what has been, too briefly perhaps, said on this subject in the text:—

"The preposition Διά . . . . . does not signify *by any one as an original cause* (for this sense is exprest by a different preposition, Ὑπο), but it denotes *through any thing as an instrument*. For the sake of illustration I shall take the first example of the occurrence of Διά in the New Testament: Mat. i. 22. 'Now all this was done that it might be fulfilled which was spoken of the Lord by the Prophet;' or, more accurately, 'which was spoken *by* the Lord *through* the Prophet.' In the first place, the preposition Ὑπο, *By*, points out the Lord as the *original author* of the communication; and, in the second place, the preposition Διά, *Through*, represents the Prophet as the *medium*, through whom this communication was conveyed to mankind. The same distinction is accurately observed in all cases (and they are very numerous), in which the New Testament writers produce quotations from the Prophets of the Old. They never introduce a prophecy by saying, that it was uttered THROUGH *the Lord* (διὰ τοῦ Κυρίου), and they seldom, if ever, say, that it was delivered BY *the Prophet* (ὑπὸ τοῦ Προφήτου), but *through* the Prophet, and *by* the Lord.

"The preposition Διά, followed either by a Genitive or Accusative case, occurs in the New Testament about 630 times. It is used to denote the *efficient cause of the production of an effect* (of course governing in these instances the Genitive), about 290 times. I have examined all the passages where it is found. I have observed that its general application, when used to point out an efficient cause, is to represent not the *primary*, but the *secondary*, or *instrumental* cause.* This sense of the word seems indeed to arise naturally from its original acceptation. It properly signifies motion *through a place*. Hence it has been transferred by an obvious process to the *way or method, by passing through which* any object

---

* "Against the universality of this rule only one passage presents much difficulty: 1 Cor. i. 9, δἰ οὗ ἐκλήθητε, '*through* whom ye were called.' But even here there is strong evidence for considering ὑπὸ as the true reading. See Griesbach. Even allowing Διά to denote the *original* cause in two or three passages, still the probability that it denoted the *instrumental* would be in any doubtful case as 100 to 1."

is attained, or the *instrument, by means of which* any end is accomplished.

"From reflecting upon the primary application of DIA in reference to *place*, its common use in Greek authors, and the distinction observed in the New Testament between this preposition and HYPO, I had formed a judgment of the Scripture testimonies concerning the Creation through Christ, before I saw the above remarks in any other author. I was afterwards much gratified to find that Origen, who lived at the beginning of the third century, who wrote in Greek, and than whom none of the ancient Fathers was more learned, more honest, or more industrious, observed the same distinction, and reasoned from it in the same manner. In his Commentary on the beginning of John's Gospel, having noticed the difference between DIA and HYPO, and having observed that in Heb. i. 2 the expression (δi $o\tilde{v}$), Through whom, denotes that God made the worlds, or ages, *through his Son*, he adds, 'Thus also here, if all things were made *through* the word, they were not made *by* the Word, but *by one more powerful and greater than the Word*.' Likewise Eusebius, the learned, accurate and laborious author, to whom among the ancients the Christian world is chiefly indebted for the testimonies to the genuineness of the New Testament writings, and who could not possibly be mistaken about the common meaning of two prepositions, which he used daily and hourly in conversation and in books, explaining the commencement of John's Gospel uses these words: 'And when he says, in one place (ver. 10), that the *world*, and in another (ver. 3), that *all things*, were made *through him*, he declares the ministration of the Word to God. For, when the Evangelist might have said, 'All things were made *by* him,' and again, 'The world was made *by* him;' he has not said, '*By* him,' but '*Through* him;' in order that he might raise our conceptions to the underived power of the Father as the original cause of all things.' Lastly, the same distinction is noticed by Philo, the Jew, who was contemporary with our Saviour, who wrote in Greek, and in several parts of his writings expresses the difference between a supreme and a subordinate creator by the opposed use of these two prepositions. See Wetstein's Note on John i. 3." (*Vindication of Unitarianism*, by James Yates, M.A., 4th ed., 1850, pp. 83-85.)

To the above quotations from Origen and Eusebius, Mr. Yates adds the Greek in a note—but we have not thought it necessary to repeat it here.

PASSAGES OF SCRIPTURE SPECIALLY NOTICED.

GENESIS.	PAGE
i. 26	96, 97
iii.	19
iii. 22	96
v. 1-3	97
xi. 7	96
xii. 6	28
xiii. 7	28
xvii.	11
xviii. 1-21	99
xx. 13	72
xxiv. 9, 10	96

EXODUS.	
vi. 2, 3	77
vii. 1	71
xx. 3	71
xxiii. 13	71
xxxi. 1-11	232
xxxii. 4, 8	72

LEVITICUS.	
v.	246
vi. 1-7	245
xvi.	246
xxiv.	246
xxvi.	246

NUMBERS.	
vi. 22-27	22

DEUTERONOMY.	
iv. 35-39	81
v.	17
v. 7	71
vi.	17
vi. 4	81, 87
vii. 9	81

	PAGE
xvii. 2 5	81
xxviii.	17
xxxii. 39-40	81

JOSHUA.	
xxiv. 26, 27	238

1 SAMUEL.	
xv. 32, 33	292

2 SAMUEL.	
i. 13-16	292
vii. 23	72
xxiii. 2	232
xxiv. 9	296

1 CHRONICLES.	
xxi. 1	20
xxi. 5	296

EZRA.	
iv. 18	97

NEHEMIAH.	
ix. 4-38	82

JOB.	
i.	20
i. 6-12	96
ii.	20
xi. 7, 8	81
xxviii.	81
xxxii. 8	232
xxxiv.-xxxix.	81

PSALMS.	
ii. 7	113
viii. 6	71
xiv.	29

	PAGE
xxv.	30
xxix. 1-11	98
xxxiii. 6	154
xlv. 6, 7	102
li.	30
lxix.	30
lxxxii. 1, 6	71

PROVERBS.	
viii. 22-30	155
ix. 1	155
ix. 13	155

ISAIAH.	
i.	74
vi. 2-8	98, 99
vi. 3	22
vii. 13-16	11
vii. 14	35, 324
ix. 1-7	12, 52
ix. 6	52
xi.	17, 49
xii.	12
xiii. 1-xiv. 27	5
xvii. 7, 8	80
xix. 3	80
xxix.	74
xxx. 22	80
xl. 3	68
xliv. 9-20	81
xlv. 1	120
xlv. 5-7	81
xlv. 11	84
xlix.	45
lii. 13-liii. 12	39, 325
liii.	47

PASSAGES OF SCRIPTURE NOTICED. 343

	PAGE
liv. 11–17	44
lxiv. 1, 9–12	12

JEREMIAH.
vii.	247
xxii. 29	99
xxiii. 5–8	49
xxxiii. 16	54

EZEKIEL.
xviii. 19	83
xxi. 27	99
xlviii. 35	36

DANIEL.
ii. 20–23	82
vii. 9–14	12
vii. 13, 14	49, 54
ix. 3–19	82

MICAH.
v. 1–6	49
v. 2	55, 68

HAGGAI.
ii. 6	68

ZECHARIAH.
iii. 1, 2	20
xii. 10	59
xiii. 7	57, 66

MALACHI.
ii.	62
iii. 1	61

WISDOM OF SOLOMON.
vi. 12–16	155
vii. 11, 12	155
ix.	83
x.	155
xviii. 15, 16	155

ECCLESIASTICUS.
xlii. 15	82

2 MACCABEES.
i. 24–29	83

ST. MATTHEW.
	PAGE
i. 23	35
ii. 6	55
iii. 3	68
iv. 3	111
iv. 14–16	52
v. 39–42	292
v. 45	182
viii. 17	40
viii. 29	112
xi. 27	112
xii. 28	235
xii. 31, 32	239
xiv. 33	112
xvi. 16–18	117, 314
xvi. 20	135
xvi. 22	49
xvi. 27, 28	65
xviii. 26–34	77
xx. 28	274
xx. 21	49
xxii. 23–33	298
xxii. 41–44	64
xxiv. 27	15
xxv. 31	15
xxvi. 56	58
xxvi. 39	119
xxvi. 31	58
xxvi. 59–66	106
xxvii. 11	107
xxviii. 19	90

ST. MARK.
i. 1	113
i. 3	68
x. 45	274
xii. 18–27	298
xii. 28–30	298
xii. 29, 30	70, 87
xv. 28	40
xiv. 27	58

ST. LUKE.
iii. 4	68

	PAGE
vi. 20–24	292
vii. 12	182
viii. 40	203
ix. 20	116
x. 22	112
xi. 20	235
xvii. 22	65
xviii. 18, 19	119
xxii. 17–20	137
xxii. 24	13
xxii. 37	40
xxii. 66–71	106
xxiii. 2	107
xxiii. 46	119
xxiv. 21	49
xxiv. 44	64

ST. JOHN.
i. 1–18	144
i. 23	68
i. 29	276
i. 49	112
ii. 17	48
iii.	135
iii. 13	166
iv.	168
v. 19–23	112
v. 30	64
v. 32–47	136
v. 44	118
vi. 28	135
vi. 38	166
vi. 69	111
vii. 16	130
vii. 39	187
viii. 28, 29	184
viii. 58	166
ix.	168
x. 24, 36	112
x. 30	206
x. 33–36	123, 186
x. 38	168
xi.	168
xi. 21, 22	185
xii. 34	49

PASSAGES OF SCRIPTURE NOTICED.

xii. 37-41	40, 64
xiv. 9	84
xiv. 26	237
xvi. 23	124, 225
xvi. 27	166
xvii.	136
xvii. 1-3	225
xvii. 3	70, 184
xvii. 5	166
xvii. 21	168
xix. 14	296
xix. 36	60
xix. 37	59
xx. 28	166
xx. 31	111

Acts.

ii. 14-22	133
iii. 13, 26	116
iv. 24	225
v. 30, 31	124
vii. 59	222
viii. 26-35	40
viii. 37	113
ix. 20	113
ix. 14, 21	228
xix. 2	93
xx. 28	188
xxii. 16	228

Romans.

i. 3, 4	197
iii.	272
iii. 25	254, 276
v. 11	276
v. 12-19	20
vi. 1-14	271
vii. 1-6	271
viii. 19-22	213
ix.	31
ix. 5	194
x.	31
x. 9	193
xi.	31
xi. 15, 25	216
xv. 4	8

1 Corinthians.

i. 1	228
iii. 11	193
v. 7	277, 279
vi. 20	273
vii. 32-40	292
viii. 6	87, 212
xv. 21, 22	20

2 Corinthians.

v. 17	213
v. 18-20	262
v. 21	276
xiii. 14	93

Galatians.

iii. 13	276
iii. 24-29	272
iii. 26	139
iv. 4	197
iv. 5-7	182
vi. 15	213

Ephesians.

i. 9	272
ii. 3	20
ii. 10	213
ii. 13-16	266, 276
iii. 9	209
iv. 8	260
v. 2	277

Philippians.

ii. 5-7	205
ii. 5-11	333
ii. 9-11	125

Colossians.

i. 15	163
i. 17-19	210
iii. 11	85

1 Thessalonians.

i. 10	299
iii. 13	299
iv. 17	299

1 Timothy.

ii. 5	298

iii. 16	201, 327
vi. 1-5, 8-10	291, 292

2 Timothy.

iii. 16	294

Titus.

ii. 13	328

Hebrews.

i. 4-9	207
i. 5-11	64
ii. 12, 13	61
iv. 12	146
iv. 15	192
vii. 27	277
ix. 11	279
ix. 26	277
x. 12	277
xi. 17	182
xii. 26	68

James.

v. 1-6	292

1 Peter.

i. 18, 19	252
ii. 24	266, 276
iv. 7	299

1 John.

i. 7	252
ii. 2	281
iii. 10	182
iv. 9	266
v. 5	206
v. 7, 8	86, 90, 204
v. 20	331

Revelation.

i. 11, 17, 18	217
ii. 26, 27	218
iii. 21	218
iv. 8-11	218, 226
v. 6-12	218
vii. 9-12	219
viii. 13	99
xix. 5, 6, 11-15	219
xix. 17-21	226
xxii. 7-9, 12, 13, 16	220

Woodfall and Kinder, Printers, Milford Lane, Strand, London, W.C.

www.ingramcontent.com/pod-product-compliance
Lightning Source LLC
Chambersburg PA
CBHW032354230426
43672CB00007B/700